IN THE FOOTSTEPS OF A PROPHET

by Jerry Savelle

In the Footsteps of a Prophet

ISBN 0-9655352-6-6

© 1999 Jerry Savelle Publications

All rights reserved. Reproduction in whole or part without written permission from the publisher is prohibited. Printed in the United States of America.

All Scripture quotation is taken from the *King James Version* of the Bible unless otherwise noted.

Jerry Savelle Publications
P.O. Box 748
Crowley, TX 76036

Dedication

I would like to, first of all, thank the Lord Jesus Christ for providing me with the wonderful privilege to preach the Gospel to masses of people all over the world for the last thirty years.

Secondly, I want to thank my wife, Carolyn, for believing in me, standing with me and allowing me to go to the world with the message that has burned within my heart. Without your confidence and support, I would not have been able to accomplish all that has been accomplished through this ministry.

Thirdly, I would like to thank my daughters, Jerri and Terri, for "giving their Dad to the world" even though it meant missing out on some of their growing up experiences. You've never regretted not having a "normal" Dad, and you have always supported me in my vision.

Fourthly, I would like to thank my parents and Carolyn's parents for believing in me both in the early days of my ministry, and right up to this present time. It was always comforting to know that I could always count on you in the hard times and in the good times.

Fifthly, I'd like to thank my staff all over the world for your dedication and your diligence. Without you, Carolyn and I could never fulfill all that God has called us to do.

Next, I'd like to thank my Board of Directors and my partners for their unwavering confidence in the call of God upon my life.

Finally, I want to thank Kenneth and Gloria Copeland for all that they have imparted into my life. This book is my tribute to you and your faithfulness in the ministry.

Table of Contents

1	Hearing the Call	11
2	The Girl Who Changed Everything	19
3	All Those Preachers Want is My Money and My Chicken!	29
4	Surrendering to the Call: February 11, 1969	33
5	A Man Named Kenneth Copeland	39
6	The Message that Changed My Life	45
7	How to Apply the God Kind of Faith	57
8	Channeling the Force of Faith	63
9	Putting the Word to Work	69
10	The Greatest Faith: My Favorite Sermon	77
11	The Power of Your Words	83
12	The Shadow of a Dog Never Bit Anybody!	89
13	God Specializes in the Impossible	99

14	Learning to Share Jesus Effectively	117
15	Kenneth Copeland and Jerry Savelle Become a Team	131
16	Living by Faith	135
17	Don't Touch God's Anointed!	139
18	Three Demands by Kenneth Copeland: Integrity, Excellence, & Be On Time	143
19	Developing an Excellent Spirit	153
20	My First Experience With Demons	161
21	The Hundredfold Principle	171
22	Seven Steps to Prayer that Brings Results	179
23	How to Transmit the Anointing	187
24	The Laws of Prosperity, Part I: Wisdom for Prosperity	197
25	The Laws of Prosperity, Part II: God's Covenant with You	203
26	The Laws of Prosperity, Part III: Laying up Treasures in Heaven	211
27	The Laws of Prosperity, Part IV: Give Your Best	219
28	The Laws of Prosperity, Part V: How to Make Heavenly Withdrawals	225

29	How to Petition God for Your Needs	*231*
30	Three Steps to Success	*239*
31	Always Be Prepared	*243*
32	Jerry Savelle-Associate Minister	*251*
33	Time to Launch Out	*255*
34	How Desperate are You for Success?	*263*
35	Things Which are Seen are Temporal	*273*
36	Preparation for Ministry	*287*
37	Ministry Standards	*295*
38	The Power of Commitment	*303*
39	The Purpose of Your Ministry	*309*
40	Establishing Covenant Relationships	*325*

Introduction

This book has been in my spirit for many, many years. I have waited patiently to tell the story that you are about to read.

This book is not just the story of my life over the last thirty years, but it contains some of the most profound lessons regarding the life of faith that Brother Kenneth Copeland taught me when he took me into his life like a son.

I shall forever be grateful to him for the tremendous role-model he has been to me, and I shall never cease to praise God for the wonderful covenant-relationship that Brother Copeland and I have enjoyed over the last thirty years.

I trust that you will find my story and the lessons that I share in this book to not only be interesting but also inspiring. It is my prayer that a revelation of the fact that God can do for you what He has done for me will become a reality in your spirit.

Use this book as a handbook or a manual to victorious living. Highlight and underline the principles that minister to you the most. And always remember that God is not a respecter of persons. Your life story is in the making. God has big plans for you.

In Him,

[signature]

1
Hearing the Call

It was 1957. Chevrolet was the hot car that every boy wanted. Blue jeans rolled up around the ankles and white T-shirts were the fad. Everything seemed so black and white. The music was good; everyone in the neighborhood knew each other; and my family was the typical "Happy Days" family stereotype. I was an average eleven year old boy, maybe a little shorter than average, but enjoying life.

One Thanksgiving weekend, my family drove from Shreveport, Louisiana, to Oklahoma City, Oklahoma, to take part in our Thanksgiving Day Family Reunion. It was a cool afternoon, and the family was all gathered around for dinner at my grandmother's home in Nacoma Park. The house was packed full of cousins and aunts and uncles all filling their plates full of traditional Southern style cooking. We had gathered like this many times before, but this year was special.

Grandma's house was very small, but whether you had to eat in the kitchen, the living room, or the bedroom, she could fit you in somewhere. One of my cousins yelled, "Bubba, let's eat by the TV." (Bubba, a nickname I inherited from my little sister, Shirley, trying to say, brother.) So, all the cousins sat around the television on the floor eating our Thanksgiving meal.

I had one cousin, Donny, on one side of me, and Joe on the other side. We were inseparable. Someone turned on Grandma's old black-and-white Philco television set, and I heard this man shouting, **"Who is this Fourth Man? I'll tell you who He is!"** I found out it was a local evangelist named Oral Roberts. I had never heard of Oral Roberts, but his sermon captivated me. He was preaching one of his most famous tent sermons called "The Fourth Man." He revealed how Jesus was manifest in every book of the Bible from Genesis to Revelation.

I was spellbound. Suddenly, just sitting there with my cousins, I heard a voice clearly say these words: *"Someday you'll do that. You'll preach the Gospel, and you'll pray for the sick."* The voice was so loud that I turned to Joe and then to Donny to see what they were saying, but they had already left. It was the Spirit of God – although I didn't know that at the time.

When I realized that my cousins were gone and that it had to be a voice on the inside of me, it frightened me. I didn't tell anybody. But I was still watching this man named Oral Roberts. Suddenly, I began to hear response from some of my relatives about what they thought about this man.

"He's fake!"

"He's a phony!"

"He paid those people to get out of wheelchairs."

Since most of my relatives were from Oklahoma, they had heard of Oral Roberts. Some thought he was great, but some were skeptics. I sat there watching people who were blind begin to see. I saw sick people healed right before my eyes.

Although I was only eleven years old, somehow, I knew it was real. Even though I had never seen anybody pray for the sick before, I knew this was not fake. I pondered those words from the Lord in my heart without telling a living soul for many, many years. *Was it truly God talking to me? Would I really preach someday? Why me?*

How It All Began

It all began on December 24, 1946, when I was born in Vicksburg, Mississippi. I was born to Jerry Wallace Savelle and Attie Snow Savelle. My dad was a veteran of World War II, serving our country in Iwa Jima and Okinawa in the U.S. Navy. My mother was a California girl who lived near the military base in San Diego. She and my dad fell in love and were married in December 1945 after he returned home from the war.

They moved to Vicksburg, Mississippi, where my dad was originally from, and they lived on his father's farm when I was born. Many years later, I was told that the day I was born, my grandmother, Vena Wallace Savelle, took me in her arms and said, "The Lord has something special for this boy." Somehow, she knew that I would do something for the Lord. My little sister, Shirley, was born May 3, 1950, and we grew up in Vicksburg until 1951.

We moved to Shreveport, Louisiana, when I was 5 years old. My mother and dad were Christians. Shirley and I were raised in a Christian home. We went to Pinecroft Baptist Church every Sunday. Mom and Dad worked in the Training Union department with teenagers, and I was in church every time the door was open. I was even voted "Mr. Vacation Bible School."

I believed in God. I believed in Jesus. In fact, I can't remember a time in my life that I didn't believe that Jesus was the Son of God. I had been taught that my whole life. I believed that Jesus died on a cross, was raised from the dead and that He was coming back. I never doubted any of that.

But you can believe all those things, and not make Him Lord of your life. That's the problem. I had not made Him Lord of my life even though I went to church every time the door was open. Being around church and being around Christians was not foreign to me, but I'd never seen anybody pray for the sick like I saw Oral Roberts do on television that day. We didn't do that in our church. I'd never seen anybody cast out devils. We didn't do that in our church. I'd never heard of speaking in tongues. We didn't do that in our church.

The only office of ministry that I was aware of was the office of pastor. As far as our denomination was concerned, the only true evangelist in the world was Billy Graham.

I couldn't really tell you anything about the Baptist doctrine. I knew we believed in Jesus, and I knew they preached about being saved. Every Sunday, our pastor preached about sin, he would give an invitation, and often I saw people get saved. I didn't really know what it meant to have a personal relationship with Jesus. All I knew was when Pastor Jerry Schmucker would give the invitation at the end, people would get up, go to the front, sign a little card, he would pray over them, and the following Sunday night he would baptize them in water. That's all I knew.

Taking the Big Step Forward

After my experience in Oklahoma, I was sitting in church one Sunday morning next to my best friend, Kenny Hennard. Pastor Schmucker preached his message on salvation, and suddenly Kenny got up and walked down to the front. I thought, *I can't believe he did that without me. We do everything together.* He didn't bother telling me what he was going to do, he just got up and walked down to the front, and the Pastor met him there and shook hands with him. Kenny filled out the card, and the next Sunday night Kenny was baptized in water.

Now I really felt like a heathen. I didn't know how long he'd been planning this. Later I found out that he had just got under conviction that morning. I can't say that I noticed a drastic change or immediate change in his life, but I knew he had done something that I had never done. I knew he had overcome shyness, fear and intimidation when he got up in front of that entire church and went forward. I wanted to do that, but I was too shy. I thought, if I walk up there, they'll think, *He really doesn't know what he's doing. He's just a kid.* But it bothered me.

A few weeks later, I was sitting next to my mother, dad and sister in church on Sunday morning. Pastor Schmucker preached, and I just knew that I had to go to the front. I didn't know what to do when I got there, but I thought that if you ever get that "feeling," then you're supposed to go to the front. And I felt that I had the "feeling."

So, I nervously got up, and I took that big step to the front. Pastor Schmucker smiled real big at me with that look, *You're doing the right thing, son.* He grabbed my hand and said in a real deep voice, "Jurry, (that's the way he pronounced my name) it's about time."

I knew that this was his sign of approval that I had taken the right step. I don't remember him mentioning Romans 10:9. He may have. I don't remember him asking me if I'd like to make Jesus the Lord of my life and explaining that to me. He might have. I do remember signing the card for membership.

And as was customary, I was baptized in water the following Sunday night. Something happened to me. I can't explain it, but I knew that something happened to this eleven-year-old boy when I got baptized in water. I later realized that I had experienced a separation. I didn't know exactly what was happening, but I knew I was being separated for something – and that frightened me. I did not want to preach. I didn't ask God for this. The last thing on my mind was preaching the Gospel. That had never entered my mind. But somehow, after I got baptized in water, I just knew that there was a separation. I knew that God had something for my life, and if I did not fulfill it, I would be a miserable human being.

I remember trying as hard as I could to be a good Christian boy right after that experience. I wasn't a bad kid; I didn't do a lot of bad things. I was just average. I loved sports – that was the passion of my life. I tried to stand up for Jesus as best as I knew how.

Praying after the Fact

In the Baptist church, I remember them telling us that dancing was wrong. But all us kids did it anyway. I remember when I went into junior high, we had a field trip one day out at Cross Lake in Shreveport, Louisiana. We were all in an open air pavilion with an old juke box playing, and kids started dancing. Kenny and I were sitting together observing it all, when suddenly, this girl walked up to me and asked, "Would you like to dance?"

For some strange reason, I blurted out, "No, thank you. It's against my religion." I couldn't believe it. Kenny couldn't believe it. This girl was pretty. I wanted to dance with her. She looked at me like, *You poor thing*! And she walked off. I looked at Kenny, and said, "Can you believe I said that?"

That was the last time I said that to a girl. We had parties, and we danced. Of course, when we got to Sunday school, they preached against it and we felt convicted. So we would ask for forgiveness and then go to the dance the very next week. I got into a habit of praying "after the fact."

I would sin and *then* I'd pray. I can remember many times getting down on my knees by my bed asking God to forgive me for something I did. It was never anything terrible, but I was under conviction all the time. The only thing I knew to do was to kneel down at my bed and ask God to forgive me.

Selfish Praying

As I began to participate more as an athlete, there were certain goals that I wanted to achieve. I remember praying about these ambitions and asking God to help me fulfill them. Most of it was selfish praying, asking God to make me the best. I never mentioned *for Your glory*; it was for *my* glory.

I had played baseball ever since Little League. I loved baseball. I decided to try pole vaulting. I had watched some of the other local schools and their pole-vaulters, and I just believed that I could break the high school pole-vaulting record. I only weighed about 90 pounds, but I was strong for my size, and I was fast, and that made me a good athlete.

The night before my first track meet, I got down on my knees in front of my bed, and I prayed. I asked God to help me break the high school pole-vaulting record and to make me the best pole-vaulter in the city. The next day, I was ready to begin my first attempt. I took off with all my speed, with the pole in my hands, and jumped with all my might. When I landed, I broke my leg. I shattered the bones in my calf in my left leg.

I didn't realize that I had broken my leg at the time. I got up limping. I was hurting, but I thought I had just sprained my ankle or something. So I grabbed my pole, went back to the other end, and took off running again. This time, I fell in the cinders before I ever got to the upright.

My friend, Larry Alexander, who was our high school high jumper, helped me up to the gym, and I got in the whirlpool. I had no idea I had broken my leg. I stayed there for about 40 minutes, and then Larry and I walked over to the baseball field to watch our team play. My coach looked at me and said, "Where have you been?"

I said, "Well, I'm a pole-vaulter now." After the game, I went home, and later my dad asked me about baseball practice. I finally said, "Dad, I didn't play baseball."

He said, "Why not?"

I said, "Well, I decided I want to be a pole-vaulter. I'm going to break the high school record in pole-vaulting."

He said, "Well, you know you're best at baseball, and you ought to stick to what you do best."

I said, "Well, you know I love baseball, and I can always do that later, but I've been wanting to do this ever since I was in junior high."

In a little while, the pain got to where I couldn't bear it anymore. I said, "Dad, I think I've broken my leg."

My dad put me in the car and rushed me to the hospital, and sure enough, I'd broken my leg. I was told I would have to be in a cast for thirteen weeks. There went my pole-vaulting career. Not only did it ruin my pole-vaulting career, but it also ruined my "praying career." I thought, *God, I asked You to help me break the pole-vaulting record, and You broke my leg!*

Praying Ceased

I had heard someone say one time, "God will break your leg to teach you something." So, I really thought God did it. I thought

God broke my leg because I didn't pray the way He wanted me to, "Let me break the high school pole-vaulting record *for Your glory.*"

That ended my getting down in front of my bed and praying. I figured there was no need in me praying anymore. That was a turning point in my relationship with God. I still went to church, but I knew it wasn't quite the same. From that moment, praying ceased in my life.

2
The Girl Who Changed Everything

I graduated in 1964 and went off to college at Louisiana Tech University in Ruston, Louisiana. The following year I transferred to Northwestern State College in Natchitoches, Louisiana. Several guys and I lived off campus, and our apartment had become a "casino." We gambled and drank all the time. If my parents had known that their precious little "Mr. Vacation Bible School" was spending most of his nights drinking and gambling, they would have been shocked. I had never tasted beer or smoked cigarettes until I went off to college. I got mixed up with the wrong crowd and began drifting further and further away from God.

On the Way to the Carousel Lounge

I drove home from college one weekend in September 1965 to meet some friends of mine. We had all graduated together and decided we would have our own little reunion at the Carousel Lounge in Shreveport one year after graduation.

Before I got to the Carousel Lounge, I drove to a car wash to get my 1957 Chevy cleaned up. I recognized a girl that I had grown up with, and she was there washing her car. We grew up on the same street, and she used to ride to school in my car with me. She was two years younger than I and was now a Senior in high school. Her name was Carolyn Creech. We talked for a few minutes, and it was good to see her. There were no Cupid arrows; she was just a friend.

Then we parted ways. I was headed toward the Carousel Lounge, but then I noticed that she was headed in the same direction. Eventually, she turned her left signal on and made a left turn. The next thing I knew, I was turning left. I was not supposed to turn left. The Carousel Lounge was straight. I didn't know where she was going. She had turned on a street that I'd never been on before.

I followed her. I didn't even know why I was following her. She pulled up in somebody's driveway. It was a strange house to me. She got out of her car, and said, "What are you doing?"

I said, "I don't know."

She said, "Why are you following me?"

I said, "I don't know. Who lives here?"

She said, "Well, one of my best friends that goes to church with me. Our Sunday school class is meeting here tonight, and we're having a prayer meeting."

I thought, *Oh, dear God. A prayer meeting!* I said, "You're having a prayer meeting?"

She said, "Yes."

I said, "This is how you spend your Friday nights?"

She said, "Yes. Just about every Friday night we either have a prayer meeting or we go out witnessing."

I thought, *What a dull life!* And I should have gotten in my car right then and drove off. But I couldn't. I said, "Well, would you like to go with me?"

She said, "Where are you going?"

I said, "No. You wouldn't like to go with me. Would you like to go somewhere else with me?"

She said, "Where?"

I said, "I don't know. Let's just drive around and talk."

So she went in and told her friends she would be back in a little while, and she got in my car, and we drove to a Dairy Queen and had milk shakes. The next thing I know, she's telling me about Jesus and how she got filled with the Holy Ghost when she was eight years old, and she had had a vision and a call from God that she was going to preach the Gospel. She said that as soon as she got out of high school, she was going to go to Bible school in San Antonio, Texas. Then she said, "And I am going to marry a man who is born again and filled with the Holy Ghost, called to preach, and we'll go to Africa."

My first thought was, *I will never turn left again as long as I live!*

I could hardly wait to get rid of her. I wanted her to drink that milk shake so fast so I could take her back. Finally, I dropped her off at her friend's house and thought, *That's the last time I'll ever see her.*

I headed off to the Carousel Lounge where my buddies were waiting, and boy, was I miserable. I was under conviction so badly, and I didn't want to feel that way. She stirred up things in me that had not been stirred up in a long time. I knew I was about to do something that was wrong, and I was convicted before I ever got there.

My friends said, "Where have you been?"

I said, "You don't want to know."

But I couldn't drink with them. I just couldn't party with them. I was miserable. So, I excused myself, and I went home. The next morning, I got in my car, and I drove back to college thinking that I would never see Carolyn Creech again.

I Can't Get Her Out of My Mind

When I got back to college, I walked into my apartment and saw my roommates lying on the floor, on the couch, and anywhere they could find. There were beer cans everywhere. They'd had another wild weekend, and this time, it bothered me. One of my roommates was from one of the richest families in Minden, Louisiana. He got everything he wanted. His mother would bring him money all the time. He didn't go to the store to buy beer; this guy had connections. The truck backed up to our apartment, and just unloaded the stuff.

When I saw this scene in my apartment, it suddenly became disgusting to me. You can't imagine the smell that was in this place. I hadn't noticed the smell before. People were passed out all over the place. It looked like the den of iniquity. I still hadn't surrendered my life to God, but suddenly, what I saw I didn't like. I did not feel right about living there; I didn't feel right about being in that environment; that's not the way I was raised.

I started gathering up my belongings, put them in my car, and I drove all over town until I found another place to live. I found this great, big house owned by an elderly lady who had rented her upstairs bedrooms out to college students for many years, and she agreed to rent one to me.

Suddenly, I realized that I couldn't quit thinking about this Carolyn Creech. I didn't want to think about her, but there was just something about her and what she said that I just couldn't get out of my mind. So, I called her.

I said, "We've got a homecoming game coming up, and the two best teams in Louisiana are going to be playing. Would you like to go to the ball game with me and afterwards to the dance?"

She said, "Well, I can't go to the dance. I don't go to dances."

I said, "Why not?"

She said, "Well, we don't go to dances."

I said, "It's against your religion?"

She said, "Well, yes it is. Now, if you want to go to the dance and you'd prefer to ask somebody that can, then don't feel badly about doing that."

I said, "Well, no. I've already asked you. So if you'll go to the game with me, then we'll just go out and eat afterwards. We don't have to go to the dance."

And she agreed. So I drove to her house to pick her up. Back then, Carolyn didn't wear very much make-up except for a little bit of lipstick. There we were going to a football game, and she looked like she was going to a Pentecostal revival. I thought, *I've made another mistake.*

We got to the game, and a former schoolmate and a future NFL Hall of Famer, Terry Bradshaw, was playing quarterback for the opposing team. He threw a touchdown pass, and his team scored. I stood up and told him what I thought about it. And Carolyn pulled me down and said, "Please don't talk like that. Do you have to talk like that? Your mother and daddy raised you better than that. I've known you since you were eleven years old. You don't talk like that."

I thought, *This is going to be a dull ball game. You can't even cuss!*

So in a little while, I reached in my pocket, and pulled out my Tampa Jewel cigar with the little wooden tip on the end. Oh, I thought I was cool. I put it in my mouth and got ready to light it, and she said, "Please don't smoke that."

I said, "Why not?"

She said, "Your mother taught you better than that. When did you start smoking? Please don't do that in front of me."

I put my cigar up and I thought, *What a dull ball game! You can't cuss, and you can't smoke.*

My buddies that I had roomed with were sitting behind me, and one of them nudged me and then slipped a little drink my way.

And Carolyn said, "Don't drink that."

I said, "Why not?"

She said, "You grew up in Pinecroft Baptist Church. You weren't raised to smoke, drink, and cuss. Your mom and dad don't do that. Why are you doing this?"

I passed it back to them and they said, "Get rid of her! She's ruining the ball game!"

I was miserable.

So, they all went to the dance, but now I have to take Carolyn to a restaurant. We were having dinner and she started talking to me about Jesus, the Holy Ghost, being a missionary, going to Africa, preaching, etc. I could hardly wait to get rid of her.

After dinner, I took her home, and thought, *That's it. I'm not calling her ever again. If I come home on a weekend, I'm not going to see her. That's it.*

That was on a Saturday night, and by Wednesday of the next week, I was skipping classes just so I could drive home to see her. I could not get her out of my mind. I found out what her last class was and showed up at the high school waiting for her. She was surprised. I was surprised. I couldn't stay away from her. And I didn't want to be with her.

Our times together were spent talking about Jesus, the Holy Ghost, missionaries, and Africa. When I would leave, I fully intended to never see her again. The next thing I knew, I would be driving home on the weekends to see her. I would try to take her to the movies, but she wouldn't go to movies. If I wanted to be with Carolyn Creech, then it was going to be in church.

Introduction to the Holy Ghost

On one of our dates, she took me to Jasper, Texas, to a Pentecostal youth revival. I saw things in that meeting I had never seen in my life. It was the first time I'd ever heard people talking in tongues. I said, "What language are these people speaking?"

She said, "That's the Holy Ghost."

I said, "What?"

She said, "That's called 'speaking in tongues,'" and she tried to explain it to me. Well, it was Greek to me.

I saw them cast out devils. It scared me. The preacher was the loudest person I had ever heard in my life. He screamed and spit on everybody. I liked my Baptist church. It was quiet. Only one person prayed at a time. Nobody lifted their hands.

But in this Pentecostal church, people had their hands lifted, everybody was shouting, praying in tongues, running the aisles, casting out devils, and the women were dancing their Pentecostal buns down! I thought, *This is definitely the last time I will ever see her again.*

But I still couldn't stay away from her. Eventually, I realized that I was falling in love with her. I realized that of all the girls I had ever dated, she was the kind of girl I wanted to marry.

Once I wrote in a letter to my mother, "If I ever get married, Carolyn Creech is the kind of girl I want to marry. I don't understand what it is about her, but I know she's the kind of girl I want to marry."

You're Marrying the Wrong Man!

In May of 1966, Carolyn graduated from high school, I finished my second year of college, and we were engaged to be married. The night before our wedding, Carolyn reminded me, "I've told you all along. I've held nothing back. I made a promise to God when I was eight years old when I got filled with the Holy Ghost, that the man I marry will be born again, filled with the Holy Ghost, preach the Gospel, and go to Africa."

I said, "You're marrying the wrong man."

She said, "No, you're *it*. The first time I ever saw you, when you moved on our street when you were eleven years old, you came riding down on your bicycle, and I was standing in the kitchen helping my mother wash dishes. I looked out the window and saw you, and I told my mother, 'Mom, there's the boy I will marry.'"

Carolyn had known that we would marry ever since she was about nine years old. I loved her. I knew I loved her, and I wanted to be with her. I just thought, *Well, I'll go ahead and marry her, and I can talk her out of all this "preaching" stuff later.*

We were married July 15, 1966, and for the next two years, it became a relationship that was tolerated. Everything in her life was centered around church; everything in my life was centered around Jerry. I was selfish, I was self-centered, and I had ambitions to have my own automotive paint and body shop and to race cars. That's what I lived for. Carolyn lived for God; I lived for me.

Starting a Family

In the latter part of 1967, we were thrilled with the news that we were going to have our first baby in the summer of '68. That same year, I received a letter from a *distant uncle,* Uncle Sam, informing me that I had to report for active duty in the military, and they shipped me off to Fort Dix, New Jersey. While I was in basic training, our first daughter, Jerri Ann, was born on August 8, 1968. I was not able to see her until she was three months old.

After I was released from active duty, I came home and was ready to go into business for myself like I had always intended. I decided that I was not going to work for the "other man" any more, and I was not going to work on wrecked cars for somebody else. I was going to do it for myself.

I opened Jerry's Paint and Body Shop in December 1968. I spent all my time at that shop while Carolyn spent all her time in church. She went to every meeting the church had. I only went after she begged me to go.

Obviously, in a marriage where you have two people with different visions and going in opposite directions, there's a possibility of that marriage perishing. Even though divorce never came up, it had become a marriage where two people were living in the same house with nothing in common. Something had to change.

3
All Those Preachers Want is My Money and My Chicken!

My mother- and father-in-law, Olen and Mary Creech, were very devoted to their church, Life Tabernacle. The pastor always called on them to have the guest speaker stay in their home. Back then preachers didn't stay in hotels very much. So whenever there was a guest speaker in Life Tabernacle Church, they always asked my mother- and father-in-law to take care of the preachers. And that always bothered me.

Carolyn and I lived in a little house next door to her parents which meant that every time a preacher came to town, I had to meet him. When I say I *had to meet them,* I was forced to meet them.

I had seen so many of these preachers take advantage of my father-in-law. My father-in-law is a giving man, he has a big heart, and he loves helping people. I think some of those preachers knew that, and when they got to his house, they took advantage of him. I used to comment about it. Before I surrendered my life to the Lord, I was very outspoken about my feelings about these preachers. So I would tell him, "I can't believe that you let these preachers do you this way. You know most of them are just religious cons. They know that you'll help them. That's the reason they want to stay with you."

He said, "I'm not the one who will suffer. If they are religious cons, they'll suffer; not me. I don't mind giving to these preachers, God always takes care of me."

It always bothered me. It seemed like every time some preacher stayed in their home, I was forced over there to meet him, and the whole family was praying that he would be the one to turn my life around. But I didn't want anything to do with them.

When I would get off work in the evening, I would be covered in bondo dust from head to toe. All I wanted to do was take a shower, put on a clean "Jerry's Paint and Body Shop" uniform and watch TV. The last thing I wanted to do was meet some preacher.

Sometimes I would come home and Carolyn had invited her family and the preacher to our house. That was even worse. I thought all preachers were fat, lazy, and wanted my chicken. I used to gripe and complain about it.

Don't Give My Money to the Preacher!

Back when I was sent to Fort Dix, New Jersey, I knew that I was going to be away for several months, and Carolyn was expecting our first child. We didn't have enough money to last while I was gone so I sold my hot rod. I had a 1965 Pontiac GTO, 389, three duces and a four speed. I used to drag race in it all the time. So, I sold it to give her enough money to live on while I was at Fort Dix.

I called home one night just to check on her, and she said, "We had a meeting at church tonight."

I said, "You did? What else is new? You have a meeting every night."

She said, "I did something tonight I've never done before in my life."

I said, "What was that?"

She said, "You know the money you gave me from the car?"

I said, "Yes."

She said, "Well, I gave most of it to the preacher tonight."

When she said that, you can't imagine how mad I got. I couldn't believe it. I said, "Carolyn, if I had known you were going to give it away, I wouldn't have sold my car. What are you going to do now? How are you going to live?"

I had no revelation of giving. I was making $80 a month with Uncle Sam.

She said, "God will take care of me."

I said, "Why didn't you tell me that before I left, and we could have kept my car?"

Oh, I was mad.

I hung the phone up, and I told a couple of my buddies, "We need to get in a card game, and quick."

They said, "Why?"

I said, "I've got to win my money back."

So we found some guys who wanted to play, and I won all my money back that she had given away. But I didn't send it to her. I held on to it just in case because I knew another preacher was coming, and she'd wind up giving it to him.

I just had this bad impression of preachers. I thought they were all alike and all they wanted was my money and my chicken.

But soon, God was going to show me that not all preachers are that way, and He was about to cause one to cross my path.

4
Surrendering to the Call:
February 11, 1969

Carolyn begged me to go to a meeting to hear a man named Brian Rudd from Canada, who was a former prison inmate, drug addict, and drug dealer who had given his life to Jesus. He was supernaturally released from prison and began traveling all over North America as an evangelist.

I promised her I would go to one service. I wasn't drinking any more, but I kept a pack of cigarettes in my pocket at all times. I wore "Jerry's Paint and Body Shop" uniforms everywhere I went, but Carolyn insisted that I wear something nicer that night.

An Eye-opening Meeting

We got to the church and Carolyn said, "Please don't carry those cigarettes into the church."

I said, "Why not?"

She said, "I don't want people to know that you smoke."

I said, "I don't care if they know that I smoke. If the truth was known, I bet half of them do. They're just hypocrites. At least I'm not a hypocrite about it."

She said, "Well, as a favor to me, would you please leave them in the car?"

I said, "Okay."

So I took my cigarettes out and laid them on the dash of my car. We went into the meeting that night, and this young man came out on the stage. I would have never dreamed he was the preacher. I had never seen a preacher like this before.

The "Hippie Movement" was going on, and this guy looked like a "hippie," and he had a blond, curly Afro. He had white, bell-bottom, hip-hugger pants with a purple shirt, and a brass cow bell around his neck.

It was the first time that Carolyn had ever told me the truth about a preacher. She said, "This one's not like all the rest." She had told me that about every new one that came to town, but this time she was right.

He began sharing his testimony, and it was a dramatic story. It was an awesome story. I was sitting on the edge of my chair listening about this man's deliverance. And right in the middle of his message, he stopped and said, "There is somebody in this room tonight that's going to get delivered of smoking."

He got off the platform, started walking down the aisle, and he walked right up to me and said, "Tonight is your night, young man, to be delivered from smoking."

I looked at Carolyn, and I said, "Did you tell him that?"

I thought she was setting me up. It made me mad. I thought she had already told him about my smoking.

She said, "Jerry, I've never met this man before. He had to hear that from God. He couldn't know it any other way unless God told him."

I said, "Well, why is God so interested in me?"

He said, "Sir, tonight's your night."

I didn't go there to get delivered. I didn't want to be delivered. I liked smoking.

He said, "Come out here in the aisle."

I stood out in the aisle. He said, "Have you got your cigarettes?"

I said sarcastically, "No. She wouldn't let me bring them in."

He said, "Well, is there anybody else in here that smokes?"

And about fifteen hands went up. And I said, "See that? I told you!"

He said, "What kind of cigarettes do you smoke?

I said, "Winston."

He said, "Does anybody in here have some Winstons?"

Some person raised their hand. He said, "Bring them to me."

This person brought their package of Winston cigarettes, and he said, "Put them in this boy's hand." They put them in my hand. He said, "Now you take them out of the package." I took them out of the package. He said, "Hold them." I held them. He said, "Break them in half." I broke them in half. He said, "Throw them on the floor." I threw them on the floor.

Now I didn't know anything about the power of words at this time. He then said, "Now point at them and say, 'In the name of Jesus, I have authority over you, and I'll never smoke again.'"

So I did it. He said, "All right, you're delivered."

So I went back to my seat, and I thought, *I'm delivered. I did not want to be delivered, and I don't feel anything.* I couldn't tell any difference.

He turned around to go back to the platform, and just before he got there, you would have thought somebody had hit him in the stomach. He just turned around and said, "Wait a minute! Come back out here."

I went back out in the aisle, and he said, "You're called to preach. You've known it since you were eleven years old. God told me that you will preach, and it won't be very long from now."

He said, "Young man, I am convinced that my trip from Canada was God sending me to tell you that you're going to preach."

Great! Now the whole church knows I'm called to preach. Nobody had known that but Carolyn. And I wasn't excited. I did not jump up and down, "Oh, hallelujah! I'm going to preach!" I was miserable. Now everybody knows it. I went back to my chair, and I didn't hear another word the man said.

We got out of that service, went back to the car, and I put my cigarettes in my pocket. Carolyn said, "You're through with those."

I said, "Well, I may be through, but I'm going to carry them. I'm not throwing them away just in case this didn't work."

February 11, 1969

The next morning, when I went to my shop, I was the most miserable human being on this planet. I opened my tool box, and there was one tray full of cigarettes and cigars. When I opened the tray, I wanted to smoke so badly I could hardly stand it. I would have lit up a screwdriver if I could have figured out a way to smoke the thing. When I lit my welding torch, the flame on the end of it reminded me of smoking. Everything I did that day reminded me. I thought, *If I can make it through this day, then I am delivered.* I made it through the day, and I never smoked again, praise God.

I started thinking, *This man said I'd be delivered, but he also said I'd preach.* And that I didn't want to do because I was doing what I wanted to do – working on cars, building hot rods, racing. *This preaching's going to foul up everything,* I thought. Oh, I fought it with everything that was in me.

I still hadn't surrendered my life to the Lord. But there was a young man who had attended Brian Rudd's meeting and had been delivered from a drug addiction. I knew him, and I knew his background in drugs.

I saw him get delivered in that meeting. Then I saw the results of his deliverance. This boy became a soul-winner. He was so on fire for Jesus, and I could not deny the miracle that had taken place in his life.

February 11, 1969, is a day that I will never forget as long as I live. Some teenagers next door to us were having a prayer meeting. The house was packed full of teenagers praying and fellowshipping together.

I was standing outside in my yard, and I could hear them praying. In a little while, the young man who had been delivered from drugs came over and started talking to me. He began sharing his testimony with me. I said, "I know who you are, and I know what you used to be, and yes, I can certainly see a difference in your life."

I couldn't deny this miracle that was standing right in front of me. It was real, and I knew it. After talking to him, I went in my house, but I couldn't sleep. Carolyn went to bed. At three o'clock that morning, I was standing in my living room a miserable human being. I finally said, "God, I heard You call me to the ministry when I was eleven years old in my grandmother's home in Oklahoma City. I've run from You, and I have fought this most of my life. I don't know if You still want me or even need me. But if You do, here I am."

I lifted both hands and I said, "Jesus, come into my life. I surrender it to You."

The next thing I knew, I began speaking in a language that I had never spoken before. I felt as though the sun was shining on nobody but me. There was such a warmth, a glow, the glory of God was in my house.

When I finally stopped praying in the Spirit, it was seven o'clock that morning. I had prayed for four hours in the Spirit. I turned around and looked, and there was my wife and my mother-in-law sitting on the couch, crying. I had no idea they were even in the room. When I saw them, I said, "Guess what happened to me?"

They said, "We know. We've been here for several hours."

Carolyn said, "You woke me up. And when I saw what was happening to you, I called my mother."

I surrendered my life to God and was ready to preach the Gospel. The next thing that happened, was a man named Kenneth Copeland came to my home town. My life was never to be the same again.

5
A Man Named Kenneth Copeland

I still had my business, Jerry's Paint and Body Shop, but I knew that it was temporary because now my ambitions had changed. I finally got in line with God's will for my life.

Shortly after I surrendered my life to God that February morning, a man named Kenneth Copeland came to my home town to hold a seminar at Life Tabernacle. I didn't get to attend the first part of the week because of my work. I had to work day and night to get the cars finished so I could shut down my business.

The last night of his meetings, Carolyn asked me to go with her, but first she wanted me to meet him at her mother and daddy's house. I didn't know Kenneth Copeland, nor had I ever heard of him. Carolyn was very impressed with his teaching and would come home every night talking about what she had heard him preach. She would make statements like, "Jerry, I've grown up in this all my life, but I've never heard the Word preached like this before."

Carolyn actually grew up attending the revivals of Oral Roberts, T. L. Osborne, and William Branham. Her pastor, Jack Moore, was one of the pioneers of the Pentecostal message in the state of Louisiana, and he knew all these men. So Carolyn grew up seeing miracles and manifestations of God. But that week she said, "I have never heard anybody like Kenneth Copeland. He's preached things this week that have stirred me up."

In my opinion, Carolyn was always "stirred up," but I could tell that something had happened to her. She was more excited about the Word of God than I had ever seen her before.

Do I Have to Meet Brother Copeland?

I had surrendered my life to the Lord, but I was still very skeptical about some preachers. Brother Copeland was staying at my mother- and father-in-law's home just as all the other traveling ministers did. So naturally, I had to go meet him. I assumed that the only reason he was staying there was to take advantage of them.

I came home from work, and my in-laws had arranged for me to meet the Copelands. That was the last thing in the world I wanted to do. Carolyn said, "Just take a shower and get dressed, and we're going to Mom's house. I want you to meet Brother Copeland and his wife, Gloria, and their children, Kellie and John."

So, reluctantly, I went over there. When I walked in the house, Gloria was sitting there in the living room with my mother- and father-in-law, and they introduced me to her. I thought she was pretty, which was unlike most of the preacher's wives I had met before.

Brother Copeland was somewhere in the other part of the house. I waited and waited, but he never came out. I thought, *I'm doing this guy a favor by coming to meet him, and he won't even come out.* Finally, I told Carolyn, "I'm going home."

She said, "Just wait a minute. He'll be here in a minute."

I didn't know how Brother Copeland conducted himself. I didn't know that he was endeavoring to hear from God. He was very disciplined about it, and he didn't like talking before he went into a service. He wanted the last voice that he heard before he went into the service to be God's voice.

I didn't know these things. Most of those other preachers that came to my father-in-law's house ate chicken right up to the time of the service. But he was different.

So I got tired of waiting on him, and I finally got up to walk out. I headed toward the back door, and just as I did, he came into the room. My father-in-law said, "Brother Copeland, I want you to meet my son-in-law, Jerry Savelle."

I turned around when I heard that, but he walked over toward the kitchen, waved at me, turned his back, and got a drink of water. I thought, *Here I'm doing you a service by coming over here to meet you, and you won't even talk to me.*

I thought, *I'm out of here.* I started back to the door, and all of a sudden, Brother Copeland said, "Hey! Wait a minute!"

I turned around, and he pointed his finger at me and looked at me with those piercing eyes, and he said, "God is going to prosper you beyond your wildest imaginations."

Then he turned around, drank his water, and went back to his bedroom.

I'm standing there thinking, *Carolyn has been talking to him!* I thought she had told him about my business, my debts and everything. I thought she had set me up again. I walked out, and I went back to my house.

When I got there, I started thinking about what he said. I thought, *Well, maybe she didn't talk to him. Maybe that was God talking through him.* And then the next thing I thought was, *Hey, I'm not going to have to go into the ministry! God's going to prosper me!*

I had never associated prosperity with preaching. I thought, *God is saying all He wants me to do is just give my life to Him. Now I can keep my business and not have to preach, and God's going to prosper me through this business.*

So, when Carolyn got home, I said, "What do you think he meant?"

She said, "Well, the first thing I want you to know is that I didn't tell him anything because I know that's what you were thinking. I didn't tell him anything. That's the first time I've ever met him, too."

I said, "Does he mean, God's going to bless my business, and I'm going to have a prosperous business?"

She said, "No."

I said, "Well, what is he talking about?"

She said, "You know what he's talking about. The ministry."

I said, "You can't prosper like he's talking about and be a preacher. If you could, then why do they all come to your daddy's house to try to get something from him?"

She said, "I don't know, but I know this man's different than the others."

We went to the service that night, but I was still a little skeptical. I thought it would be like all the other services that Carolyn had taken me to.

Who Does He Think He Is?

After the singing, the pastor came forward and said, "Now before Brother Copeland speaks to us tonight, our choir is going to sing one more song. And then immediately after they finish their song, Brother Copeland will be speaking."

This church was known for its music. They had a phenomenal choir, and the pianist, Anna Jean Price, actually studied piano with Van Cliburn. So they began singing a song that I had heard all my life in the Baptist church. And when they finished, Brother Copeland walked up to the pulpit, grabbed the sides of it like he was riding a motorcycle, pointed his finger to the choir director and said, "Don't ever sing that song in my presence again. It is embalmed with unbelief!"

All of a sudden, I became a crusader. It made me mad. I leaned over to Carolyn and said, "Who does he think he is? We can sing anything we want to in our church."

All of a sudden it's "our" church. I said, "We can sing whatever we want to in our church. He can't tell us what we can sing. I thought you said this man was great. He can't come in here and tell us what we can't sing in our church."

She said, "Jerry, just be quiet."

Before he preached his sermon, he started picking the verses of that song apart and showed us how they didn't line up with the Word of God. Well, he got my attention. I believe to this day, that God had him do that for me. I could hardly wait to hear what he would say next. Carolyn was right. I had never heard anything like this before, and he was not like all the rest.

6
The Message that Changed My Life

To this day, I have the outline of the sermon he preached that night that absolutely changed my life forever. It was a message simply called, "The Word of Faith."

I had never heard anything like this in my life. He explained the life of faith where you could understand it. He made the Bible come alive. Prior to that, I thought it was just a history book and a story book. But he made the words jump off the pages and into your heart.

His sermon changed my life that night. I went home with a whole new outlook. I was stirred up.

The next morning when I went to my shop, I couldn't think about anything else but what I heard the night before. I sent my helpers home. I said, "Go home, guys. We're not working today."

They said, "Why not?"

I said, "I don't know. I just can't work on cars today. Just go home. Take the day off."

They said, "You've got customers coming for their cars."

I said, "I'll call them. They can come get them tomorrow. Just go home."

God Can Make Champions Out of Failures

I shut the overhead door to my shop. I locked my office door, walked up to my desk, and picked up a Bible that Carolyn had put in there when I first opened that shop that I had never read. For some reason, I just felt like I needed total privacy that day. I went into the little restroom and sat on the floor with that Bible trying to find those Scriptures that Kenneth Copeland preached the night before. All day long I sat there with my Bible, crying like a baby, asking God, "Is this real? Is what he said real? Will it really work? If so, that's what I want with all my heart."

I said, "Lord, I'm a failure. I've failed at my business. I've failed at my marriage. What can You do with a failure?"

I will never forget what I heard the Lord say that day. He said, "Son, don't worry. I am a Master at making champions out of failures."

By the end of that day, I was a new man.

Now, all of a sudden, I wished I could have been in that entire seminar and heard everything Kenneth Copeland said. I had 9,000 questions, but now Brother Copeland was gone. He was back in Fort Worth while all this was happening to me.

Learning to Receive

When I got home that night, a lady from the church, who was a friend of Carolyn's, came over.

She said, "I was praying today, and God told me to bring you something."

I said, "What?"

She said, "Kenneth Copeland was here last week, and he recorded his messages. God told me to bring you the tapes of those services. Here's the seven tapes from those meetings."

And she reached in a bag and handed me these seven-inch reels that had messages on each side. And she said, "God told me that if you'll listen to these, it will change your life forever."

I said, "Well, I appreciate this, but I don't know how I'm going to listen to them. I don't have a tape player."

She said, "I'll be back."

She left, and came back with a huge tape player. They did not have cassettes back then. This tape player was big, and it had speakers attached to it.

She said, "Forgive me."

I said, "Why?"

She said, "God told me to give you my tape player too, but I was hoping that you already had one so I wouldn't have to give mine away."

I said, "Well, I can't take your tape player."

I was not accustomed to people giving me things. I was Mr. Independent. You couldn't give me anything. If I couldn't earn it with my own hands, then I didn't want it. I said, "No, I'm not taking this."

She said, "Well, God told me."

I said, "I don't care. I can't take this."

She said, "Well, let me loan it to you. And you listen to these tapes."

So I said, "Okay. I'll borrow it until I listen to these tapes."

I set that tape player up in our guest bedroom, and I put a

little desk in there, got a notebook, and I would listen to those tapes at night after Carolyn would go to bed. The first tape I listened to was the last message of the series, "The Word of Faith." That's the one I had heard him preach, and I wanted to hear it again.

I got so excited. It was almost unbelievable. It was almost too good to be true. You have to understand, there were not many Word of Faith preachers around at that time. This man preached a message that you didn't hear in most churches.

I began hearing things that I knew were going to change my life forever. So I got the idea that I would listen to those tapes over and over again. If he said something that I didn't understand, I could stop the tape and make him say it again. I would listen to a message, rewind it, and listen to it over and over again. After I'd done all fourteen of those messages that way many times, I began to understand it. The Word was coming alive in my heart.

I started outlining every sermon. I would write it all down, and then I would type my outlines on my little typewriter. I still have that original notebook that I started back in 1969.

I wrote down the key points that Brother Copeland made in his messages, and then I would endeavor to put them to work in my own life. In this book, you will find several of my original outlines. These were the most important things that ministered to me, and I believe they will minister to you as well. Read these outlines, study them, re-read them and meditate on every point until it becomes a revelation to you.

The Word of Faith

A.   **Faith is the substance.**

        1.   **Hebrews 11:1-3** -- *Now faith is the substance of things hoped for, the evidence of things not seen. For by it the elders obtained a good report. Through faith we understand that the worlds were framed by the word of God, so that things which are seen were not made of things which do appear.*

2. Faith is the substance of things hoped for.

3. Faith causes the world of hope to become a reality.

4. What God says is true, and faith will cause it to come to pass.

5. Without faith, hope has no substance. Therefore, hope alone will produce no results.

Most of my life I heard Christians talk about "hoping and praying," but Brother Copeland stated that hoping and praying alone will not produce results. He said it takes faith to get results.

6. Some say you can't believe in things you cannot see, but you do it every day.

Brother Copeland asked the congregation this question. *How many of you in here have a brain?* They all lifted their hands, and then he asked: *When was the last time that you saw it?*

I thought, *Yes, you can believe in something you cannot see.* Then he asked this question. *Now let's see it on a spiritual level. How many of you believe that your names are written in the Lamb's Book of Life?* Everybody lifted their hand. He then said, *Would someone stand up who has recently seen the Book? Have you seen the Book? No. So you can believe in something you cannot see?*

The point he was endeavoring to make is, faith is the evidence of things not seen.

Hebrews 11:1 Amplified says, *Now Faith is the assurance (the confirmation, the title deed) of the things [we] hope for, being the proof of things [we] do not see and the conviction of their reality [faith perceiving as real fact what is not revealed to the senses].*

Brother Copeland paraphrased it like this, **. . . *faith is the title deed of the things hoped for, the evidence of things not yet revealed to the five physical senses.***

I will never forget when I heard that. It really made an impact in my life. Faith is the title deed of the things hoped for, the evidence of things not yet revealed to the five physical senses. Even if I can't see it, feel it, or touch it, that doesn't mean that it doesn't exist. I can't touch God physically, but He does exist. I can't feel the Holy Ghost physically, but He does exist. I can't see the angels with my natural eyes, but they do exist. He was introducing to me a whole new lifestyle.

B. **Faith-filled words.**

    1. **Hebrews 11:3** -- *Through faith we understand that the worlds were framed by the word of God, so that things which are seen were not made of things which do appear.*

        Genesis 1:1-3 -- *In the beginning God created the heaven and the earth. And the earth was without form, and void; and darkness was upon the face of the deep. And the spirit of God moved upon the face of the waters. And God said, Let there be light: and there was light.* (**God made the world with the words of His mouth.**)

    2. **When you understand that you have the ability to speak faith-filled words just like God, then this is the key to victorious Christian living.**

    3. **1 John 5:1-5** -- *Whosoever believeth that Jesus is the Christ is born of God: and every one that loveth him that begat loveth him also that is begotten of him. By this we know that we love the children of God, when we love God, and keep his commandments. For this is the love of God, that we keep his commandments: and his commandments are not grievous. For whatsoever is born of God overcometh the world: and this is the victory that overcometh the world, even our faith. Who is he that overcometh the world, but he that believeth that Jesus is the Son of God?*

C. **Faith is released through the words of your mouth.**

    1. **Your words should have the same power behind them as if Jesus had spoken them.**

    2. **Matthew 12:36-37** -- *But I say unto you, That every idle word that men shall speak, they shall give account thereof in the day of judgment. For by thy words thou shalt be justified, and by thy words thou shalt be condemned.*

The power of words. They'll make you; they'll break you. They'll bring victory; they'll bring defeat. They'll bring healing; they'll bring sickness.

D. **You can have what you say.**

   1. **There is a miracle in your mouth. Mark 11:23** -- *For verily I say unto you, That whosoever shall say unto this mountain, Be thou removed, and be thou cast into the sea; and shall not doubt in his heart, but shall believe that those things which he saith shall come to pass; he shall have whatsoever he saith.*

This was the first time that I ever heard Mark 11:23. It made a profound impact in my life.

   2. **Matthew 12:34** -- *. . . for out of the abundance of the heart the mouth speaketh.*

Brother Copeland gave an illustration to show how this works. He said that the night before, when he arrived at the church, he went into the bookstore, and there were two ladies working there.

While he was looking around, one of the ladies spoke to the other one and said, "My, I can hardly talk today. My throat is so sore, I think I'm losing my voice."

The other lady said, "What did you say? I can't hear. I think I'm going deaf!"

Brother Copeland had been preaching all week long on faith-filled words; you can have what you say; death and life are in the power of the tongue; and one of these ladies is losing her voice, and the other one's going deaf. So he used them as an illustration showing that out of the abundance of the heart the mouth speaks.

He said, "For some of you, it doesn't make any difference what the Word says. You're going to talk like you've always talked anyway."

He said, "If God turned the volume up on the power of their words, then these two ladies together would be deaf and dumb."

I will never forget what an impression that made on me. I was realizing that a lot of the torment that I had been going through, and the problems I had been experiencing, had been a result of my mouth. Nobody had ever told me that before. Nobody had ever told me that the biggest problem I had in my life was my mouth. But now it was beginning to make sense. This message was getting down into my spirit and changing the way I talked.

3. **Psalm 91:2-3** -- *I will say of the Lord, He is my refuge and my fortress: my God; in him will I trust. Surely he shall deliver thee . . .*

Brother Copeland said, **"Even David in his day knew this spiritual law: You can have what you say."**

4. **1 Samuel 17:46** -- David said to Goliath, *This day will the Lord deliver thee into mine hand; and I will smite thee, and take thine head from thee; and I will give the carcases of the host of the Philistines this day unto the fowls of the air. . .*

Brother Copeland said, **"David said what he would do; God honored his words, and with his words he slew Goliath."**

I always thought it was that rock that slew Goliath, but Brother Copeland pointed out that it started with his words.

E. **Put a guard on your mouth.**

    1. **Never confess sickness, disease, poverty, failure, lack, or want.**

    2. **Proverbs 6:2** — *Thou art snared with the words of thy mouth.*

    3. **Confession brings possession.**

    4. **Begin to believe that everything you say will come to pass,** and you'll stop saying some of the things you used to say.

F. Talk the Word of God.

   1. If you can't talk the Word, shut up!

   2. Your words are either filled with faith or doubt and unbelief.

   3. Words are vehicles. They're carriers of either faith or doubt and unbelief. *(handwritten: seed containers)*

G. Faith demands action.

   1. James 2:17 – *Even so faith, if it hath not works, is dead, being alone.*

   2. **It's not enough just to say it, it has to have corresponding actions.**

   He gave this illustration. "If somebody came running in this church tonight, screaming 'The building's on fire! The building's on fire!' everybody who believes that would have corresponding actions. You would get up and run out. If you don't believe it, and you're only moved by what you can see or what you can smell, then you'll sit around and look for the smoke, or try to smell the smoke." He said, "If what they were saying was the truth, then your unbelief is going to be very costly. So there must be corresponding actions. If you're going to say, *By His stripes I am healed,* then act healed. Talk health; talk the Word; get up and do something you couldn't do before."

   3. **Hold fast to your confession. Hebrews 10:23** -- *Let us hold fast the profession of our faith without wavering; (for he is faithful that promised).*

   4. **Faith comes by hearing, and hearing by the Word of God.** The more Word you put in your heart, the greater your faith will become.

   That's the message that changed Jerry Savelle's life thirty years ago! And it's still working in my life today. When I read these notes, I can picture myself sitting there at that desk, in that bedroom on Trainy Lane in Shreveport, Louisiana. I never dreamed at that time that God would send me around the world to proclaim this same message. Or that He would use me to touch the lives of hundreds of thousands of people.

Consuming the Word

I was hungry for God. I sat there at that desk, listening to those tapes over and over and over. Every message became a revelation to me, and I couldn't get enough. I had never had anything to affect my life like this before.

Our second daughter, Terri Lynn, was born on September 30, 1969. Shortly after Terri was born, I shut my business down. I studied the Word just like it was my job. I knew how devoted I was to my job. So, I spent eight, ten, twelve, seventeen hours a day studying those seven tapes.

I moved into that bedroom like it was my place of business, and I spent no less than eight hours a day in the Word. I came out at noon, had lunch with the family, went back in there at 1:00, came out at 5:00, had dinner with the family, and then played with my daughters. When they went to bed, I went right back into that bedroom, listened to those tapes, and studied until I would fall asleep.

Those tapes became my university. I couldn't get enough information. I was hungry for God; I was hungry for knowledge; I had a quest to live by faith like Brother Copeland talked about on those tapes. I wanted to preach more than I wanted to do anything else.

I just believed that if it would work for Kenneth Copeland, then it could work for me. As I kept listening to those tapes, he often referred to a man named Kenneth Hagin. I didn't know who Kenneth Hagin was, but it became obvious that Brother Copeland had learned most of this from him. He saw it work for Kenneth Hagin, and he believed it would work for him too. And it did. In fact, it will work for anyone who will dare believe it.

I dissected those fourteen messages until I had outlines on every one of them. I listened to them until it was no longer just Kenneth Copeland's revelation, but it became Jerry Savelle's revelation.

I did that for three solid months. I totally immersed myself in those messages. And at the end of those three months, I came out of that bedroom with the fire of God in my eyes, the Word of God in my heart, the power of God in my hands, and I was ready to preach.

I didn't start preaching in the churches because there wasn't a church that wanted me. I went to the streets. My first sermons were in the streets to drug addicts, prostitutes and alcoholics. I saw all those messages actually work right there in the street. God started giving me such phenomenal results in the streets that the churches started hearing about it, and the next thing I knew, they wanted me in their church. Here I was, a nobody, with no formal training, but God was honoring His Word in my life with signs following.

I encourage you right now, no matter how knowledgeable you may be in the Word already, to read that outline on "The Word of Faith" as if you've never heard it before. Read it over and over again. There may be some truths that you have let slip in your life, and now it's time to pick them back up and start applying them again. Put the Word of Faith to work in your life and watch God bring phenomenal results to you just as He did for me.

Handwritten note: We R. in the financial situation today because of the idle words we have spoken in the past.

* giving much & receiving little.

7
How to Apply the God Kind of Faith

The focus of this book is not for you to simply read my life story, but to learn the principles that changed my life from being a failure to becoming a champion for Jesus. I want to show you through my personal life, by example, the challenges I overcame by putting these spiritual laws to work. These outlines that I'm sharing with you are what gave me a story to tell.

The Proving Time

When I began studying Brother Copeland's tapes, I was approximately $30,000 in debt. My business debts were about $15,000. I owed about $12,000 on my home, and then personal bills were another $4,000.

In 1969, if you're $30,000 in debt, that is a lot of money. And then when you decide that you're going to lock yourself in a bedroom and study the Bible, and you've got all these debts – it looks like an impossible situation to overcome.

My dad and I had always been extremely close. He taught me to work and to work hard. He told me that a man that won't work is worse than an infidel. If you don't work, you don't eat. And he got really concerned when I quit my business to study the Word.

When God told me to leave my business, I was concerned about my bills. I was concerned about my family and putting food on the table. So I asked Him about it. I said, "Well, God, how am I going to get my needs met while I'm studying the Bible?"

He said, "If you will put Me first place, and put My Word first place, I will take care of you."

He didn't say *don't work,* He just said, "If you'll put Me and My Word first place, I'll take care of you."

And consequently, I would get a call every once in a while, and somebody would say, "Jerry, I need for you to work on my car."

Even though I didn't have my shop anymore, I worked on several cars just out in my carport. And that would be enough to sustain me, to keep the bills paid and keep food on the table.

Every once in a while, I would have someone ask me to come do odd jobs like carpentry work or something. For instance, my father-in-law asked me to come help him finish a house that he was building. I'd never worked on a house. I didn't know anything about carpenter work.

I said, "Well, I'll be happy to help you, but I just want you to know that I don't know one board from another, nor one nail from another. That's not my expertise, but I'll be happy to help you. I'll burn trash for you. I'll haul lumber. I'll do whatever you need me to do."

And I did. I went out there, and I worked on that house with him. When I got home, I was tired. I had my dinner, fellowshiped with my family, and when they went to bed, I got my eight hours in of studying the Word of God. I may have had to stay up all night to do it, but I had made a commitment to God that I would be faithful to study the Word, and I stuck to it.

At the end of that week, I received one of the greatest blessings. My father-in-law said to me, "God told me to give you half of my commission." Hallelujah! It reduced my debts tremendously.

It was enough for me to go in and pay off a lot of my bills. God was sustaining me. God was meeting my need.

I never missed my eight hours in all that time. And when I didn't have something to do in the way of physical labor, then I would spend twelve, fifteen, seventeen hours a day in the Word. God honors faithfulness.

This next outline is from a message Brother Copeland taught entitled, "Applying the God Kind of Faith." You may read some of the same things from the first outline, but repetition is how you get the Word in you. Make your own notes next to these outlines and study them over and over again.

Applying the God Kind of Faith

A. Have the faith of God.

    1. Mark 11:22 – *And Jesus answering saith unto them, Have faith in God.*

    2. The literal Greek says, "Have the faith of God."

    3. **Jesus is telling us that we can operate in the same kind of faith in which God operates.**

    4. If we can't, then Jesus would have never said, "Have it."

    5. The understood subject in this sentence is "you," meaning "you" can have the God kind of faith.

B. Who can have the God kind of faith?

    1. Romans 12:3 – *For I say, through the grace given unto*

me, to every man that is among you, not to think of himself more highly than he ought to think; but to think soberly, according as God hath dealt to every man the measure of faith. **This verse tells us that God has dealt to every man the measure of faith. (That is, every born-again person).**

2. **Ephesians 2:8** — *For by grace are ye saved through faith; and that not of yourselves: it is the gift of God.*

3. **The God kind of faith is God's gift to you.**

4. **You receive this faith at the New Birth.**

5. **It begins with a measure, but it can increase. Romans 10:17** — *So then faith cometh by hearing, and hearing by the word of God.*

C. **Faith is released through the mouth.**

1. **Romans 10:8-10** — *But what saith it? The word is nigh thee, even in thy mouth, and in thy heart: that is, the word of faith, which we preach; That if thou shalt confess with thy mouth the Lord Jesus, and shalt believe in thine heart that God hath raised him from the dead, thou shalt be saved. For with the heart man believeth unto righteousness; and with the mouth confession is made unto salvation.* With the mouth, confession is made unto salvation.

2. **In Mark 11:23, Jesus said the word "say," three times. He said the word, "believe," once.** The point is, **Keep saying it until you believe it.** In other words, the emphasis was on the "saying." And if you say it enough, you'll begin to believe it.

D. **Examples of this kind of faith in the New Testament.**

1. **Mark 5:21-24.** Jairus said, "Come lay Your hands on my daughter, and she shall be healed." He released his faith through his words.

2. **Mark 5:25-34** — *And a certain woman, which had an issue of blood twelve years, And had suffered many things of many physicians, and had spent all that she had, and was nothing bettered, but rather grew worse, When she had heard of Jesus, came in the press behind, and touched his garment. For she said, If I may touch but his clothes, I shall be whole.*

And straightway the fountain of her blood was dried up; and she felt in her body that she was healed of that plague. And Jesus, immediately knowing in himself that virtue had gone out of him, turned him about in the press, and said, Who touched my clothes? And his disciples said unto him, Thou seest the multitude thronging thee, and sayest thou, Who touched me?

And he looked round about to see her that had done this thing. But the woman fearing and trembling, knowing what was done in her, came and fell down before him, and told him all the truth. And he said unto her, Daughter, thy faith hath made thee whole; go in peace, and be whole of thy plague.

The woman with the issue of blood **said,** "If I but touch His clothes, I shall be made whole." She released her faith through her words.

3. **Faith-filled words changed the laws of sickness, disease, and death.**

E. **Faith will not work above the level of your confession.**

1. **Proverbs 18:21** — *Death and life are in the power of the tongue.*

2. **Avoid making negative confessions by filling your heart with the Word of Faith.**

Faith Works Every Time

These basic principles that I'm sharing with you will work whether you need $100 or whether you need $100,000. Why? Because faith couldn't care less about the amount. It just goes to work removing the circumstances that are hindering you from experiencing victory.

If you've got adversity in your life today, then I challenge you to use these outlines that I'm giving you. Go back and check up on what you've been saying. Ask God to give you supernatural recall of everything you've said, and you'll be surprised at what's been coming out of your mouth. Remember, you can have what you say.

In a faith-filled atmosphere, it's easy to talk the Word. But under pressure, what are you talking? Use these outlines as your checklist. That's what I've done for thirty years, and it works every time.

8
Channeling the Force of Faith

During those three months of studying the Word, I just had to find an outlet – somewhere to share what I was learning. The churches didn't want me, so I took it to the streets. The churches thought I had gotten too caught up in this "faith stuff." It seemed that they wanted me saved but not radical.

Taking It to the Streets

I would sit out in front of a bar and would wait for someone to stagger out so that I could share Jesus with them. When someone staggered out, I grabbed him and sat him down on that curb next to me. I'd preach everything I had learned on those tapes. Not one time did one of those drunks say, "We don't believe it that way. That's passed away. That's not for us today."

In fact, the first man that I preached to had just come out of a bar, and he was drunk. I preached for about one hour to him. But he never heard a word I said. He was asleep on my shoulder. But the second hour, he began to sober up, and he began to listen to what I said. The third hour, I got him born-again, filled with the Holy Ghost, and delivered! Then he went in that bar and brought all his buddies out and lined them up on the curb. I stood in front of them, and preached to 15 or 20 drunks. I led every one of them to the Lord, invited them to church, but some of the churches didn't want them.

They didn't smell very good, they didn't look very good, but they had experienced a miracle in their lives. They had heard some Good News probably for the first time in their lives.

I had never done drugs. I didn't know one drug from another. But I remember the Lord telling me, "It's not your knowledge of drugs that will win these people. It's your knowledge of Me. Tell them about Me."

So I'd get right in the middle of these drug addicts and drunkards. I would just share Jesus with them from my heart and win many of them to the Lord.

I was having such phenomenal results in the streets with young people getting delivered and set free, that their parents noticed a drastic change, and began to call me. They would ask, "Who are you? What do you do? We know other kids that need help." The next thing you know, I am going all over Shreveport to people's homes praying for their children. Then, I began getting invitations to preach in jails. My home had become a haven for kids who wanted to get delivered from drugs. My ministry began as a result of me taking what I had learned from Kenneth Copeland and preaching it in the streets.

What's In Your Heart Will Come Out

Later, when I first went to work for Brother Copeland, he was to speak in a meeting in Colorado. I normally went ahead of him to set up everything, driving his Buick Wild Cat Station Wagon. We carried almost everything Kenneth Copeland Evangelistic Association owned in the back of that station wagon.

The local Full Gospel Businessmen's Association had agreed to help sponsor the meeting. So when I got there, they asked me, "Would you like to come to our dinner banquet tonight?"

I said, "Yes, I'd be happy to."

They said, "Well, we don't have a speaker; would you like to speak?"

I thought, *Would I! Do you have any idea what you have just asked?*

Brother Copeland had a Bible course on reel-to-reel tapes called "The Believer's Basic Bible Study." It contained 64 messages. I had listened to every one of them many times. I had outlined every one of them. And I could preach every one of them.

And when they said, "Would you like to be our speaker tonight?" I preached all 64 messages in one service!

When Brother Copeland got there, I said, "Sir, we don't need you now, I've already preached everything you know!"

You can do the same thing. Take these outlines, study them until it becomes your revelation and then preach them word-for-word. You'll begin to have your own testimonies, your own experiences and illustrations that will eventually help someone else.

There are hundreds of thousands of people getting born again every day that have never heard anything like this in their lives. Don't assume everybody's already heard these basic truths.

Don't wait until you come up with your own sermon hot off the press. Get these basic but powerful revelations down in your spirit and then preach them to anyone who will dare to listen.

The following is another outline from those fourteen messages by Kenneth Copeland that I studied for three months. Read it, study it and then put it to work in your life.

Channeling the Force of Faith

A.   Faith is always now.

    1.   **Hebrews 11:1-3 (Amplified)** – *Now faith is the*

assurance (the confirmation, the title deed) of the things [we] hope for, being the proof of things [we] do not see and the conviction of their reality [faith perceiving as real fact what is not revealed to the senses].

    2. Romans 4:17. God speaks of things that are not as though they were.

    3. The world says, "I'll believe it when I see it," but faith says, "I believe it, then I'll see it."

    4. "Libraries make swelled heads, but the Word of God makes enlarged hearts." (A quote from Smith Wigglesworth.)

    5. Feed your heart God's Word; faith comes by hearing the Word continually. (Romans 10:9).

B. What faith is NOT.

    1. Faith is not the product of reasoning.

    2. Faith is not produced from the head; it comes from the heart.

    3. Faith is not a product of the mind; faith is produced in the spirit of man.

    4. Faith IS the product of the re-born human spirit. (Ephesians 2:8).

C. The force of faith.

    1. Faith is a spiritual force that can change things in the natural, material realm.

    2. The head reasons, but the heart acts.

    3. When the heart acts, it releases faith, and that faith will move mountains.

    4. When you feed your spirit God's Word on a daily basis, it always produces the force of faith.

5. The words of your mouth release the force of faith.

6. A fearless confession comes from a Word-ruled heart.

7. God's Word in your mouth becomes just like the Word in Jesus' mouth.

8. A doubting heart is a sense-ruled heart.

9. Your hand is the carrier of the strength that is in your arm. The words of your mouth are the carriers of the faith that is in your heart.

D. Faith-filled words.

1. Faith-filled words are the most powerful things in the universe.

2. Fear-filled words can make you sick; faith-filled words can make you well.

3. Faith-filled words will create.

4. Faith-filled words will bring the impossible to pass.

E. Hope has no substance.

1. To only hope to get healed has no substance; faith is the substance of things hoped for. (Hebrews 11:1).

2. When you give substance to your hope, then the Holy Spirit causes it to become a reality.

3. You must say what you believe. (Mark 11:23).

4. Get to the place in your life where you believe everything that you say will come to pass.

5. Begin to put a high premium on words.

F. Your words will make you or break you.

   1. *Proverbs 6:2 — Thou art snared with the words of thy mouth.*

   2. **Come to the place in your life where you begin to believe that your confession of God's Word is more real than your problem.**

   3. Put God's Word first place in your life.

   4. Get rid of the "buts" in your vocabulary. Stop saying, "I know the Word says it, but you don't understand my problem."

   5. Confession brings possession.

My heart rejoices to this very day when I read these outlines. This is where it all started for me. Now it's time for you to begin your new walk of faith!

9
Putting the Word to Work

I can remember reading these outlines, sitting there in my bedroom for hours, and then endeavoring to put them to work in my life. I heard Brother Copeland say on one of those tapes that once when he was ministering in a particular city, a lady called him and said that her baby was dying. He said that the anointing of God just came on him when he heard her say that, and he shouted very boldly, "That baby will live and not die!"

Then he gave the illustration that this had happened to Brother Hagin when a relative called him and said someone was dying. Brother Hagin just shouted out, "They'll live and not die, in the name of Jesus. I'm saying it according to Mark 11:23. They'll live and not die."

It turned out that the person didn't die. Brother Copeland simply did what he learned from Brother Hagin. He reported how the baby lived and was growing up healthy and normal.

I heard that illustration so many times listening to those tapes over and over. Not too long after that, the young people at our church were going to have a party at a lake on a Saturday afternoon.

They asked Carolyn and me to act as chaperones with some other adults. And so we went.

We were all having a great time out at the park when suddenly, some teenagers came running up to me and said that there was a man in the parking lot crying saying that his baby was dying.

They told the man, "Just a minute!" And they came and got me. So I ran over to the man and noticed he was slumped over his steering wheel, and he was crying. I said, "Sir, can I help you? What's the problem?"

He said, "My baby's dying! My baby's dying! I don't know what to do!"

I said, "Where do you live?"

He said, "About two miles from here."

I said, "Where's the baby?"

He said, "With my wife."

So, I said, "I'll go with you. We'll pray."

He said, "You will?"

I said, "Yes. We can pray. God can change this. All things are possible to him that believes."

Everything that I had been listening to started coming up out of my spirit. I had put God's Word in my heart in abundance.

I looked at him. Even though I didn't try to copy Brother Copeland or Brother Hagin, I'd heard them say it so many times, "Out of the abundance of my heart my mouth spoke." I pointed my finger at him, and I said, "Sir, the baby will live and not die. Let's go."

We drove out to his house. This man lived in poverty. It broke my heart to see how these people lived. We went into this house that was just barely standing. It was pitiful. There was hardly any furniture in it, and what furniture there was, was falling apart. I walked into this man's bedroom, his wife was lying on an old spring that had no mattress on it, just a blanket with this baby. The baby was swollen up, dying. I don't know what was wrong with the baby, but it was obvious that the baby was dying.

I walked over and laid my hands on that baby, and I began to shout, "The baby will live and not die in the name of Jesus! According to Mark 11:23, I can have what I say, and I say in the name of Jesus, this baby will live and not die! I know you folks don't understand this, but just say what I say. Point your hand towards this baby and say, 'The baby will live and not die; the baby will live and not die.'"

The anointing of God absolutely consumed that place. They started crying, and I led them both to the Lord. The baby started getting better right there in our presence. Years later, I got a picture from that couple, and that baby was about four or five years old, doing well, and never had another problem. I saw the Word work right before my eyes!

Brother Copeland learned these things from Brother Hagin. He outlined all of Brother Hagin's tapes. He set up a desk in his garage, listened to Brother Hagin's tapes day and night, outlined them, and then went out and preached them, word-for-word, just like Kenneth Hagin.

I heard how Brother Copeland did that, and I saw the results in his life. I wanted what I saw, so I did the same thing. God is no respecter of persons. What He's done for one, He will do for another if they will believe.

Faith will work for anyone – it will work for you. Make a decision right now that you're going to fill your spirit with God's Word and watch what God will begin to do in your life.

Are you ready for the next outline? Here it is. Study it carefully until it becomes a revelation to you.

Real Bible Faith, Part I

A.   Victory that overcomes the world.

1. **1 John 5:1-5.** *This is the victory that overcomes the world, even our faith.*

2. According to these verses, victory belongs to me.

3. My faith is my method of victory over the world.

B. The three most common questions asked by Christians.

1. Who has the right to victory?

2. How do you get victory?

3. Will victory come to me?

4. The answers are found in 1 John 5:1-5.

C. Always go to the Word of God for your answer.

1. **John 17:17** -- *Sanctify them through thy truth: thy word is truth.* **Jesus said thy word is truth.**

2. The definition of "truth" is "the highest form of reality that exists."

3. God's Word is more real than my problem.

D. How real Bible faith works.

1. Real Bible faith always wants to know what God thinks.

2. Real Bible faith always wants to know what the Bible says about my problem.

3. The Bible will never tell you that you can't have it or that you can't do it.

4. The Bible always says it's already yours. Now receive it.

5. You can't receive it if you don't know it belongs to you. God's Word is His will for your life.

E. Will God do it for you?

1. Everything Jesus did at Calvary was for your benefit.

2. God looks at you through the Blood of Jesus.

3. In the eyes of God, you're not the sick trying to get healed; you are the healed protecting your health.

F. How real Bible faith is released.

1. **Luke 17:6** – *If ye had faith as a grain of mustard seed, ye might say unto this sycamine tree, Be thou plucked up by the root, and be thou planted in the sea; and it should obey you.*

2. **Faith-filled words dominate.**

3. **There's nothing wrong with your faith – just release it.**

Brother Copeland said that a woman came to him one time and said, "Brother Copeland, I don't understand why I don't have victory over this situation in my life. I have all the faith in the world."

He said, "That's your problem, Lady. You've still got it."

She hadn't released any. You've got to release it. You can have $100,000 in your bank account, but if you never write any checks, then it won't do you any good. You may have a heart full of faith, but it won't do you any good until you release it.

4. **Jesus gave you this faith. He will develop it.** *wow!* **Hebrews 12:2** – *Looking unto Jesus the author and finisher of our faith.* **The literal Greek, "finisher" is translated "developer."**

5. **All your faith needs is to be fed; feed it daily.**

Romans 10:17 — *So then faith cometh by hearing, and hearing by the word of God.*

G. **Don't base your faith on your feelings.**

    1. Your feelings will change, but the Word always remains the same.

Real Bible Faith, Part II

A. Real Bible faith never fails.

    1. **1 John 5:1-5** -- *Whosoever believeth that Jesus is the Christ is born of God: (4) For whatsoever is born of God overcometh the world: and this is the victory that overcometh the world, even our faith.*

1 John 5:1-5 became my life story. It became my motto. It represented everything that I knew that my ministry would become. I had 1 John 5:1-5 printed on my very first business cards, and to this day, I close my television program with this, "Your faith will overcome the world!"

I heard Brother Copeland say it on all seven of those tapes. You can see how those verses, hearing them over and over repeatedly, got down into my spirit and began to form my future. I realized that a revelation of this kind of faith, and knowing that I had it already inside me, and that it just needed to be developed was going to produce a victorious Christian lifestyle for the rest of my life.

    2. **The Apostle John is telling us that our faith is our method of victory over everything Satan throws our way.**

    3. **Mark 9:23** -- *. . . all things are possible to him that believeth.*

B. **We are not of this world.**

    1. We are residents of the Kingdom of God.

2. **Luke 12:31** – *. . . seek ye the kingdom of God; and all these things shall be added unto you.*

3. **Luke 12:32** – *Fear not, little flock; for it is your Father's good pleasure to give you the kingdom.*

4. **Colossians 1:13** – *Who hath delivered us from the power of darkness, and hath translated us into the kingdom of his dear Son.* **So we are not of this world.**

5. **This world has no authority over us.**

C. **Victory is NOW.**

1. Don't put off a victorious life until you get to heaven when you can have it now.

2. **Matthew 6:10** – *Thy will be done in earth, as it is in heaven.*

3. God's Word is His will for your life NOW.

D. **Real Bible faith works for whosoever.**

1. **Mark 11:23** – *. . . whosoever shall say unto this mountain, . . .*

2. **Mark 16:17-18** – *These signs shall follow them that believe. . .*

3. Begin declaring "'Whosoever' meaneth me."

E. **Believing demands action.**

1. If you refuse to act on the Word, then you really don't believe it.

2. **Acting on God's Word makes Jesus vitally real in your life.**

3. Be a doer of the Word. **James 1:22** – *Be ye doers of the word, and not hearers only, deceiving your own selves.*

4. **Luke 6:46** — *And why call ye me, Lord, Lord, and do not the things which I say?*

5. **John 3:21** — *But he that doeth truth cometh to the light, that his needs may be made manifest, that they are wrought in God.*

6. **James 2:17** — *Even so faith, if it hath not works, is dead, being alone.*

F. Faith is fed by the Word of God.

1. **Romans 10:17** — *So then faith cometh by hearing, and hearing by the word of God.*

2. **Faith is put into force by acting on God's Word.**

3. **Matthew 12:34** — *. . . for out of the abundance of the heart the mouth speaketh.*

Keep the Word in your heart and in your mouth.

4. **No Word equals no faith. No faith equals no victory.**

You can take these very same outlines and do what I did. Consume them. Study them. And then apply them. God will confirm His Word in your behalf with signs following.

10

The Greatest Faith:
My Favorite Sermon

This is my all-time favorite sermon by Kenneth Copeland. I studied this outline over and over again. It opened my eyes to so many truths about the Word of God, and I believe it will do the same for you.

The Greatest Faith

A. Your faith will overcome the world.

1. 1 John 5:1-5 — *Whosoever believeth that Jesus is the Christ is born of God: and every one that loveth him that begat loveth him also that is begotten of him. By this we know that we love the children of God, when we love God, and keep his commandments. For this is the love of God, that we keep his commandments: and his commandments are not grievous. For whatsoever is born of God overcometh the world: and this is the victory that overcometh the world, even our faith. Who is he that overcometh the world, but he that believeth that Jesus is the Son of God?*

Almost every outline begins with 1 John 5:1-5.

    2.   **John 16:33** — *. . . In the world ye shall have tribulation: but be of good cheer; I have overcome the world.*

    3.   **It is not trials that perfect your faith; it's the Word of God.**

    4.   **It's what you do with your faith in the midst of trials that determines your outcome.**

B.   **Understanding the three parts of man.**

This revelation absolutely revolutionized my thinking as much as anything I had ever heard on those tapes. I had no idea that I was three parts: spirit, soul, and body. I had never heard that before in my life. What a revelation!

    1.   **Man is a spirit. He has a soul, and he lives in a physical body.**

    2.   **You don't *have* a spirit; you *are* a spirit.**

    3.   **The spirit is the real you.**

    4.   **1 Thessalonians 5:23 talks about God sanctifying you wholly, spirit and soul and body.** *And the very God of peace sanctify you wholly; and I pray God your whole spirit and soul and body be preserved blameless unto the coming of our Lord Jesus Christ.*

    5.   **The physical body eats physical food and produces a force called strength.**

    6.   **The mind eats mental or intellectual food and produces a force called willpower. The soul is made up of the will, the mind, the emotions, and the thinking faculties.**

    7.   **The spirit feeds on spiritual food which is called the Word of God and produces a force called faith.**

I could completely understand that. I could see that when I feed my body properly, then I'm going to be strong. I could see when I feed my mind properly, I'm going to have willpower. Then I could see if I feed my spirit the Word of God, I'm going to have faith. Isn't that a powerful revelation? I'd never heard that before in my life.

C. **Fear is faith in reverse.**

    1. **Worry is the foundation of fear.**

    2. **Meditating God's Word is the foundation of faith.**

    3. **Worry is nothing more than meditating on the wrong things.**

    4. **Worry produces fear, and fear will make you sick.**

    5. **Meditating God's Word produces faith, and faith will make you well.**

D. **An example of the greatest faith.**

    1. Matthew 8:5-13 -- *And when Jesus was entered into Capernaum, there came unto him a centurion, beseeching him, And saying, Lord, my servant lieth at home sick of the palsy, grievously tormented. And Jesus saith unto him, I will come and heal him.*

    The centurion answered and said, Lord, I am not worthy that thou shouldest come under my roof: but speak the word only, and my servant shall be healed. For I am a man under authority, having soldiers under me: and I say to this man, Go, and he goeth; and to another, Come, and he cometh; and to my servant, Do this, and he doeth it. When Jesus heard it, he marvelled, and said to them that followed, Verily I say unto you, I have not found so great faith, no, not in Israel.

    And I say unto you, That many shall come from the east and west, and shall sit down with Abraham, and Isaac, and Jacob, in the kingdom of heaven. But the children of the kingdom shall be cast out into outer darkness: there shall be weeping an gnashing of teeth. And Jesus said unto the centurion, Go thy way; and as thou hast believed, so be it done unto thee. And his servant was healed in the selfsame hour.

I wrote in my Bible right out beside **Matthew 8:5-13, Speak the Word only.** The man said, speak the word only and my servant shall be healed.

    2.   **Jesus says the greatest faith is faith that needs no other evidence outside of "speak the Word only."**

    3.   **The greatest faith is becoming Word of God-minded.**

    4.   **The greatest faith is confidence in God's Word and its authority alone.**

    5.   **Confidence in God's Word always brings results. God honors His Word.** (Isaiah 55:11, Jeremiah 1:12).

E.   **The lowest faith.**

    1.   **John 20:26-29** — *And after eight days again his disciples were within, and Thomas with them: then came Jesus, the doors being shut, and stood in the midst, and said, Peace be unto you. Then saith he to Thomas, Reach hither thy finger, and behold my hands; and reach hither thy hand, and thrust it into my side: and be not faithless, but believing.*

Thomas had earlier declared after the disciples had told him we've seen the Lord, "I will not believe unless I can see and feel."

    2.   **Here Jesus is saying, "If you have to feel it first or see it first, that is faithless."** (Author's paraphrase.)

    3.   **The lowest faith is always based on feelings.**

4. **Feelings change; the Word never changes.**

5. **2 Corinthians 5:7** — *(For we walk by faith, not by sight:).*

6. **If you can only believe what your five physical senses give evidence of, then you're operating in the lowest faith.**

What is the greatest faith? It's when you can say, "I need no other evidence outside of God's Word."

You and I can have this kind of faith if we spend time in God's Word every day of our lives.

11
The Power of Your Words

During those three months, I acted on everything that I was learning. I was learning how to talk right. Carolyn and I made a declaration and an agreement with one another just like Kenneth and Gloria did, to correct each other if one of us made a negative confession.

We had never heard anything like, **your words have power.** We used to talk negatively just like everybody else. But when we started getting a hold of these principles that I'm sharing with you, we made an agreement with each other. If either one of us heard the other talking negatively, then we'd say immediately, "All right, that's your confession. I come into agreement with it. It'll come to pass."

Carolyn might say something like, "Jerry, we're never going to get out of debt."

I'd say, "Carolyn, that's your confession. I'm in agreement with it. We'll never get out of debt."

She would say, "No, I bind those words."

Or I'd say something like, "That nearly scared me to death."

And she would say, "All right, that's your confession. You'll die, and I'm coming in agreement with it."

I'd say, "No, no, no. I bind those words!"

What were we doing? We were training one another. Now what you've got to be careful of is that you don't get mad at your partner for correcting you. We had that a few times.

When you begin cleaning up your vocabulary, you don't just stop talking negative. You must also learn to replace all those negative words with the Word of God. So we started filling our hearts with God's Word. We began watching what we said by putting a guard on our mouths.

Don't Say That!

There were times when we didn't use a whole lot of wisdom. We wouldn't confess sickness and disease, and if one of our babies had some kind of symptom of sickness, we didn't talk it. We talked the Word. We laid hands on them, and we anointed them with oil, but we wouldn't speak anything negative over them. But when family members or friends would come over to visit, they might say, "Oh, your baby is sick."

It never dawned on us that this was not a revelation to them. I would just jump on them. "DON'T confess that in my house! If you can't talk the Word, get out of here!"

I ran people off. I was trying to protect my faith, but I did not use a whole lot of wisdom in it. I had to go apologize to those people because they weren't studying what I was studying. They didn't know these things. I hurt them many times when they were just concerned. Then I'd have to go apologize to them and explain what was happening in my life. Later, they began to get hold of this.

I can tell you one thing, I was sincere in everything I did. But there were a few times, I was sincerely wrong.

God knew that Carolyn and I were hungry. He knew that we wanted Him more than we wanted anything in our lives. He covered our mistakes, and gave us grace and mercy. He corrected us when we needed it, and, praise God, we began to grow. It changed our lives, and we have not been the same since. I'm still acting on these same principles today.

Here is another sermon by Brother Copeland that impacted my life in those early days of my Christianity.

The Bible's Secret of Words

A.   **Bridle the tongue.**

    1.   **James 3:2-8** – *For in many things we offend all. If any man offend not in word, the same is a perfect man, and able also to bridle the whole body.*

Behold, we put bits in the horses' mouths, that they may obey us; and we turn about their whole body.

Behold also the ships, which though they be so great, and are driven of fierce winds, yet are they turned about with a very small helm, whithersoever the governor listeth.

Even so the tongue is a little member, and boasteth great things. Behold, how great a matter a little fire kindleth!

And the tongue is a fire, a world of iniquity: so is the tongue among our members, that it defileth the whole body, and setteth on fire the course of nature; and it is set on fire of hell.

For every kind of beasts, and of birds, and of serpents, and of things in the sea, is tamed, and hath been tamed of mankind:

But the tongue can no man tame; it is an unruly evil, full of deadly poison.

    2.   **A man that is able to bridle his tongue is able to bridle his whole body.**

3. You can't bridle the tongue with the same power that you can tame the animals. It takes the supernatural power of God.

4. God's supernatural power is in His Word.

5. Speak the Word continually, and you'll bridle the tongue.

6. **Proverbs 4:20-24** — *Put away from thee a froward mouth.*

7. A froward mouth is a disobedient, out of control mouth that is not under the conviction of God's Word.

B. The ability of words.

1. The Bible places a very high premium on the words of your mouth. **Hebrews 11:3** -- *Through faith we understand that the worlds were framed by the word of God, so that things which are seen were not made of things which do appear.*

    Genesis 1:1-4 -- *In the beginning God created the heaven and the earth. And the earth was without form, and void; and darkness was upon the face of the deep. And the spirit of God moved upon the face of the waters. And God said, Let there be light: and there was light. And God saw the light, that it was good: and God divided the light from the darkness.*

2. **Matthew 12:37** — *For by thy words thou shalt be justified, and by thy words thou shalt be condemned.*

3. Your eternal salvation is based on the words of your mouth. **Romans 10:9-10** -- *That if thou shalt confess with thy mouth the Lord Jesus, and shalt believe in thine heart that God hath raised him from the dead, thou shalt be saved. For with the heart man believeth unto righteousness; and with the mouth confession is made unto salvation.*

4. God has put the whole plan of redemption and its ability to work in your life on the words that you speak.

C. The power of faith-filled words.

1. Faith-filled words dominate the laws of sin and death.

2. Faith-filled words control the operations of Satan and his forces.

3. All that Satan can do is not strong enough to overcome faith-filled words.

D. Words are vehicles.

1. Words will carry doubt, fear, unbelief, sickness, disease, poverty, lack and want.

2. Words carry faith, health, prosperity, victory, and success.

3. Words can kill and words can heal. Proverbs 26:22 – *The words of a talebearer are as wounds, and they go down into the innermost parts of the belly.*

4. Words have the ability to go into the innermost chambers of a man's heart.

5. **Hebrews 4:12** -- *For the word of God is quick, and powerful, and sharper than any twoedged sword, piercing even to the dividing asunder of soul and spirit, and of the joints and marrow, and is a discerner of the thoughts and intents of the heart.* **The Word of God can change the thought and the intent of a man's heart.**

6. Words can govern the lives of men even after the person who spoke them is dead. *wow!*

E. Fill your words with faith.

1. Fear-filled words can stop a man's heart, but faith-filled words can make it normal.

2. Your words are the carriers of your faith or your fear.

3. What you talk about the most represents what's in your heart in abundance.

4. Get rid of fear-filled words just like you got rid of profanity.

5. No matter how severe your circumstances may be or how impossible your problem may seem, faith-filled words will change them.

6. Faith-filled words will sustain you.

F. Faith-filled words are the most powerful weapons in the world of the spirit.

1. Faith-filled words can do in the spirit realm what a physical weapon can do in the world of the natural. *Wow!*

2. Satan is a spirit being. You can't hurt him with physical weapons, but faith-filled words wound him deeply.

3. This is why God's Word is called the Sword of the Spirit.

4. Stop wasting words. Speak only those things that are beneficial to a victorious Christian life.

12
The Shadow of a Dog Never Bit Anybody!

In the church that Carolyn grew up in, the people loved God with all their hearts, but there was a lot of Pentecostal tradition. Brother Copeland stepped all over those traditions every time he came. He was so bold, and he pulled no punches. He made no apologies for what he believed, and that impressed me. He'd say, "I know I'm stepping on your religious toes, but just sit there, and God will heal them!"

He would say, "If you went to the doctor and he cut you open, and you screamed, 'Ow! That hurts!' You wouldn't get up and run off the operating table. Give him the courtesy to sew you back up. If you people will just listen to me, I'll sew you back up."

I loved the way he preached because he was the first preacher I had ever heard that wasn't double-minded, two-faced and feeble. You knew exactly where this man stood all the time. He never cried about his life. Most of the preachers that Carolyn took me to hear would say, "This is a faith ministry, but if you don't give, we're going under."

I thought, *Oh no. Another hour on the offering, and who knows how long on the sad stories.*

At the close of the very first service that I attended of Brother Copeland's, his closing remarks were these: "If you believe it, it will work. If you don't, it won't. Good night." And he walked off. He was so matter-of-fact about everything. I could tell by the way he talked that he truly believed what he preached. He lived it every day, not just on Sunday.

In June of 1970, Brother Copeland was driving back to Shreveport, Louisiana, to conduct another seminar at our home church. While driving his 1969 Pontiac Bonneville, he had an accident on the way over. He blew out a tire, and it caused him to damage the left fender, both front and rear doors, and the quarter panel on his car.

He was scheduled to be staying with my mother- and father-in-law when he arrived in town. So when he got to their house, he asked my father-in-law, "Doesn't your son-in-law work on wrecked cars?"

Olen said, "Well, he did, but now he's preparing for the ministry."

He said, "Do you think he could repair my car while I'm in town?"

So my father-in-law called me, and he said, "Brother Copeland's had an accident in his car and wants to know if you could repair it while he is in town."

I said, "I'd be happy to. Just tell him that I don't have my shop, but I can repair it in my carport if he doesn't mind me doing it that way. I'd be happy to do it for him while he's in town."

So during the day, I worked on Brother Copeland's car. Sometimes Brother Copeland would come over and watch me. I would be grinding on the quarter panel, and look up, and he would be standing behind me, watching me. This is the man that I had been listening to his tapes day and night for three months. The man on the tapes was standing behind me.

I felt like Moses had just showed up at my house. I was trying to work on his car, and there's Kenneth Copeland standing right behind me, looking over my shoulder.

I Had 9,000 Questions That I Wanted to Ask

I had so many questions about faith! Here's the man who was teaching me how to live by faith, and now he's right here. So finally, I put that grinder down and I said, "Brother Copeland, do you mind if I ask you a question?"

He said, "No. Go ahead."

I said, "Brother Copeland, I have been listening to your tapes for the last three months. I have nearly worn them out. I've listened to them dozens of times. I've taken notes, and then I've listened to them again and taken more notes. In fact, I have outlined all seven of those tapes. Now, there's one thing that I have learned how to do during these three months."

He said, "What's that?"

I said, "I have learned how to walk in divine health. I don't have a problem with healing. I got a hold of that and have a revelation that I am redeemed from the curse, and that by His stripes I am healed. I'm not having any problem with healing."

He said, "Great. What's your question?"

I said, "My problem is that I'm in debt, and I'm believing God to get out of debt. I believe that My God shall supply all of my need according to His riches in glory by Christ Jesus, but I don't have a clue as to how!" I said, "Brother Copeland, how do you talk God into meeting your needs financially?" (I thought you had to talk God into it.)

I said, "I heard on your tape where you believed God to get out of debt, and within eleven months, God got you completely out of debt. How did you talk God into that?"

He just laughed, and he said, "Well, it's not a matter of talking God into it. God's already done all He's going to do about your financial well-being."

I said, "You're kidding!"

He grinned, and he said, "No. What I'm saying is, this same Jesus who went to the cross for you to purchase your healing has already purchased your prosperity, too. You don't have to talk God into anything. God already did it 2,000 years ago."

Well, that gave me some hope. I said, "Okay, but I've got these bills. I've got these debts. I'm not afraid to work. I'll work, but I know I'm supposed to be in full-time ministry. How do you get to the place where God supports you while you're in the ministry because I've never done this before? Most of the preachers that I've ever seen were always begging for money. You don't seem to do that."

"The Shadow of a Dog Never Bit Anybody"

And then I'll never forget what he said. He looked at me, and he said, "Jerry, the shadow of a dog never bit anybody."

He didn't explain to me what that was supposed to mean. He just walked away.

He left me standing there. I thought, *The shadow of a dog never bit anybody? That's the dumbest thing I've ever heard in my life! What has that got to do with my needs getting met?*

I asked him about God meeting my needs, and he started talking about dogs. I thought, *That's the craziest thing I've ever heard.* So I grabbed my grinder, and I went back to work trying to figure out what in the world he meant.

"Your Problem Is Your Big Mouth"

Later that night, I went to the service to hear Brother Copeland preach. I had my notebook out, I had my Bible, I was ready, "Let her rip, Brother Copeland."

I was sitting there waiting for him to start preaching. He was sitting on the platform, and all of a sudden, he motioned for me. When he did that, I turned and looked behind me thinking he was pointing at somebody else. I turned back, and he said, "You, come here."

I thought, *Oh, God, what have I done? God must have showed him some ugly thing that I've done. He's going to tell the whole church.* It scared me. I had no idea what he was about to do.

He took me into the room where the choir kept their robes, and he said, "Did you figure out what I told you today?"

I said, "No, Sir. I haven't. The last thing you said was, 'The shadow of a dog never bit anybody.'"

He grinned and said, "You don't know what I meant by that?"

I said, "No, Sir. I don't. It's been bothering me all day."

He said, "What I meant by that is this. Shadows cannot hurt you. The dog can bite you, but his shadow can't. Satan is throwing shadows at you. Symptoms of defeat, symptoms of failure – they're only shadows, and they have no strength. They cannot hurt you if you'll stand on God's Word, and resist the temptation to give up. Now there's one more thing that I want to tell you, your biggest problem is your big mouth."

Then, he turned around, walked off and left me in that closet. I was outraged! I thought, *I cannot believe this. I am probably the only person in this church who really believes in him, and he has the audacity to say that my problem is my big mouth?* It made me mad.

I went back into the service, but I cannot tell you one word that he preached because I was fuming on the inside. I thought, *If he only knew the hours I have spent in those tapes. And then he has the audacity to tell me that my problem is my big mouth?!* I never heard a word he preached.

I got back home, and I was still mad. I walked into that guest bedroom where I had been studying, and I looked at those tapes, and my notebook, and I picked up that first tape, "The Word of Faith," that was on a seven-inch reel. I walked outside, and I said,

"Well, here's what I think of you, Mr. Copeland!" And I rolled it down the street.

I watched the tape unwind as it rolled down the street. I walked in the house, and I got another tape. I went outside, and I was just about to roll tape number two down the road. But before I could, the Spirit of God said, "Son, there goes the answer to your problem!"

I said, "Lord, did You hear what he said to me? He said that my problem was my big mouth! God, I have been watching my words, I have learned about a positive confession. Why would he say that about me?"

And I'll never forget what God said. He said, "I'm about to give you supernatural recall of everything you've said since you prayed and asked Me to meet your need."

I said, "What do you mean by supernatural recall?"

He said, "I keep a record, son. Everything you said has been recorded, and now I'm going to play back everything that's come out of your mouth since you first asked Me to meet your need."

And I heard my words. I literally heard everything I had said. While I was in the Word, I would say, "My God supplies all my need according to His riches in glory." But under pressure, when the bills came, and I didn't have the money, and I didn't know where I was going to get it, I heard myself saying, "Oh, dear God, am I ever going to get out of debt? How will I ever pay this off? Dear God, we're going broke."

That's a double-minded man. The Bible says a double-minded man is unstable in all his ways, and that man can't expect to receive anything from the Lord.

So when God gave me supernatural recall of everything I said, I realized that what Brother Copeland had said to me was true. I said, "Lord, it's true."

And the Lord said, "Son, your problem's your big mouth."

I said, "You got that from Brother Copeland."

He said, "No, son; he got it from Me."

I ran down the road and gathered up my tape, and I rolled it back on the reel. You should have seen that tape. It looked ten times bigger than it was before. I thought, *Oh, God. I just rolled my answer down the road!* Never again did I get mad at Brother Copeland for telling me the truth.

The Vocabulary of Silence

The next day I continued to work on Brother Copeland's car, and then went to the service again that night. Brother Copeland spoke to me again after the service, and said, "Did you get a revelation of what I told you last night?"

I said, "Yes, Sir, I got a revelation. Did I ever get a revelation! It was my big mouth. You're right."

He said, "That's not what you wanted to hear, was it?"

I said, "No, Sir, I did not want to hear that." I didn't tell him I rolled his tape down the road, but I said, "God spoke to me and corrected me, and I got the message."

He said, "Now, I'm going to give you another revelation."

Now I'm thinking, *I don't know if I want any more revelation from him because every time he gives me a revelation, it hurts.*

He said, "Learn the vocabulary of silence."

And then he walked off and left me with that. He had a habit of giving you these nuggets, give you time to think about it, and then he would explain it later.

Learn the vocabulary of silence. I had never heard that phrase in my life. I could not imagine what that meant. But then later he explained.

He said, "What I'm telling you, Jerry, is this. If you can't talk the Word, then shut up. If you have to walk around putting your hand over your mouth every time you feel like talking something contrary to God's Word, then do it. Refuse to let it come out. Learn the vocabulary of silence."

In other words, if you can't talk the Word, then don't talk at all.

And he said this, "You're going to find that when you start putting this to work, you may go for about two weeks with nothing to say. But you'll learn to put a guard over your vocabulary. The bottom line is this: Every miracle you experience in your life is connected to the words of your mouth."

Jerry Savelle & Kenneth Copeland Will Be a Team

Towards the end of that seminar, I completed the repair of Brother Copeland's car, and now it was time for the last service. I was sitting there ready for him to preach, I had my vocabulary revelation, I had my big mouth revelation, I had my tapes rolled back up, they were working fine, everything was cool – I was excited. I could hardly wait for him to preach.

He started preaching, and he stopped right in the middle of his sermon, and he said, "Jerry, stand up."

I thought, *Oh God, what's he going to do?* It scared me. Every time he said, "Jerry, stand up," I thought that he was going to reveal something to everybody that I wasn't too proud of. It never dawned on me that it might be something good.

He said, "Now, you people know Jerry Savelle. He's Olen Creech's son-in-law. Jerry's been preparing for the ministry, and he's going into full-time ministry." Then he said, "Jerry, while I was praying today, God showed me something, and it concerns you."

I thought, *Praise God! Wow! God's talking to him about me in his prayer time! Wow! It doesn't get any better than that!* Then I thought, *What'd He say?*

That's me ... born December 24, 1946.

Carolyn's parents, Olen and Mary Creech with Carolyn.

Carolyn Ann Creech at two years old.

As a young school girl, Carolyn always knew she would serve God.

SCHOOL DAYS 1954-55

Our Wedding Day, July 15, 1966.

One of our dates to a Homecoming football game at Northwestern State University.

My parents (far left), Carolyn's parents and us at our wedding.

He said, "Jerry, God showed me this afternoon in prayer that you and I will be a team, and we will preach the Gospel around the world together for the rest of our lives."

I sat down, and he continued preaching. He just took up right where he left off. I never heard another word he said. I sat there thinking, *Did he say what I thought he said? God showed him that he and I would be a team? We would preach the Gospel around the world?* I had never dreamed of getting out of Louisiana! And I certainly never dreamed of becoming his partner in ministry. I counted it a great honor to be in the same building with the man, and now God's saying we're going to be a team. *We'll preach the Word around the world together for the rest of our lives?*

Before the service was over that night, he walked over to me and said, "Now, it's going to be your responsibility to believe God for the perfect timing for this team to begin."

He told me to listen to God and to spend a lot of time praying in the Spirit. He also told me to not let people distract me. He said to protect my time with God. And so I did. I'm sure that you can imagine just how exciting my prayer time became.

13
God Specializes in the Impossible

The next time that Brother Copeland came to Life Tabernacle, I was now a front-row believer. I was no longer hiding in the back fighting being there. No, I was eager to hear every word that came out of Kenneth Copeland's mouth. I knew that my life was being changed progressively, and I couldn't get enough of God's Word.

Brother Copeland was the first preacher I'd ever heard of who conducted his meetings as "Seminars." I understood "Seminars," and I could identify with that more so than I could "Revivals." I had gone to seminars in my business to learn different paints or materials that were being introduced to the automotive industry.

I went to restoration seminars because I was restoring antique cars and classic automobiles. It may be for just one day, but they drilled you. They gave you lots of information, and they repeated it until you got it.

Well, that's the way Brother Copeland's meetings were. He didn't call them "Revivals," he called them "Faith Seminars." I had never seen a preacher take one verse and preach on it for seven days, but he did. And by the time you got out of his meeting, you had been to a seminar. You felt like you had just finished a semester of college. That really made a strong impact on me.

Satan Comes Immediately to Steal the Word

The thing I remember most about the morning sessions in this particular meeting was his teaching from Mark 4. He shared about how that once the Word is sown, Satan comes *immediately* to steal the Word. For the first time, it became a reality to me that the reason I was coming under attack was because of the Word that was in my heart.

Draw a Line in the Spirit

I'll never forget him saying, "Draw a line in the Spirit," and he acted as though he drew an imaginary line on the platform. He put Satan on one side, and he put God on the other. Then he said, "Think of John 10:10. Jesus said, 'I have come that you might have life and have it more abundantly.' That's on the God side of this line. On the other side of this line, the thief comes to kill, steal and destroy. That's Satan's side. Don't put God on Satan's side, and don't put Satan on God's side. Draw the line in your life. If it has anything to do with killing, stealing, and destroying, Satan's behind it. If it has anything to do with life and living it more abundantly, God's doing it."

Oh, that made a powerful impression on me. I had been told by "religious" people that God made me sick; God wrecked my car; God did all these terrible things to teach me something. Well, I didn't know anything about God. And deep down in my spirit, I thought, *What a terrible God! Why would anybody want to serve a God Who will kill your children, make you sick, or wreck your car just to teach you something?*

I remember thinking, *I'm a father. I have children, and I've got better sense than to treat my children that way. And you mean God's not any smarter than me?* I thought, *If He's doing His children this way, then that's child abuse.* I will never forget when Brother Copeland drew that imaginary line, there was a line drawn in my life. And from that moment forward, anything that happened to me, if it had anything to do with life and living it more abundantly, then I gave God the credit. If it had anything to do with stealing, killing and destroying, then I immediately identified that with Satan. And I'm telling you, it made a major difference in how I approached life from that moment forward.

Brother Copeland is an Extremist — Be Careful!

Not everybody in the church was thrilled with this great revelation. Brother Copeland was really stepping on some religious toes. Most people who are religious-minded are going to fight for the right to be sick, thinking they're being humble before God.

But there I was soaking it up. I thought his preaching was the greatest thing I had ever heard in my life. That's the reason some of the congregation got really concerned about me. They loved me, but they were concerned that I was getting sidetracked and that I was going to be deceived with "heresy." Some considered this kind of preaching heresy. Every once in a while, some of them would take me aside and say, "Now, Brother Jerry, we know you love God. We know you're sincere. We know you have a lot of zeal. We believe in you. We know God's called you to preach. We know that's what you want to do with all your heart, but be careful of this faith stuff. Don't get too far out with this faith stuff."

And that's when I heard for the first time, "Be careful about following Kenneth Copeland."

And I'd say, "Why? He represents everything I want to be in the ministry."

And then I heard this for the first time: "Brother Jerry, he's an extremist. Be careful. He's an extremist. He doesn't preach the whole counsel of God. He's an extremist."

I didn't even know what that meant. But I decided to look in the dictionary and see if I could find the definition of "extremist." And when I saw the definition, I liked it. Then I applied it to what Brother Copeland preached and I thought, *I like it even better.* And the next time somebody said, "He's an extremist," I said, "That's exactly what I want to be!"

"Oh, Brother Jerry, please don't be deceived!"

I said, "No, I want to be an extremist."

"Do you know what an extremist is, Brother Jerry?"

"Yes," I said, "I want to be extremely blessed! Extremely healed! Extremely successful! Extremely prosperous! I want to go beyond the norm!"

"That's not what we're talking about, Brother Jerry! He doesn't preach the whole counsel of God!"

Later, after I went to work for Brother Copeland, I heard him say one time in a meeting, "People accuse me of being an extremist, and they say I don't preach the whole counsel of God." I thought, *Oh, I'm going to get an answer here.* So I got my notebook out, and I was ready to hear what he was going to say.

He said, "You're right. I don't preach the whole counsel of God." It got silent. He said, "And the main reason I don't is because I don't know the whole counsel of God! But the part I know, works! Do you know *anybody* who preaches the *whole* counsel of God? We're all still learning."

Then he made this statement. "Folks, if you've got a heart problem, don't go to a foot specialist. If you've got problems with your feet, don't go to a dentist. My assignment is to teach you faith. I am a faith specialist. Now, most of you have got problems with faith, so you're in the right clinic."

That made good sense to me.

You're a Threat to the Devil

So, I learned that Satan's not blessing folks, and God's not making them sick. If it's got anything to do with blessing your life and giving you life and more abundantly, then God's behind it. If it's kill, steal, and destroy, Satan's behind it. Now if you draw that line in your life, I'm telling you, you're going to begin to enjoy a victorious Christian life.

The last morning of this meeting in 1970, he continued to teach that Satan comes immediately to steal the Word. I realized in those sessions that when I come under attack, it's because I'm dangerous to the devil because of the Word that is in my heart.

Brother Copeland said, "Satan could care less whether you live or die. If you die and go to heaven, he doesn't care. You're out of the way. If you die and go to hell, he doesn't care. You're out of the way. It's while you're alive with the Word of God in your heart on planet Earth that really disturbs him because you're a threat to his operations."

Satan Came and Attacked My Baby!

Carolyn and I were sitting in the service during that last morning session when suddenly, we heard a scream from outside the auditorium. It sounded like a child screaming. It never crossed my mind at that moment that it might be one of my children. Our children were very young at the time. Jerriann was not quite 2 years old, and Terri was nearly 8 months old.

I was so locked into what Brother Copeland was preaching, that it didn't dawn on me that it might be one of my babies. In a little while, the scream got closer and closer to the auditorium. All of a sudden, the door flew open, and a nursery attendant came running and shouting, "Brother Jerry! Brother Jerry!" I turned and looked, and she had Terri, my youngest daughter, in her arms.

Faith vs. Fear

Terri was screaming at the top of her voice, and I noticed there was blood all over the nursery attendant, and blood all over Terri. I didn't know what was wrong, and fear broke out in that auditorium. Brother Copeland had been preaching all week about faith, and all it took was one situation, and the atmosphere of faith left, and fear came.

I got up, and walked toward the nursery attendant, and she handed Terri to me. I noticed that blood was coming out of the end of her fingers, but I still didn't know what had happened. The nursery attendant explained that while Terri was crawling around in the nursery, her fingers got caught underneath a rocking chair, and the attendant rocked over them completely cutting them off.

When I realized two of my baby's fingers were cut off behind the first joint, fear tried to rise up in me. This is my baby! She was screaming with pain. Blood was pouring out of the end of her little fingers like turning a water faucet on.

And all of a sudden, I realized that we were about to find out what Jerry Savelle really believes. Anybody can say, "Amen, Hallelujah, Praise the Lord," while everything's going well, but now we are about to find out what we really believe when tragedy strikes. We're about to find out what this entire congregation believes. We're also about to find out if Kenneth Copeland really believes this.

I turned and looked at Brother Copeland there on the platform. He hadn't said a word yet. He saw panic break out in the church. And I'll never forget the thought I had: *If his actions and his words don't line up with everything he's been preaching this week, then he does not really believe this.* We were about to find out what he believed.

It's one thing to preach this "faith stuff," but when Satan attacks in the middle of your meeting, we're going to find out if this is just something you read out of a book, or do you really believe it.

I'll never forget what he did. He walked off that platform, walked over to Carolyn and me and the baby, then he held her little fingers and laid his hands on them, and said very calmly, "In the name of Jesus, I command the bleeding to stop and the pain to cease." He didn't shout or scream. He didn't panic. He acted like this was something he did every day.

He took his hand off her, walked right back to the platform and said, "Now. Let's get back to Mark 4." And he kept teaching. Instantly, the baby stopped crying; instantly, the bleeding stopped; and instantly, she laid her head over on my shoulder, closed her eyes and fell asleep.

I went out of the auditorium and into the men's restroom to wash the blood off her fingers. I could see that her fingers were cut off at the first joint. While I was washing her fingers off, fear tried to rise up again. This is my child. Can you imagine this happening to an eight-month-old baby? While fear was trying to rise up in me, I heard the Holy Spirit reminding me of Jude 20, "Praying in the Holy Ghost, building up your most holy faith."

I started praying in tongues, and the more I did, I noticed fear left and faith came. I was holding the baby in one arm, and I flipped through my Bible with the other hand to find Mark 11:23. This had become a valuable verse to me, and I said, "Jesus, You said that whatsoever I say, if I believe it in my heart and not doubt, it will come to pass. I will have whatsoever I saith."

Then I flipped over to Deuteronomy 28, and I found the verse under the blessings of Abraham that says, "Blessed shall be the fruit of your body." I said, "Jesus, this little girl is the fruit of my body."

Then I lifted my Bible up to God, and I said, "I am holding fast to these Scriptures, and I declare in Jesus' name that my God will restore my baby's fingers."

I put that Bible down, and then I wrote in the back, "My God will restore my baby's fingers." I dated it, and I signed my name to it as a point of contact to release my faith.

While I'm doing all this, I heard a knock on the door. I said, "Come in." It was the nursery attendant. She came in and said, "Brother Jerry, I went back to the nursery to clean up, and I found these on the floor." And she handed me my baby's fingers.

When she put those two little fingertips in the palm of my hand, fear tried to rise up again. And I just did what I had done before. I started praying in tongues, and the fear left, and faith came. Then I held those fingertips up to God, and I said, "In the name of Jesus, according to Mark 11:23 and Deuteronomy 28, my God will restore my baby's fingers." I put those fingers in a piece of tissue, and I put them in my shirt pocket.

Don't Run FROM God; Run TO Him

Now, this is not the time to run *from* the Word; this is the time to run *to* the Word. Faith *comes* by hearing the Word. I needed all the faith I could get. I went back into that auditorium, and I sat back down where I had been seated before. The baby was asleep in my arms with no pain. People couldn't believe it. I mean, she'd just had two fingers cut off, and there she was asleep on my shoulder.

I sat there until Brother Copeland finished his sermon. I knew I had a crisis to deal with, and it was going to take the Word of God and my faith to overcome that crisis.

As soon as that service was over, some people came up to me and said, "God must have done this to teach you something, Brother Jerry, and we don't know why God cut your baby's fingers off, but we know it was for His glory."

I thought, *The audacity! Here I am, standing for my child, you have just heard Kenneth Copeland tell you to draw a line in the Spirit, and you're saying God did this to one of His children?* I just finally said to them, "I don't receive that."

Then Brother Copeland came off the platform, and said, "Now, Jerry, I know you're believing God, and I know your faith will produce victory. You've got what it takes, but I'm going to advise you to take her to the doctor, because you can't leave her fingers exposed like that. You take her to the doctor right now and have them examine her." He said, "I don't know what they're going to tell you to do, but you can't leave those fingers exposed. Now, this doesn't have anything to do with you being a man of faith by taking her to the doctor. You need to get some medical attention."

I said, "All right."

She'll Never Have Fingers Again!

So Carolyn and I got in our car and drove to the clinic. A physician named Dr. Strain saw her, and he said, "This is not something I can take care of. I'm going to call the Willis Knighton Hospital, and refer you to Dr. Simon Wall, one of the top plastic surgeons in the state of Louisiana."

So, we arrived at the hospital, and when we walked in, the nurses saw what had happened and couldn't believe that this child was not crying. Dr. Wall looked at Terri's fingers, did X-rays, and then he came back and told us, "All I can do is take a skin graft. I'll take a piece of skin from her hip, and I'll cover those fingers. There is no way that we can reattach the fingers. They won't grow back. She'll always have two little nubs on the end of those fingers. They'll never be normal again."

And we watched as our baby's fingers were dropped in a jar to be thrown away.

God Will Restore Our Baby's Fingers!

He gave us his professional opinion. I said, "Sir, I appreciate that, and I know you know what you're talking about. However, I believe God will restore my baby's fingers."

Actually, he thought I was in shock because I kept saying, "God will restore our baby's fingers." Finally, he went over to Carolyn, and said, "I'm trying to tell you, but your husband doesn't seem to understand. It is medically impossible that your child's fingers will ever be normal again."

She said, "Sir, we understand what you're saying. But what you don't understand is we have faith in God, and we believe God will restore our baby's fingers."

He said, "That is medically impossible."

I said, "Sir, you do what you can do. You take the skin graft. If that's all medical science can do, we accept that. But we do not accept that it is impossible for her fingers to be restored. Go ahead and do the skin graft, and God will take up where you leave off."

He said, "It's impossible."

God Specializes in the Impossible!

I said, "We believe it is possible. We know you don't understand this. We're not arguing with you, and we're not trying to say you don't know your business. You know your business. They tell me you're the best in the state. So do what you know to do, and then God will take over from there. My God specializes in the impossible."

He took a piece of skin from her hip and covered the two fingers. They recommended keeping Terri in the hospital over night, so I told Carolyn, "You stay here tonight with Terri, and I'm going back to that meeting because if there's any one thing we need right now, it's faith. Whatever I hear Brother Copeland preach, I'll come back and preach it to you, and then our faith will continue to be strong so we can stand against this."

Attack Satan with the Word

So, I drove to the church, and all the way over there, Satan was screaming at me: "Impossible! Impossible!" I could hear the doctor's word: "Impossible! Impossible! Impossible!"

I couldn't stand it anymore. I rolled the windows down as I was driving, and I was determined to shut the devil up. I screamed at the top of my voice, *"In the name of Jesus! My God will restore my baby's fingers!"* Then I shouted, *"God, if I could get my hands on Satan, I'd break his neck for what he's done to my baby."*

And I heard the Spirit of God say, "Son, if you could get your hands on Satan, you couldn't hurt him. He is a spirit. If you really want to hurt him, you're going to have to do it with spiritual weapons. The spiritual weapon I've given you to do it with is the Word of God. Put the Word on him, son!"

I started quoting every Scripture I could think of all the way to the church. I went from Genesis to Revelation. And when I got to the church, I was ready for the Word so I could go back and battle the adversary until I won.

Brother Copeland asked me what was going on, and I told him. He joined hands with me and agreed that God would restore our baby's fingers. When the meeting was over, I went back to the hospital, shared with Carolyn everything I heard Brother Copeland teach, and we stood our ground and continued to believe for a miracle.

The next morning we took the baby home, and the doctor reminded us, "I know when you came in yesterday this was a very traumatic experience for you, but I just want to reinforce what I said yesterday. This is medically impossible."

Speak Only the Word

We took the baby home, and from time to time, people from the church would come to check on her. Many times, we just had to bind their words after they left. I finally learned not to correct them because they didn't know any better. However, we were determined that we were not going to have any unbelief in our house.

We didn't turn the television set on. We didn't read the newspaper, and we didn't listen to people who refused to talk the Word. When Carolyn and I talked to each other, we talked the Word. Every moment of the day we talked the Word. We would not allow any unbelief and doubt.

A few days later, I received a letter from Brother Copeland, and he said that he was standing in faith with us believing that God would restore our baby's fingers. And then he wrote, "And while I was praying today, God told me to send you my personal study Bible with my personal notes."

He wrote this message in that Bible:

> *To Jerry Savelle, to me a very special brother in Christ Jesus.*
>
> *Dear Jerry, Please accept my study Bible as your own.*
> *Use it to the glory of our Lord.*
> *Your friend and brother in the ministry of Jesus,*
>
> *Kenneth Copeland*
> *August 30, 1970.*
>
> *Jesus is Lord!*

I thought I had just received the Ark of the Covenant.

Inside were personal, hand-written notes from Kenneth Copeland's own personal study time. This was the Bible he used when he started preparing for the ministry. I went through and read all his personal notes, and it charged my faith to a higher level. That Bible and his personal note to me and the fact that he was standing with me meant more to me than you can ever imagine.

After a couple of weeks, we were told to bring the baby back to the doctor. He cut the bandages off to check the progress, and when he looked, he said, "Well, one of the skin grafts looks to be doing fine, but the other graft doesn't seem to be taking."

Carolyn said, "Well, I'll pray."

And before he could say, "No, that won't work," she laid her hands on Terri's fingers and said, "In the name of Jesus, skin graft, take! You do what you're supposed to do!"

And then she confessed again, "And God will restore my baby's fingers."

The doctor reluctantly wrapped them up again, and said, "Bring her back in two weeks."

Now it has been four weeks since the incident, and we had totally immersed ourselves in the Word of God. We hadn't turned the television set on. We were not interested in what the world had to say. We had a situation that needed undivided attention. We didn't want our child going through life missing two fingers.

We took the baby back, and the doctor was pleased with the grafts. They looked good, everything was going well, but he said, "Let me remind you that these fingers will never, never be normal. She's always going to have these two little nubs."

One week later, we took her back, and when Dr. Wall unwrapped the bandages, he said, "This is amazing. These fingers appear to be growing." But then he declared, "But they'll never be normal, and they'll never have fingernails."

Carolyn said, "No, Sir, God will restore our baby's fingers."

He said, "Bring her back in a week."

Faith Without Works Is Dead

The night before we were scheduled to take her back, we received a little card in the mail announcing that a man named Kenneth Hagin was going to be preaching in Tyler, Texas, which was about 100 miles from our home.

I didn't know Kenneth Hagin, but I'd heard Brother Copeland refer to him on his tapes and in his sermons. When I got that card in the mail, I thought, "Faith cometh by hearing, and hearing by the Word of God." If this is the man that helped develop Kenneth Copeland's faith, then this is a man I need to hear. The only problem was, during this six weeks' time while we were believing God for our baby's fingers to be restored, the engine was barely running in the old car that I had, a '64 Oldsmobile with over 100,000 miles on it. I didn't have a car that worked. I didn't have a way to Tyler, Texas, but I knew we were supposed to be there.

So I told Carolyn, "We're going to go to that meeting tonight."

She said, "How are we going?"

I said, "I don't know, but God is going to provide a way somehow. We've got to be in Tyler, Texas, tonight. The Bible says faith without corresponding actions is dead."

She said, "Well, what are we going to do?"

I said, "We're going to get dressed, we're going to get the babies dressed, and then that's as far as we can go. We're going to sit here in our living room, dressed in our clothes for church, with our Bibles under our arms, and we're going to believe that God will arrange for us to get there somehow."

It looked like the dumbest thing in the world. Carolyn, myself and the two babies were all dressed up, sitting on the couch, with our Bibles under our arms, it was getting closer and closer to time for the service, and we still had a hundred miles to drive.

Suddenly, the phone rang, and it was a lady named Sharon Seward, who had come to some of the home Bible studies that I was doing. She said, "Brother Jerry, have you ever heard of Kenneth Hagin?"

I said, "Yes, through Kenneth Copeland."

She said, "I got this card in the mail stating that he's going to be in Tyler tonight. Don't you think that's a meeting we should be in?"

I said, "I think we should."

She said, "Well, I just talked to a man today about buying a car that I'm interested in, and he told me that I could drive it to make sure it's what I'm looking for. I asked him if it would be all right if I drove it to Tyler, Texas, and he said it was fine. Brother Jerry, I just had a strong impression that you and Carolyn are supposed to go with me. If I come over in this car and pick you up, would you go to Tyler with me?"

I said, "I believe that's God! Come on! In fact, we are dressed and ready. You just come right on."

I turned around and told Carolyn, and she and I began to rejoice and praise God.

Sharon got to our house and said, "Brother Jerry, would you mind driving?" I drove the car to Tyler, and all the way over there, we talked the Word. We preached to one another. We also decided to believe for front row seats.

We arrived at the meeting hall, and it was packed out with about 200 people. An usher came to the door, and he said, "We don't have any more chairs. It's full."

I said, "You don't have any more chairs?"

About that time, another usher came up and said, "Wait a minute! I found some more chairs."

He said, "Where are we going to put them?"

And the other man said, "The only place I can see to put them is in front of the front row."

We all turned and looked at one another and winked at each other. We knew that we were in the right place at the right time. The praise and worship was already taking place, and I assumed it was Kenneth Hagin leading. I soon found out it was Buddy Harrison, Kenneth Hagin's son-in-law, who later became one of my closest friends. Buddy said, "Now let's welcome Brother Hagin to the platform."

Brother Hagin walked to the platform, opened his mouth, and I thought, "That can't be Kenneth Hagin!" I thought the way Brother Copeland talked about Kenneth Hagin that he would have a deep, powerful voice. Instead, he spoke in a soft, high-pitched voice, "Open your Bibles to Mark 11:23."

His voice didn't line up with my image of him. But by the time Brother Hagin got through preaching that night, Carolyn and I were just beside ourselves. What he told us to do from Mark 11:23, we had been doing for the past six weeks. We knew we were on target. We *knew* that our miracle was at hand. In fact, when that service was over we thought, *we don't even need a car to get home.* We were so high in the spirit.

We walked back to his book table, and saw about ten or twelve books by Kenneth Hagin that only cost about fifty cents a-piece, and we could not buy one book. We didn't even have fifty cents to spare. I looked at all those books, and I was like a kid in a candy store. Oh, I wanted them so badly, but I didn't have fifty cents to purchase even one of them. We started to walk out, and Sharon said, "Brother Jerry. Did you see all those books?"

I said, "Yes."

She said, "Do you think we should have those?" (She said *we*.)

I said, "Yes."

She said, "Now Brother Jerry, you've been teaching me what you've learned from Kenneth Copeland. Why don't I buy each one of these books. You read them, and then you teach them to me."

I said, "That sounds like God to me!"

And she bought one of each of those books for me to take home.

God Restored My Baby's Fingers!

The next morning, we took the baby back to the doctor as scheduled. He cut the bandages off her fingers, and before Carolyn and I could see anything, he lifted both hands and screamed, "My God!"

I looked over at her fingers, and I said, "No, Sir, not your god; *My God!* My God! My God restored our baby's fingers!"

God restored our baby's fingers to normal. They were the normal length, and they even had fingernails back on them.

This man could not believe it! He was the top plastic surgeon in the state of Louisiana. This miracle is documented. God restored those fingers.

You can't even tell that those fingers were ever cut off except for two little scars underneath those nails. And to this day, I believe that God left those scars there for me as a token of my covenant. Over the years, any time Satan would say, "Impossible, impossible, impossible," I would say to Terri, "May I borrow your fingers?"

She would hold her little fingers up, and I'd say, "Satan, look at this. What did you say? Impossible? Look at this! Don't run off, you started this. Look at this! God did it and if He did the impossible once, then He can do it again!"

What an impact that made on our lives. That miracle marked us for the rest of our lives. God showed us that He is the God who specializes in the impossible. And He's been doing it for thirty years in our lives.

14
Learning to Share Jesus Effectively

When Brother Copeland was at our church, he told me about a man in California named Dave Malkin, who was known for winning souls. He said, "Jerry, I really feel in my heart that God wants me to send you out there to meet this man. When I go home, I'm going to call Dave, and then I'll call you back and let you know what I find out. But I really feel impressed of the Lord that you need to meet Dave Malkin. You need to spend some time with him, because I believe he can make an impartation into your life that will be a great blessing to your ministry."

So he and Gloria went back to Fort Worth, and a few days later, I got a phone call from him. He said, "Jerry, this is Kenneth Copeland."

I said, "Yes, Sir."

He said, "I called Dave Malkin. Dave said you can come any time you want to. Now, Jerry, God told me to pay your expenses out there, and to tell you to stay as long as you feel like you need to stay until you learn what God wants you to learn through this man. So when can you go?"

I said, "Well, I can go any time."

He said, "Well, Dave tells me that there's going to be a lot of people on the beach on the Fourth of July, and he and his team intend to invade Pismo Beach with the Gospel. There's going to be over 100,000 hippies at Pismo Beach. Can you go then?"

I said, "Yes, Sir. I can go."

A New Adventure in Faith

So, I left around the First of July and flew to Los Angeles, California. That was an experience in itself. I was a country boy from Louisiana, born in Mississippi. I didn't know there were cities as big as Los Angeles. I didn't know there were airports as big as LAX, and I didn't know a soul there. I took a young man with me named Don Burton, who had been delivered from drugs. He and I had been doing some witnessing together.

Dave Malkin met us at the airport and drove us to his home. I had never met a man more excited about Jesus in all my life than Dave Malkin.

We stopped and had lunch at a Denny's restaurant, and Dave led the waitress to the Lord. Then, he led the busboy to the Lord, and he led the cashier to the Lord. I had never seen anybody who was so bold, and not intimidated by anything or anyone. No matter what they said to him, he had an answer, and it was fresh and full of life and joy. I was amazed. I'd never seen anybody win people to Jesus so quickly and so easily.

All the way to his house, he was telling us about the great adventure we were about to have, and how he would teach us and train us.

That evening we arrived at Dave's house. There were over one hundred former hippies, drug addicts, prostitutes, and alcoholics gathered up in his house along with Don and me. To this day, it was one of the most wonderful experiences I'd ever had. I'd never seen so many young people so on fire for Jesus.

He had them share their testimonies, and they were absolutely amazing. One guy had been addicted to heroin for 21 years and was totally delivered. Some had been in prison, some were delivered from witchcraft . . . everything you can imagine. Needless to say, the glory of God was present, and I was enjoying every minute of it.

The next day, we packed up and drove to Pismo Beach. We camped out in a little church that opened its doors to Dave Malkin's ministry and allowed us to sleep on the pews, on the floors, anywhere we could find a place. The next morning, we hit the beach.

We invaded Pismo Beach. There were over 100,000 hippies at Pismo Beach on Fourth of July weekend in 1970. And we had 113 turned-on-to-Jesus, Spirit-filled, tongue-talking, God-loving, soul-winning believers who were ready to invade that beach. We baptized hundreds of people in the Pacific Ocean after they had been born-again that weekend.

A nationwide magazine later wrote an article about this new thing that was happening in California, and they called it the "Jesus Movement."

I spent thirteen days with Dave Malkin learning how to win people to Jesus one-on-one. I returned home from that trip higher than a Georgia pine tree. I went to my church and told them what I had learned. Now I was ready to put to work in my town what I had learned in California.

I said, "God, what do I do? I've got this fire in me for the young people in my city. What do I do?"

Starting a Home Bible Study

He said, "Bring them to your home. Set up home Bible studies all over town where these kids can meet."

And so, we did. We formed a team of young people, and we went witnessing every day in Shreveport. Every night we had a Bible study at a different house and taught them the Word of Faith.

We set up what we called "stations" all over town. I learned it from Dave Malkin. We learned that if we would set up teams to be in the same place every day that people would begin to expect us to be there. Many times, people we had talked to weeks before would come back asking us to pray for them.

What I learned in those thirteen days with Dave Malkin was shaping my future as an evangelist. I realized that my ministry was centered around winning people to Jesus. It began to set a course for my life. Thank God that Kenneth Copeland was sensitive enough to the Holy Ghost to send me to Dave Malkin for thirteen days.

We began to have many new converts who needed to be taught the Word. You can't just win them to Jesus and then never teach them how to grow in the Lord. What do I do now? I'm not a teacher. I knew how to win souls. So I would take my tape player to the Bible study, and I would have all these kids sit on the floor, and I'd say, "Tonight, we're going to listen to Kenneth Copeland preaching 'The Word of Faith.'" I'd turn the tape on, and I'd say, "Now at any time you might have a question, raise your hand, we'll stop the tape, and listen to it again."

I started sharing with them the same things that I had learned from Brother Copeland. Eventually, the Lord said, "Now, leave the tape player at home and you teach them."

I thought, *Dear God. I don't know if I can teach this like Brother Copeland.*

He said, "Out of the abundance of the heart, the mouth will speak. Do you have it in you in abundance?"

I said, "I do."

He said, "Then don't be afraid. Stand up, and it will flow out of your mouth in abundance."

That started a whole new dimension of my ministry. I was an evangelist, but I was becoming a teacher. I had the privilege of developing my teaching ministry in home Bible studies. The churches still didn't want me yet, but I had Bible studies all over Shreveport. The anointing to teach had come into my life.

Bible Correspondence Course

I shared with you how Brother Copeland sent me his Bible, but he also sent me a little book that was to further change my life by E. W. Kenyon, called *The Blood Covenant*, along with several other books. I still have my original in my archives. Eventually, I signed up to take the Bible correspondence study course. They would send me a lesson in the mail, and then they would send an exam. I would send it back, and they would grade me on that lesson.

There wasn't a JSMI Bible Institute or a Rhema Bible College back then, so my Bible study came from E. W. Kenyon's Living Bible Studies. Then I graduated to the advanced course. I was hungry.

My Own Personal Bible School

Brother Copeland sent me a number of books to study. He sent me everything that he had in print. I have kept all my notes for thirty years, every book, every tape, everything that has made an impact on my life and now I know why – so I could share it all with you thirty years later.

I was preaching in the streets, then I started preaching in the home Bible studies. Then churches began to hear about the results we were having in the streets and the home Bible studies, and occasionally, a "brave" church would call me and invite me to come and speak.

Jerry Savelle, Youth Minister

At first, they only invited me to speak to the youth. So I began holding youth meetings in churches. I would share with them everything that I had learned from Dave Malkin about soulwinning. I would say to them, "The only way you will be allowed to come to my meeting is if you listen to me for one hour, and then you have to go with me in the streets and apply what you've learned."

Sometimes, we would start out with ten to fifteen people, and wind up with eighty-five to one hundred young people hitting the streets every day winning souls. It was wonderful!

Meanwhile, Brother Copeland began to hear about the success I was having in the youth meetings in the churches there in our city. Sometimes while he would be in a church somewhere, the pastor would ask him, "Do you know anybody who can stir up our youth?"

And he'd say, "I know the man. Jerry Savelle. I'll give you his number."

I wasn't even working for Kenneth Copeland yet, and he was already recommending me to various churches. I received my first call to go to a church outside of my own home town in Oklahoma City, and Brother Copeland had recommended that the pastor call me.

I went to Oklahoma City, and the youth meetings were very successful. They got so excited about soul winning. It was awesome. While I was there, the pastor was very impressed with what had been accomplished. We had tripled the number of youth that were attending the services from when I first arrived. So, the pastor asked me if I would like to go to work in that church as the Youth Director.

He offered me a salary, an apartment that my family and I could live in, and it all sounded so good. I told him, "Let me go back home and pray about it, and then I'll call you."

So, I went home, and Carolyn and I prayed about it, and we thought that it could be good training for us. I knew Brother Copeland said that he and I were going to be a team, and it was my responsibility to believe God for the perfect timing for that team to begin. I had no idea when it would begin. So, I thought, *This would give me some more training before I go to work for Brother Copeland.* It looked good. It sounded good. It felt good. But I still couldn't get it settled in my spirit that it was God's will for me even though outwardly everything looked good.

One day, I was praying about it. I hadn't called the pastor back yet, and I got a call from Brother Copeland. He said, "How did your meeting go in Oklahoma City?"

I said, "Brother Copeland, we had a tremendous time there. We were able to get these youth excited about soulwinning, and now there are three times as many young people in that youth department than there was when I got there."

He was excited about that. He said, "Well, I've been talking to my pastor here in Fort Worth, Harold Nichols, and I'm doing a meeting here next week. I just feel like you and Carolyn should come over here and be in this meeting. I want you to meet Pastor Nichols because I believe you need to come do the same thing in his church."

I said, "All right. Praise God, we'll come."

So, we drove to Fort Worth, and we didn't know a soul in that town other than Kenneth and Gloria Copeland. We knew we couldn't just assume we were staying with them. Yet, we didn't have any money for a hotel.

We drove to Fort Worth and arrived just in time for the evening service. Brother Copeland had already been preaching at Grace Temple for several days. After the service, he introduced us to Pastor Harold Nichols, and Brother Nichols said he wanted to talk to me before we left town about coming to his church and doing a meeting with the young people.

So, after the meeting that night, Brother Copeland went home, everybody in the church went home, and we didn't know where we were going. In fact, we made peanut butter and jelly sandwiches that we'd brought from home and baby food for the babies. So, that first night, we ended up sleeping in our car in the parking lot at Grace Temple.

We didn't feel sorry for ourselves. We didn't say, "Oh, poor ol' us." No, we were so happy. We just knew that we were getting closer and closer to the perfect will of God for our lives. And it's not really that bad when you sleep in the parking lot because the next morning, you get the best seats. You're the first ones there.

Go to Kenneth Copeland's House!

The next day after Brother Copeland preached, he invited us to go have lunch with him. Of course, once again, we were just amazed that he would invite us to lunch. We followed the Copelands to El Chico's Mexican Restaurant. We were sitting there having our meal thinking, *Oh, dear God, I hope he doesn't ask for two checks because we don't have any money.* It sounded like he was paying for it, and we hoped so.

Thank God, when the check came, he said, "Give me the check," and he bought the meal. We were so relieved. I thought I was going to have to wash dishes before I could get out of there.

As we walked outside, he said, "Where are you folks going?"

We said, "Well, we're just going back to the church until time for the service."

He said, "Man, that's five hours from now. Why don't you come home with us?"

I thought, *Go home with Kenneth Copeland!*

He said, "Come on. Go home with us." Then he said, "I won't get to spend much time with you because I have to prepare for the service tonight, but come on home with us, and you can just make yourself at home. I've got books you can read, tapes you can listen to, whatever you want to do."

I said, "Are you sure?"

He said, "Yes. Come on, go home with us."

So we followed them to their house. Brother Copeland showed us his study where he kept his books and tapes, and he said, "Now you just sit in here and do whatever you need to do. I'm going to pray and prepare myself for the service, so I won't be seeing you until time to go to the service."

I said, "I understand, no problem."

So, he and Gloria went off to the bedroom, and Carolyn and I were sitting there in Brother Copeland's study. I was pulling books out, and reading little personal notes he'd written in the margins of the books. I thought, *This has got to be the Holy of Holies!* Every once in a while I'd say, "Carolyn, pinch me. Is this really happening to me?"

We were just two kids hungry for God, and the next thing we know we're in Brother Copeland's house. This was the man who brought the message that changed my life. I thought he was the most godly man I'd ever met. I'd never met anybody like him. And there I was sitting in his study, his chair, reading his books in his house. That's the favor of God!

Ask Kenneth Copeland Any Question You Want

In a little while, Brother Copeland came out of his bedroom and walked in the study and said, "While I was in there praying, God told me to spend some time with you."

I said, "He did?"

He said, "Yes. You've got some questions. So, I'm going to spend about an hour with you, and you just ask me any question you want to ask."

Well, I had been studying the Gifts of the Spirit. They intrigued me. I saw Brother Copeland operating in the Word of Knowledge and Discerning of Spirits, and I didn't understand a lot about it. I said, "Well, Brother Copeland, can you explain to me the Gifts of the Spirit? How do you get to the place where God will use you in that? I see Him using you, and I want to be used by God. But how do you get to the place where God will allow you to do that?"

He gave me a one-hour Bible lesson on the Gifts of the Spirit. I remember him saying, "Now, Jerry, whose Gifts are these?"

I said, "Well, they're yours when God gives them to you."

He said, "No, it's the Gifts of the Spirit. They're His Gifts. These are not my Gifts; I'm only the vessel. They're the Gifts of the Holy Spirit. Man is only the vessel. He's only the instrument."

"Jerry, You're Just a Delivery Boy!"

Then he used this phrase: "Jerry, when I'm operating in the Gifts of the Spirit, all I am is God's delivery boy. That doesn't make me anything; it's still God; it's His Gifts; all I am is the delivery boy. I'm the vessel. Now what you need to be praying is this: God, make me a vessel. Let me be a vessel."

Then he said, "When God is allowing you to operate in those Gifts, who is that Gift for? You or the person that is in need?"

He explained that the Gift is not for me; it's for the person in need. It's for the person who needs healing; it's for the person who needs a Word of Knowledge. He said, "Jerry, you're just a delivery boy. It's not your Gift."

That really opened my eyes. I said, "Brother Copeland, the Bible says that we are to earnestly covet the best Gifts. What does that mean?"

He said, "Well, what is the best Gift?"

I looked down at that list trying to determine which one was the best Gift, and he knew what I was doing. I said, "Well, I don't know. Which one's better than the other?"

He said, "The best Gift is the one that's needed at the time."

Oh, that blessed me. He said, "If there's someone who needs a Word of Knowledge, then you don't want to be operating in the Gifts of Healing. You want to be operating in the Gift of the Word of Knowledge. The Gift of the Word of Knowledge becomes the best Gift because it's the Gift that is needed at that moment."

He was opening up a whole new world to me. It caused me to realize that I didn't have to be somebody special; God could use

me. All I needed to do was just desire to be a vessel, keep the vessel pure, and God would use me in these Gifts.

Brother Copeland laid his hands on me and prayed, "God, You see the hunger in Jerry. Use him. He wants to be a vessel. Use him as a vessel."

Then, he left to go prepare for the service. Carolyn and I went back in the study, and we were just overwhelmed that he would come out of his prayer time to instruct me. We felt so honored.

Prophesy, Jerry!

So, we went back to church that evening, and I could hardly wait to hear Brother Copeland preach. He began ministering, and suddenly, right in the middle of the sermon, he said those frightening words again, "Stand up, Jerry."

My first thought was, *I've done something wrong, and he's going to tell this whole church. I don't even know these people, and they're going to find out something about me that they didn't know.* Then I thought, *That's foolish. It might be something good, like we're going to be a team.*

He said, "Stand up, Jerry."

I stood up.

He said, "Now, folks, this is Jerry Savelle. He's from Shreveport, Louisiana. I met Jerry when I was preaching over there, and he's preparing to go into the ministry. Now, I've been teaching and instructing Jerry when I have the opportunity. Jerry really wants to be used by God in the Gifts of the Spirit. Now, Jerry, God showed me while I was preaching that there is a prophecy that is to go forth in this service tonight, and it's in you. So just go ahead and give it out."

Then he said, "Prophesy, Jerry!"

Instantly, fear rose up on the inside of me. I looked at him, and I said, "No."

He said, "It's all over you, son, go ahead and give it out. Just yield to the Holy Ghost. Give it out."

I said, "No."

I was afraid that I would send somebody to Africa, and they were supposed to be in Germany, and if they died, it would be my fault because I sent them to the wrong country. That's the first thing that came into my mind.

I said, "No."

Brother Copeland was on the platform. I was out in the audience. He's saying, "Prophesy!" I'm saying, "No."

He said, "Prophesy! It's all over you, son!"

There was something going on inside of me, there were words on the inside of me, but I was afraid to release them because I was afraid I was going to make a mistake. And he kept saying, "Go ahead, son."

I said, "No."

He came, and he laid his hands on me. He said, "Now, go ahead and prophesy."

I said, "No."

Then, he said to the congregation, "Now, let me explain what's going on here. God is all over this man, and he knows it, and he wants to be yielded to God, and he wants to be a vessel. But he's afraid he's going to make a mistake."

He said, "Is that right, Jerry?"

I said, "Yes, Sir. I don't want to make a mistake."

He said, "Jerry, the greatest mistake you'll ever make is being afraid to make a mistake."

He said, "Jerry, if you make a mistake, I'm here to correct you; I'm here to help you; God's here to help you. This is the way you're going to learn. Now, you told me you used to play baseball. Did you play at your best the first time you ever played? No, you just kept doing it until you got better at it. Now you just release what's on the inside of you, and if there's anything wrong with it, I'm here. I'll help you. I'll correct you."

Well, he made me feel better, but I still said, "No."

He said, "You're not going to do it?"

I said, "No, Sir, I can't. I'm afraid I'll make a mistake."

He said, "I know that's what's stopping you."

I said, "I just can't do it. You do it."

He said, "Well, I can give it. I know exactly what God wants to say. I'll tell you what I'm going to do. I'm going to give it out, and at any time you want to jump in and finish it, you do so. Now when I start, you don't have to say it out loud, but you go ahead and say what you're sensing on the inside of you."

I said, "I'll do that quietly, but I'm not going to do it out loud."

So he started, and once he started, the same words he said were the words I heard on the inside of me. I didn't finish it for him out loud, but I repeated every word under my breath. I said everything he said at the same time he said it. I never got loud enough where anybody else could hear me. But the fact that I was saying the same thing he said really built my confidence.

And, of course, he talked to me after the service and encouraged me, and he said, "You're on target, God wants to use you. Now you just learn to be bold and get rid of that fear. God will use you."

I learned some valuable lessons from that experience. Later, we returned home to Shreveport, and I called the pastor in Oklahoma City, and told him that I couldn't come back to Oklahoma City because Pastor Harold Nichols in Fort Worth had asked me to come and do the same thing in his church with his youth. I said, "I don't know what this means, but I'll call you after this meeting is over."

Jerry Savelle, Ordained Minister

Pastor Harold Nichols invited me back to his church to conduct a youth rally. It was a powerful meeting. During that time of ministry, Brother Copeland said, "I want to ordain you, and Brother Nichols will assist me."

So, Brother Copeland and Pastor Harold Nichols ordained me in Fort Worth, Texas, in the spring of 1971.

Nothing was said about Brother Copeland and me becoming a team. I went back home, and I called the pastor in Oklahoma City, and I said, "Sir, I don't feel like I can make a commitment to come to work for you. Something has happened, and I don't want to miss God."

He said, "Well, would you at least come and do another meeting for us? Come and take up where you left off and do another meeting?"

I said, "I'd be happy to do that."

I drove back to Oklahoma City, and we had another tremendous meeting with the youth. After the meeting was over, I drove back to Shreveport, and when I walked in the door, Carolyn said, "Brother Copeland called. He's in Lompoc, California. He's going from there to Jacksonville Beach, Florida, to hold a meeting, and he wants you and me to be in that meeting." I was about to go on my first crusade with Kenneth Copeland.

15

Kenneth Copeland and Jerry Savelle Become a Team

It was May 1971. We got in our car, which was barely running, and we believed God that it would make it to Jacksonville, Florida, to join Brother Copeland. I worked on that thing all the way to Jacksonville. In fact, I think that there is still a greasy spot in Montgomery, Alabama, that I left there in 1971.

We met Brother Copeland in Jacksonville, and he said, "I'm doing morning, afternoon and evening services, and after my services, I want you to invite all the people in this meeting who want to learn how to win souls to join you. I want you to conduct a soulwinning seminar with them, and then take them to the streets, take them to the beach, and teach them how to win people to Jesus."

I said, "Okay."

After Brother Copeland would preach in the morning, I would invite people to stay and allow me teach them about soulwinning. We went to the streets between services and put the Word of God to work.

We went to the beach, and we won as many people, one-on-one, out on the beach, as Brother Copeland did in the meetings every night. There were over two hundred people who came to Jesus in the services. We won that many one-on-one on the beach.

Joining Brother Copeland in Prayer Time

Before that meeting was over, Brother Copeland asked me to join him in his prayer time one afternoon. I met him in his room, and while we were praying, he said, "Have you been praying about the team coming together?"

I said, "Yes, Sir. Every day I pray for the perfect timing. I don't know what that means or when that time is, but I'm praying for the perfect timing just like you told me."

He said, "Well, when can you move to Fort Worth?"

I said, "As soon as I leave this meeting."

He said, "Then I think it's perfect timing, don't you? I believe this was the beginning of what God wants you and me to do —work together in these meetings. You move to Fort Worth just as quickly as you can."

Headed for the Promised Land – Fort Worth, TX

We left that meeting and went back to Shreveport. Carolyn and I made arrangements to move, and we headed for our Promised Land: Fort Worth, Texas . . .

We had everything we owned in our Oldsmobile and a little U-Haul trailer. On the way to Fort Worth, some of our belongings blew out on the highway, and I was so embarrassed that I just kept driving. It was nothing but junk anyway.

When we got there, once again, we didn't know anybody but Kenneth and Gloria Copeland, and we knew we weren't moving in with them. We didn't know where we were going, and I didn't have very much money. I knew where Brother Copeland's office was, so I drove there. Brother Copeland's dad, A.W. Copeland, was there in the office. He said, "We're glad you're here, and we know that it's God's will for you to be here. Now where are you folks going to stay?"

We said, "Well, we're going to go look for a place right now."

We left and drove around that area to find something close to the office. We found a little old two bedroom wood frame house on Stanley Street. It was a pitiful little place, but it was all we could afford.

The next day, I was to report to the office for my first day of work as an employee and a team member of Kenneth Copeland Evangelistic Association. I could hardly wait to get there. I knew that God had sent me here, and I was prepared to serve this great man of God for the rest of my life.

16
Living by Faith

My first day of work at Kenneth Copeland Evangelistic Association, Brother Copeland announced to me, "Now, in the natural, I can't afford you. If you ever get paid, it will be because you use your faith."

I thought, *Dear God. I'm not even going to get paid unless I use my faith. I don't have any money as it is!* He then told me that the next day, we would be leaving for a series of meetings, and I was to drive the station wagon. Our first meeting was in Portsmouth and the second was in Norfolk, Virginia.

We were scheduled to be gone for almost three weeks, so I went home to tell Carolyn. We had two little babies with no refrigerator, no stove, no dining table – basically nothing but an empty house to live in.

I had three dollars left after I paid a deposit on the house, paid the first month's rent, and turned the utilities on. That night, Brother A. W. Copeland called and said, "I want to come by and see where you folks live."

He came by and saw that we didn't have anything. So, he went right then and bought us a used stove. Praise the Lord, Carolyn had a stove to cook on.

Then, a man that we had met at Brother Nichols' church heard that we had moved in only a block away from him. So, he stopped over and said, "Is there anything we can do for you folks? Do you need anything? We're so glad you're here."

I said, "Well, thank you very much. We appreciate your offer."

He said, "Is there anything you need? Do you have all the furniture you need?"

I said, "Well, we could use a refrigerator."

He said, "Well, I have a camping trailer, and it's got a little refrigerator in it." He said, "I'll let you use that until you can get one of your own."

I said, "That would be a blessing. I appreciate it."

We had a little refrigerator that could only hold a carton of milk for the babies, maybe some bologna, and an ice tray or two. But we were so thankful that God was meeting our needs.

We had a refrigerator, a stove, and Carolyn decided that she could make it with that. When I got ready to leave the next morning, you talk about hard. I wanted to call Brother Copeland and tell him that I couldn't go on this meeting. I couldn't leave my family with only three dollars.

So finally I told her, "Carolyn, this is the hardest thing in the world for me to do." I felt like such a failure. I was supposed to be the provider for my family. I had always worked hard. I made good money in what I did before. I was a good provider. I had provided her with a nice home in Shreveport; now I had her in a dump.

I said, "I know we're in the will of God. I know we're right where God wants us to be, and it hurts me more than anything to leave you and the babies with three dollars. But I just know that somehow God's going to see us through."

She put her arm around me, and she said, "Jerry, you're right where God wants you to be. I'm right where God wants me to be; and God is going to take care of me. I don't want you to have one worried thought. God will take care of us. Now you go, do what God's called you to do, and we'll be praying for you."

I drove off that morning praying in tongues because there was nothing else that I could do in the natural, and I had to literally cast the care of it over on the Lord.

Wednesday night came, and Carolyn and the babies went to Grace Temple. When it came time for the offering, Carolyn took her three dollars out, and put it in that offering. We had learned about sowing and reaping. She told herself, "Three dollars is not going to carry me for three weeks, so since this doesn't meet my need, it's now seed."

That was an act of faith on her part to put the only money she had to her name in the offering that night completely trusting that God would multiply her seed sown. She got back home that evening, and as she was taking her coat off to hang it in the closet, she reached in her pocket to get something and found a $20 bill in there. Somebody at that church had put a $20 bill in her pocket before she left that building.

She was shouting, "Praise God, this faith stuff works!" We were down to our last three dollars. She sowed it, and God supplied. For three weeks while I was gone, she never went without. She didn't have abundance, but she didn't go without. The kids didn't go without. God took care of them. We were truly learning to live by faith.

17
Don't Touch God's Anointed

I traveled to my first meeting as a staff member for Kenneth Copeland Evangelistic Association. What an experience! But something very unusual happened in that meeting. After the first night's service, two men who went on the trip with us asked me if I'd like to come to their room for pizza. So I went to their room, and while I was sitting there fellowshiping with them and eating, both of these men started speaking against Brother Copeland. They talked about the things that he'd preached that night and how they didn't agree with what he said. They didn't like the way he did things in the ministry. I couldn't believe it. I couldn't believe that I was in a room listening to men who actually worked with him, but were talking about him this way. I knew it was wrong for me to be there and listen to that, so I got up and excused myself. I went back to my room.

I never said a word to anybody about this. I never saw Brother Copeland except when I drove him to the meetings, and I knew not to talk to him. That was a rule; you weren't supposed to talk to Brother Copeland before a meeting. You didn't start the conversation. If there was any talking, he started it. And so I never said a word to him.

But when I got home, I told Carolyn about it. I said, "I can't believe that these men talk about him that way."

My first day back at the office after we returned home, I noticed that those two men were there, but then I heard the secretary say, "Brother Copeland is coming in at 1:00, and he wants to see you both."

I didn't think anything about it. I just figured it was business. Well, at 1:00, Brother Copeland came in the office, and he called for those two men. I was in the back office running tapes, and in a little while one of the men came up to me, and said, "Bye."

I said, "Bye?"

He said, "I'm leaving. I just got fired."

I said, "Fired?"

He said, "Yes. I'll see you around."

I noticed the other guy walked out with his head down, and then I heard the secretary say, "Brother Copeland wants to see you."

I thought, *I'm going to be fired! I just got started, and I'm going to be fired!* I didn't know what they got fired for, but I thought maybe it had something to do with what was going on in that meeting in Portsmouth.

So I went to his office, and he said, "I understand that you were with those two men in the meeting in Portsmouth one night after the service."

I said, "Yes, Sir, I was."

He said, "I picked up in the Spirit that these men were talking against me. I heard their conversation in the Spirit, and that's the reason they're no longer here. Did you join in their conversation?"

I said, "No, Sir, I didn't say anything. I'm not just trying to protect my job, but I didn't say anything. I got up and left."

He said, "I believe you."

He said, "We will not tolerate strife in this ministry."

So I became, at that moment, *the* road crew for Kenneth Copeland Evangelistic Association. The staff now consisted of one secretary, one bookkeeper, Brother Copeland's father, Brother Kenneth Copeland, Gloria, and Jerry Savelle. My job was to make all the tapes, set up all the meetings, drive the car, set up the sound system, do the preliminaries, introduce Brother Copeland, and afterwards, take him back to the hotel.

What did I learn from that lesson? *Stay out of strife! Don't touch God's anointed. It can cost you everything.*

The Apostle Paul wrote to the Corinthian Church, "I have seen your behavior while I was in prayer. Even though I am not with you in the flesh, I'm there in Spirit. I see your conduct."

I learned from Brother Copeland that even though I may not be around my staff twenty-four hours a day, seven days a week, and even though I may be half way across the world, I can see their conduct. I can hear their words in the spirit. And I don't keep people in my ministry who get into strife. Don't ever talk against God's anointed men and women. Even if you don't agree with the way he or she does things, keep your mouth shut. Pray for them. But don't touch God's anointed!

18
Three Demands by Kenneth Copeland:
Integrity, Excellence & Be on Time

Brother Copeland had three demands: he demanded integrity, he demanded excellence, and he demanded that you be on time. I personally had never been around anybody that was so demanding in those areas. I had been taught that you keep your word, but I'd never seen anybody push it quite as far as he did.

My Most Memorable Meeting with Kenneth Copeland

In one particular meeting in Omaha, Nebraska, in 1971, we were holding our meeting in a brand new Hilton Hotel. During the services, I would get so full of the Word and so charged up that I just had to go share it with somebody. I couldn't just go back to my room and sit there. So, I went to the streets between services, and I would find somebody to preach to. Most of the time, it was to alcoholics.

After one meeting, I went out into the street trying to find somebody to witness to, and I came across a homeless man who was an alcoholic. I started following him and found out he lived in a boxcar near the train station. So, I started witnessing to him. He didn't want to hear anything that I had to say, and he started walking off. So I just followed him. He kept turning around and saying, "What do you want?"

I said, "I want to talk to you about Jesus."

He said, "I don't want to hear about your Jesus."

I said, "Well, it's too late. I'm going to tell you whether you want to hear it or not."

I kept following him, and he would turn around and tell me to go away and to leave him alone. I just kept following him. He was a little short guy, and he told me that his friends called him "California Shorty" -- he was originally from California. So I ended up in a boxcar with California Shorty and about five other homeless men. I was sitting, witnessing to him, and of course, the other guys were aware of what I was saying. In a few moments, one of them pulled a gun on me and said, "We don't want to hear this."

I thought, *They don't want to hear this! What am I doing here? This guy's going to blow my head off if I don't shut up!* But then there was a boldness that arose. Now I'm not telling you to go out and do this. What I'm saying is, God protected me at that very moment. He saw my heart. He saw my sincerity, and He just protected me. The guy could have shot me. I could have laid there in that boxcar, and not been found for days. Brother Copeland had no idea where I was. He just knew that I was probably in the streets witnessing.

So, I told the guy, "Well, you know, you can shoot me, but my spirit will never die. I'm here to tell you about Jesus. He loves you. You don't have to live like this anymore."

And something I said during the course of that conversation got to him. He put the gun away, and one of them came up to me and asked me to pray for him. When I prayed for him, he cried. When he started crying, it affected the other guys. Eventually, I led every one of them to the Lord.

I invited them to go back with me to the afternoon meeting, and we arrived a little early. I told them to just sit in the lobby of the hotel. I had five homeless men sitting in the lobby of this brand new hotel.

The hotel manager approached me and said, "What are these guys doing here?"

I said, "I just led them to the Lord."

He said, "Well, they don't look like they've just come to Jesus."

I said, "It's not the outward appearance that's changed. It's the inward man."

He said, "We can't have this."

I said, "They need to be in this meeting."

He said, "Take them into the meeting room. Don't let them sit out in the lobby."

So I took them into the meeting room. When the service started at 2:00, I did the preliminaries, I prayed over the meeting, and I introduced Brother Copeland. Those guys were sitting on the front row, and I went down and sat down next to them.

When Brother Copeland saw them, he said, "Well, Jerry, who are these men? I see you've been out witnessing again."

I said, "Yes, Sir. I've got five men here who just received the Lord this afternoon."

So he had them all to stand, and everybody applauded for them. And then Brother Copeland started preaching on "Seven Steps to Prayer that Brings Results."

In the course of his message, he said, "You folks need to learn how to talk to God just like you talk to your best friend. Don't get so religious. Don't talk Elizabethan English if that's not the way you normally talk. God understands Texan. God understands Nebraskan. God understands you right where you are. So just talk to Him like you talk to your best friend."

Well, ol' California Shorty hadn't been in church before. So he just stood up and shouted, "Hey, God! This is California Shorty. Do you remember me?"

And the whole place broke up. Brother Copeland thought that was one of the funniest things he'd ever heard.

Well, California Shorty and his group ended up bringing more guys to the services. He became an evangelist!

One evening, Brother Copeland was preaching on the "Reality of Righteousness" and there was a guy in the service who got upset with the message. He didn't like it. He thought, "There's none righteous, no, not one!" He just couldn't stand it, and he got up and said something and walked out.

Brother Copeland didn't pay any attention to it; he just kept preaching. Well, California Shorty got up and walked out. I thought, *I wonder where he's going?* So I got up and followed him. When I got outside, I noticed the guy who had shouted at Brother Copeland was on his back on the floor, and California Shorty was on top of him, and he was about to slug the guy. He'd knocked him on the floor, and was right on his chest about to hit him. He said, "You don't talk ugly about my preacher! You understand? That's my preacher!"

I said, "California, that's not the way we handle this, man!"

He said, "That's the way we do it in the street."

I said, "Yes, but you're not in the street anymore!"

Here he was, less than twelve hours old in the Lord, and he was already a "defender of the faith." That was one of my most memorable experiences in Omaha in 1971.

Be On Time

As I've previously mentioned, I would go out witnessing every day after the morning services, and I knew I had to be back around 1:45 p.m. to pick up Brother Copeland at the hotel. He *demanded* that you be on time. Being on time was a *must.* If he said,

"Pick me up at 1:45," then you were there at 1:43, not 1:46. He was such a stickler about this.

What he was endeavoring to do was to train people to develop their own integrity, and then they wouldn't have any problem believing in God's integrity. There was no legitimate excuse for being late. You just knew not to be late, and above all, never make Kenneth Copeland late. He was very adamant about that.

I had never made him late before. I understood that. I appreciated that demand he was placing on my life because it produced discipline. It was bringing me into a new dimension of excellence in my own life. I appreciated it, I didn't question it, and I was glad to do it.

But on one particular afternoon, it was about 1:30 p.m., and so I thought I would go by the Hilton Hotel first, just to make sure the sound system was working before I went by to get Brother Copeland. When I got to the hotel, the sound system was gone. The chairs were gone. I couldn't even find the sound system. We were having a meeting in thirty minutes, and everything was gone!

I went through the hotel trying to find out what was going on, and finally I found a maintenance man, and he said, "We thought the meeting was over."

I said, "What did you do with our equipment?"

He said, "I locked it in a closet."

I said, "You've got to unlock it. I've got to get it set up now."

Talk about a dilemma! I didn't know which was worse: making Brother Copeland late or getting him to the meeting with no sound system and no chairs. I was trying to figure out what do I do. So I thought, *I'm in trouble either way. If I go get him and bring him back to the meeting room and he sees the equipment gone and the chairs removed, he's going to be upset about that.* So I thought, *priority here is to get the room set up.*

I Made Kenneth Copeland Late

I found California Shorty and his gang in the lobby, and they helped me again. By that time, it was five minutes to 2:00, and I ran outside, jumped in the car, and drove about three blocks to where Brother Copeland was staying. When I turned the corner, Brother Copeland was not on the curb like he normally was. He was **out in the street** waiting on me. I could see him a block away out in the street with his watch in his hand. When I pulled up, he got in. He was silent at first, and that was worse than anything. I'd rather he had just said, "Get out of the car, I'm going to run over you twice."

Silence hurts sometimes more than words! I knew he was like a volcano on the inside. You could feel it. He wouldn't say a word. But then he decided to talk, and now I wished he would have stayed silent. He got all over me for making him late. And he never even asked me for an explanation why.

We got to the service, and he apologized to the people for being late. He said, "I have never been late for a service since I've been in the ministry, and I'll never be late again."

Then he started preaching. I was sitting out there in the audience. The devil was trying to take over my mind and my thoughts. I thought, *I have proven my loyalty to him up to now. He could have at least asked me why. He should know by now that surely I have a legitimate excuse! But he never asked!*

Satan was trying to drive me out of the will of God over something foolish.

I can tell you everything Kenneth Copeland has preached in every meeting I've ever been in, but not that one. I wasn't listening. I was listening to the thoughts that were running through my mind.

I thought, *As soon as this meeting's over, I'm telling him I'll catch the next bus out of here.* That's what I was thinking. And that's what I was prepared to do.

As soon as that meeting was over, I took him to the car, and drove him back to the apartment without saying a word.

When I turned the corner and went down that street where I had seen him standing earlier, he said, "Jerry, I need to apologize to you."

He said, "I didn't even ask you why you were late. I just jumped on you because you made me late. I should have known better. You had to have had a legitimate excuse. You've never made me late before. What happened?"

I explained what happened and how I chose to set the auditorium up first, but apparently, I had made the wrong decision.

He said, "No, it was the right thing to do, and I apologize. Forgive me."

That really blessed me, and I asked God to forgive me for allowing Satan to control my thoughts.

Brother Copeland did the honorable thing and that impressed me. It marked me for life. Occasionally, Brother Copeland will say when he introduces me in a convention, "Jerry Savelle is the only man who has ever made me late." We get a big laugh out of it now.

Brother Copeland didn't just teach me through his words, he taught me through example. Working for him was my "Bible School." I shall never cease to thank God for that wonderful opportunity.

Demand Excellence and Integrity

Brother Copeland always said, "If you don't keep your word even in the small things like showing up on time, then you're going to think that's the way God operates. Because if you don't develop your own integrity, then you can never develop a trust in God's integrity."

People tend to think God is like them. They don't keep their word, so they think God doesn't keep His. But the first lesson in learning how to trust God's integrity is to develop your own. It's a must if you are going to enjoy a successful life of faith.

I will never forget when Brother Copeland held his Bible up in one of those early meetings and said, "This is not just a 'book.' This is God's Word. His Word is His Bond. You are what He says you are. You can do what He says you can do. And you can have what He says you can have."

Then he said, "When you get to the point in your life where you believe God's Word just like you do the word of a doctor, a lawyer, or your very best friend, then you'll never struggle with your faith again."

That's powerful.

Oral Roberts demanded excellence and integrity in his ministry. While Brother Copeland worked for him, he saw that and put it to work in his own life later. He not only demanded it in his own life, but also in the lives of those who worked for him.

Brother Copeland would never accept a "that's good enough" attitude. He would never accept "Well, we can get by with that." He *demanded* excellence. He demanded 100 percent commitment, and he demanded that we represent Jesus first class. He was not very popular in some religious circles because to them he was too radical.

In some religious circles, there was this "poor ol' us" mentality. They never strived for the best. They didn't think they could have the best. They didn't believe that God wanted them blessed and prosperous. Brother Copeland did, and he preached it with boldness.

I determined that if there was ever a time when I would launch out into my own ministry, then I would put these same principles to work in my ministry. I saw the results that they produced in his life, and that's what I wanted in my life.

Look at the following Scriptures regarding excellence and integrity.

Daniel 6:1-4 says, *It pleased Darius to set over the kingdom an hundred and twenty princes, which should be over the whole kingdom;*

> *And over these three presidents; of whom Daniel was first: that the princes might give accounts unto them, and the king should have no damage.*
>
> *Then this Daniel was preferred above the presidents and princes, because <u>an excellent spirit was in him</u>; and the king thought to set him over the whole realm.*
>
> *Then the presidents and princes sought to find occasion against Daniel concerning the kingdom; but **they could find none occasion nor fault**; forasmuch as he was faithful, neither was there any error or fault found in him.*

In the time in which you and I live, there is a greater demand for us to be people of integrity than ever before. As you well know, the credibility of preachers is at an all-time low. People make jokes about preachers all the time. It's sad when you turn on the television, and one of the late night talk show hosts is using stories about ministers in their monologue.

The world seems to think we're a bunch of cons. They think we say one thing in the pulpit, but we live our lives another way away from the pulpit. Well, where did they get that idea? Many preachers have projected that kind of image.

The only way we can change what the world thinks about preachers today is with integrity and excellence.

If you give your word, then back it. If you tell somebody you're going to do something, then do it.

In these Scriptures, we see that they couldn't find any fault in Daniel. Apparently, they looked. Apparently, his life was under scrutiny. But they found him faithful and honest. What a great testimony.

We've all made mistakes; we all have shortcomings. I'm sure if you looked close enough, you would find something in all of us. But they couldn't find anything in Daniel. They found that he was faithful. He had an excellent spirit. That's what you and I should strive for.

19
Developing an Excellent Spirit

Where does excellence begin? Where do you begin developing excellence in your life? You may not have connected this with excellence, but here it is.

Proverbs 17:27 says, *He that hath knowledge spareth his words: and a man of understanding is of an excellent spirit.*

You Have Two Ears and One Mouth: Be Quiet & Listen

You'll find that people who possess an excellent spirit are not big talkers. They don't waste words. I personally have a problem being around people that just talk all the time, and mostly about themselves. It's not enjoyable to me to be around preachers who talk about everything they're doing as if nobody else is doing anything, and as if God's very fortunate to have them. It appears that they think the world would all go to hell if it wasn't for them. That's not an excellent spirit.

He said, *He that hath knowledge spareth his words.*

It became a revelation to me that a man who has an excellent spirit spares his words. He doesn't talk a lot. There's another verse in Proverbs 10:19 that says, *In the multitude of words there wanteth not sin...* In other words, when there's a lot of talking going on, you can count on it, sin's going to show up. It may show up in the way of exaggeration or lying. You can find people who just talk, talk, talk, and nobody else can get a word in, and eventually, they're going to start exaggerating or lying.

I love preaching. When I'm preaching, my biggest problem is finding a place to stop. But away from the pulpit, I am a quiet man. I don't talk a lot. One of my best friends, Buddy Harrison, was that way before his "homegoing." Buddy and I spent entire days together, hardly saying anything to each other, and yet we would have a wonderful time.

If you're going to develop an excellent spirit, then watch your words. Don't just talk all the time. That's the reason God gave you two ears and one mouth. Listen twice as much as you talk.

Proverbs goes on to say, *A man of understanding is of an excellent spirit.* The Amplified Bible says, *a cool spirit. A man of understanding has a cool spirit.* You are "one cool dude" when you operate in excellence.

Understanding is the result of hearing and comprehending truth. Once you understand truth, then you must commit yourself to live by it and establish an unwavering stand. That's excellence.

Your Gift Makes Room For You

Let's see how Daniel developed this excellent spirit in his life.

Daniel 1:8 says, *But Daniel **purposed in his heart** that he would not defile himself with the portion of the king's meat, nor with the wine which he drank: therefore he requested of the prince of the eunuchs that he might not defile himself.*

Daniel made a commitment to the things that he had seen in God's laws. This is what I observed in Brother Copeland's life. He demanded of himself to live by every revelation he received from God's Word.

When I went to work for Brother Copeland, he constantly talked about Kenneth Hagin in his sermons. He spoke about the impact that Kenneth Hagin's teachings had made in his life. Even though I had been to one Kenneth Hagin meeting in Tyler, Texas, I had never actually met Brother Hagin. Then shortly after I went to work with Brother Copeland, Brother Hagin came to Fort Worth for a meeting. After the service, Brother Copeland was talking to Brother Hagin, and I was standing right next to him. But somehow, he just failed to introduce me to Kenneth Hagin. They were engaged in conversation, and I guess it just didn't occur to him to introduce me to Kenneth Hagin. I didn't say, "Brother Copeland, tell him I'm your right-hand man. Make sure I meet Brother Hagin."

I wanted to meet Brother Hagin. I'm not going to lie to you. I thought it would have been a great honor to meet Kenneth Hagin. I just wanted to shake hands with him, and tell him how much I appreciated his ministry. But I wasn't going to push myself on him.

Years later after I had already left Brother Copeland's organization, I was invited to speak in his first Believers' Convention along with Kenneth Hagin and Charles Capps. I shook hands with Kenneth Hagin just before I was scheduled to preach. A few months later, his son, Kenneth Hagin, Jr., called me and said, "Daddy wants you to speak at our Camp Meeting this year."

My first real introduction to Kenneth Hagin, and he asked me to speak at his Camp Meeting. Now, that's a whole lot better than forcing myself on him, or trying to use "my connections" with Kenneth Copeland to meet him. My gift made room for me.

Don't Be Self-Promoting

God was proving to me that you don't have to be self-promoting, you don't have to compromise your convictions, and you don't have to play "religious politics."

Daniel purposed in his heart that he would operate in excellence of spirit. Have you ever purposed something in your heart? Have you ever made a firm decision and refused to compromise? That's what produces excellence of spirit. You have to make decisions based on the truths that you see in the Word of God, commit yourself to them, and then refuse to compromise.

There are some things that you're going to have to determine and purpose in your heart if you're going to operate in excellence. Don't wait to do them when the pressure is on. Do it now. You can count on it, the pressure will come. But if you've already made your decision, then you're ready for whatever Satan brings your way. If you make a decision in your personal life to do something, then stick to it, come rain or shine, and God will honor your uncompromising stand.

Honor Your Word

Imagine yourself inscribing your word or your vows in tablets of stone. If your decision was to not borrow money, then imagine yourself writing this in tablets of stone: "I will not go in debt." And the first time there is an opportunity to compromise, then just go pick up your tablet of stone and keep it before you so you don't break your vow.

Proverbs 20:7 says, *The just man walketh in his integrity.*

Proverbs 11:3 says, *The integrity of the upright shall guide them.*

Psalm 26:1-2,11 says, *Judge me, O Lord; for I have walked in mine integrity: I have trusted also in the Lord; therefore I shall not slide.*

Examine me, O Lord, and prove me; try my reins and my heart.

But as for me, I will walk in mine integrity.

Brother Copeland was a man of integrity and his demand for it marked my life. I can remember him saying often, "If you tell somebody you're going to do something, then do it."

God Will Uphold You

Psalm 41:12 reveals to us that God upholds those who walk in integrity.

Psalm 41:12 says, *. . .thou upholdest me in mine integrity, and settest me before thy face for ever.*

God keeps you in front of His face when you walk in integrity. I like that. It sounds as if people of integrity are very special to God.

God Will Protect You

Integrity will preserve you in time of trouble.

Psalm 25:20-21 says, *O keep my soul, and deliver me: let me not be ashamed; for I put my trust in thee. Let integrity and uprightness preserve me; for I wait on thee.*

Too many of God's preachers today are compromising their integrity. And one of the reasons preachers compromise their integrity is their desire to be successful. You can see it in every field or endeavor. You see it in the political world. There are some honest men that go into politics, men of integrity, and once they get into that arena and realize that they're a little fish in a big pond, they wind up compromising their ethics, their standards, and their integrity. Why? In order to be successful. It begins to look as though it's the only way to achieve the success that they desire.

There are honest businessmen that from time to time are presented with opportunities that are unethical, but in their desire to be successful, they are willing to compromise their ethics. There are preachers that do the same thing. They haven't demanded excellence in their lives.

You have to be careful that you don't start accepting things you once rejected. Don't allow things in your life that you purposed in your heart you wouldn't do. Sometimes things that were once considered wrong, now become tolerable. You can't do that. You can't begin to justify your actions when they compromise your convictions.

> Job 27:3-6 says, *All the while my breath is in me, and the spirit of God is in my nostrils;*
>
> *My lips shall not speak wickedness, nor my tongue utter deceit.*
>
> *God forbid that I should justify you: till I die I will not remove mine integrity from me.*
>
> *My righteousness I hold fast, and will not let it go: my heart shall not reproach me so long as I live.*

That's a powerful statement. This is a man saying, "I will not compromise my integrity. For no reason whatsoever, I will not compromise my integrity."

Don't Compromise Integrity

When you refuse to compromise your integrity, God will preserve you, God will take care of you, and God will keep you in front of His face.

Job 31:6 says, *Let me be weighed in an even balance, that God may know mine integrity.*

When was the last time you said, "Hey, God, I'd like to present myself to You today. I'm asking You to weigh me. See if You can find any wrongdoing in my life." That's what Job was saying. He said, "I present myself to You. Weigh me in the balance. Check out my integrity."

God protects those who walk in integrity even when they make mistakes. We see an example of this in Genesis 20:1-6. Remember the king that approached Abraham and Sarah, and the king thought that Sarah was Abraham's sister? He took her into his tent and fully intended to commit a sexual act with her. God stopped him and said, "Don't touch this woman. This is Abraham's wife."

And the king said, "I didn't know. I thought she was his sister."

And God said, "Because of your integrity, I stopped you."

So even though he was about to make a mistake, he did it in ignorance; he didn't do it maliciously so God protected him.

If you walk in integrity, God will protect you.

Watch Your Conduct

Ephesians 4:1 (NAS) says, *I, therefore, . . . entreat you to walk in a manner worthy of the calling with which you have been called.*

Paul is admonishing us to be very conscious of our conduct and our behavior. Be careful how you project yourself to others. Your life and your ministry are open books. People are reading chapters out of your life and ministry everyday, and first impressions do count.

In closing this chapter, I'd like to share with you the three greatest enemies of the ministry which Brother Copeland taught me many years ago.

1. The spirit of lust.

2. The spirit of greed.

3. The spirit of pride.

These three things will attempt to get you to compromise your integrity, but you must make a quality decision not to yield to them.

The spirit of lust. There are many ministries that have been destroyed or at least they're certainly not making the impact they once did because they didn't reject the spirit of lust. Satan knows where people have weaknesses, and he uses it to his advantage. You must be on guard at all times and build yourself up in the Word to the point that lust is no longer attractive to you.

The spirit of greed. There are ministries that no longer exist because of greed. Remember it is the love of money that is the root of all evil. A foolish man lets money destroy him; a wise man uses it as a tool for reaching more people for Jesus.

The spirit of pride. There are ministries who have hit bottom because of pride. The Bible says, pride comes before a great fall. Don't ever allow yourself to get to the point that you think more highly of yourself than you ought to think. If you ever get that attitude, you're headed for a fall.

Now that you are aware of these enemies, guard yourself against them. Don't allow yourself to be caught up in lust, greed, or pride.

See to it that you do not fall into Satan's trap in those areas. Develop a spirit of excellence. I attribute the success in my life and ministry to the fact that I have held on to these qualities which I learned from Kenneth Copeland thirty years ago. They will produce victory and success in your life every time.

20
My First Experience with Demons

Some of my most memorable crusades with Brother Copeland were in Omaha, Nebraska, and Springfield, Missouri, when I witnessed an increase in the Anointing of God for ministering to the sick . . . and my first experience with demons!

Something New

The meeting in Omaha was one of the first times we began to see people falling out under the Power of God. It was new to us. It wasn't commonplace back then. Brother Copeland prayed for the sick at all the meetings. I usually stood by him with one hand stretched out toward him and one toward the person he was praying for. And as he walked down the line, my job was to stay with him and just pray in the Spirit as he prayed for the people. I didn't touch him, and I didn't touch the people. I just prayed.

But in this Omaha meeting, something started happening that hadn't happened that often before. They started falling out. Of course, my first reaction was to grab them. I looked at Brother Copeland because I thought he was hitting them or something. I didn't know what was going on. I couldn't understand why they were falling down.

Is all this Legitimate?

It was all new to me. We hadn't seen that happen too many times. Brother Copeland said that he had seen it happen in Brother Hagin's meetings a few times, but it was relatively new.

So I said, "Well, what do you want me to do in the way of assisting you? Am I supposed to catch these people, or just let them fall?"

Some of them would fall, and their head would hit a chair or something. The first thing I thought of was, *Dear God, we're going to be sued.*

When it started happening more and more, we decided that maybe I should stand behind the people instead of next to him and just be there to assist them. So that became the new phenomenon in the meetings when we had the prayer lines. I became a "catcher." We didn't have a biblical term for it so we called it "catcher."

Brother Copeland started searching through the Word to gain more insight into it, and he found several illustrations. For instance, when God appeared to Abram in Genesis 17, it says, "Abram fell on his face." There were several accounts in the Word of God when people came into the presence of God, they couldn't stand up. They fell. We saw it in Jesus' ministry. There were times when He would minister to someone, and they would fall. I don't know if Peter was called a "catcher" or not, but we know that there were times that under the Anointing of God, they would fall.

So Brother Copeland began to teach me that it was the presence of God, and that in the presence of God sometimes people just can't stand up.

It seemed like in every meeting it was happening. It almost got to the point where it seemed like a badge of spirituality. If the preacher didn't have people falling, he wasn't anointed. And it's a shame that it got that way. And then, of course, people took it upon themselves to just start falling, and some of them got very dramatic with it. Some would even look and make sure there was a catcher first. Sometimes women held their hats as they went down. So you began to wonder when it was legitimate and when it wasn't.

Then it got to the point to where people thought they *had* to fall in order to receive something from God. So there had to be more and more teaching on it. Brother Hagin began to teach a lot about it. But the thing that was important to me was that we were entering into a new dimension of the Anointing of God.

Something else that happened during those meetings that I had never seen before, was Brother Copeland started praying for people who had one leg shorter than the other. We would actually watch that leg grow out right before our eyes. It got to where that became kind of a commonplace thing in the meetings. He didn't just do it because it worked in one meeting. But there were times when the Spirit of God would say to him, through a Word of Knowledge, that there was someone there with one leg considerably shorter than the other.

My job was to take a chair up front for the person to sit in, and Brother Copeland would have them scoot all the way to the back, sit up straight, then he'd pick up their legs with their feet pointing straight up. Many times, it wasn't just a little quarter of an inch short, it was three or four inches short.

Brother Copeland would take those feet and say, "I command in the name of Jesus for this leg to be lengthened and come out normal." And I would watch as the shorter leg would actually grow to meet the other foot completely! That was my Bible School. I was watching the power of God work right before my eyes just like it did in the Bible.

"Jerry's Never Done This Before"

I'll never forget the first time he had me do it. I thought, *Oh, dear God, what if it doesn't work?* He was endeavoring to make a point to the people that he was not pulling on their legs. He was not making this happen. It wasn't a gimmick. So, one time he said, "Now, Jerry's never done this before. Jerry, come up here."

He had me get down by their chair, hold their legs up, and then he instructed me. He said, "Don't ever lay your hands on someone or speak a word until you're ready to release your faith. Don't waste words, don't waste actions, and don't lay your hands on them until you're ready to release your faith. And then make sure every word is filled with faith, and make every action go in line with getting results."

So, he said, "Now you command that leg to be lengthened in the name of Jesus."

I did it, and the leg grew out right there in my hands with me holding it. That person got up and walked around with no limp. And that began to happen more and more frequently.

I've noticed in thirty years of ministry, that for everything that is true, there's always going to be a counterfeit. For everything that is really of God, Satan's going to try to foul it up, or pervert it. It's amazing how God will start out doing something, and then man comes up with a way to foul it up, abuse it and misuse it. Kenneth Copeland never did that.

From time to time, Brother Copeland would even have somebody come out of the audience to help him so the audience would know that it was not fake. He was proving that it was not a gimmick or a put on, but it was the true healing power of Jesus at work.

"Not Now, Lady!"

Another experience that marked my life forever took place in a meeting with Kenneth Copeland in Springfield, Missouri, in 1972. Brother Copeland preached on the "Authority of the Believer," which made a powerful impression on me.

The second sermon he preached was entitled, "Substitution and Identification," and he showed in this message how that everything that Jesus went through at Calvary, He did in our place. He was made to be sin that we might be made the Righteousness of

God. He was our Substitute. We don't identify with sin, we identify with righteousness. It was a powerful message.

Then he preached, "Redeemed from the Curse." That was one of my favorite sermons. When I found out that I was redeemed from every sickness and every disease, it made a powerful impact on my life.

Then one evening, he taught on "The Authority in the Name of Jesus." He showed us the three areas in which Jesus' name gained its authority. He obtained His authority through conquest, because it was conferred upon Him, and by inheritance.

So, there I was learning all those powerful, life-changing lessons, taking notes (that I still have to this day), and consuming every word that came out of his mouth. You have to understand that in 1972, we didn't have an abundance of tapes and books, nor did we have twenty-four hour Christian television.

Most people were finding out for the first time that they had authority over the devil. Some people planned to use their authority when they got to heaven. And Brother Copeland would come back and say, "What are you going to do with all that authority you're saving up? The devil's not even going to heaven! You will be walking around looking for a fight, and there's nobody to fight. You need to exercise that authority while you're in the earth."

The last morning service that we had at the Howard Johnson's Hotel, I got up and I led the people in prayer, then I introduced Brother Copeland. I went back to where I had my little tape recorder, put my headset on, and then Brother Copeland said, "Turn me on, Jerry."

I turned the recorder on, made sure I was getting a recording, and as soon as that was done, then I put the headset down, got my Bible open, my notebook, and prepared to take notes. Brother Copeland was preaching on faith and prayer from Mark 11:23 and 24. He was just about to make a point, when suddenly, this lady stood up, and started waiving her hands, "Brother Copeland! Brother Copeland!"

He said, "Not now, lady, please, just a moment. When I get through, I'll talk to you."

She yelled, "No, Brother Copeland! I can't wait! I can't wait!"

He said, "Lady, please, let me finish this statement and then I'll talk to you."

She said, "I'm sorry, Brother Copeland! I have something from God. I've just got to tell it!"

As Brother Copeland described it later, it was like throwing a wet blanket over the service. Some people thought Brother Copeland was being rude to this lady. When, in fact, she was being rude by interrupting the service. But some of the people were not perceiving it that way.

Brother Copeland finally got very blunt with her and said, "Well, lady, you've ruined the anointing, what is it?"

She said, "I've just got to say something. God showed me something." She opened her little notebook where she had written one line on each page. She would read that line, and then she'd flip the page and read another line. She didn't say anything that Brother Copeland hadn't already said. It was nothing more than notes that she had taken from what he was preaching.

I'm thinking, *Why did she have to interrupt him to tell us this?* He stood there in his *Copeland stance,* you know, with those piercing eyes just looking at her. I was sitting there listening to her, and then I moved my chair around so I could see what he was going to do – this was my Bible School. I figured it might happen to me some day, so I wanted to see how he handles this.

All of a sudden, she threw her notepad down, bent her knees, stretched her arms out like a bird, walked out into the middle of the room, and in a totally different voice than what she was speaking in before, she said, "I see You, Jesus," and she pointed to the corner of the room behind Brother Copeland. I got out of my chair and looked in that corner. If Jesus was in the corner, I wanted to see Him.

She said, "I see You, Jesus. You told me You would come down today, and I would mount up on Your wings, and we would soar away together!"

Then she got real weird. Different sounding voices started coming out of her mouth, and my lightening-fast mind said, "That's a demon!" I thought, *Oh, boy, I'm going to get to see how Brother Copeland handles a demon. Brother Copeland, the man of God, the prophet, is going to deal with this, and I'm going to get to sit here and watch what he does.* Brother Copeland listened to her for a minute; people got up and moved away from her; it was frightening to most of the people – including me. I was right out on the edge of my chair waiting to see what Brother Copeland would do.

Jerry, Get Her Out of Here!

All of a sudden, he turned around and said, "Jerry, get her out of here!"

It scared me! I said, "You've got to be kidding! I don't want to go anywhere with that woman!"

He said, "Did you hear me? I said, get her out of here, get her delivered, and don't you leave her until she's free."

I had this pitiful, "Please, Mr. Copeland, I don't want to go" look on my face. He turned around there again and said, "I said, in the name of Jesus, get her out of here, get her delivered, and don't you come back until she's free."

She was running all over the room like a bird. So I got up reluctantly, and I grabbed one of her "wings." She jerked away from me and almost slapped me with her hand. Then she ran to the back of the building. I turned around to look at Brother Copeland with this frightened look, and he said, "Get her out of here."

So, I'm chasing this woman down, running all over the building trying to catch her! Of course, everybody in the building was watching. Finally, I grabbed her again with both arms. She was swinging trying to break lose, and I dragged her over to a door. I didn't know where the door led to, so I opened the door, and it was the parking lot. I thought, *I don't want to take her out there. Dear God, people driving by will see me out there. Plus it will give her more "runway" to take off from!*

I shut the door, and I dragged her across the other side of the room, I opened the door, and it went into the kitchen of the hotel. I couldn't take her in there. I looked at Brother Copeland like, "Where do I take her?" He just pointed, "Get her out of here!"

So I went to the back of the building, and there was a door. I opened it, and it was the cloakroom where you hang your coats. I thought, *I don't want to get in here with her! I don't know what she's going to do next.* I turned around once again waiting for answers from Brother Copeland, and he's still pointing at me, "Get her out of here!"

Use the Name!

Finally, I took her into that closet. I couldn't even find a light. There was no light. I could tell Brother Copeland was wanting me to shut the door, so, I shut the door behind me. While I'm shutting the door, she broke lose and started flapping her wings, and hangers went everywhere. She hit me under the chin, knocked me against the wall, and she kept flying around in that closet.

It sounded like we were killing each other in that closet! It was dark; I could barely see her. Finally, I felt a hand hit me in the face, and it knocked me down. The next thing I knew, this woman was on top of me. I was thinking, *Oh, dear God, if Brother Copeland opens this door and sees this woman on top of me in the floor -- I'm fired!*

I finally rolled her off of me and pinned her arms down. I thought, *What do I do now?* Then, I heard, "Use the Name." I thought, *"What Name?"* The Spirit of God said, "The name of Jesus. There's authority in the Name! Use the Name!"

All of a sudden, I had a revelation of who I was in Christ Jesus. I realized that I have power and authority over demons. I remembered that there's nothing more powerful than the name of Jesus. I started calling those spirits out in the name of Jesus. The woman went through all kinds of convulsions, and it was the weirdest thing I had ever been through in my life. But in a few minutes, she just stopped fighting me, and I said, "Now you say the name of Jesus."

She said, "Jesus."

I said, "Now thank Him for your deliverance."

As she praised God, she was filled with the Holy Ghost and started speaking in tongues. When I opened that door, everyone was gone, including Brother Copeland. I didn't know how long I had been in that closet, but she was delivered. I wanted to tell Brother Copeland, but he was gone.

I found out later that she was from a mental institution and had been brought to the meeting by some of her friends. They were waiting in the parking lot for us to get out of that closet. They were amazed at the transformation in her life. I went back to my room, and in a little while, I got a phone call from Brother Copeland. He said, "How'd it go?"

I said, "I'm black and blue, but I got her delivered! Hallelujah!"

He said, "Well, what did you learn?"

I said, "I learned there's *authority* in the name of Jesus just like you preached last night."

That was my first major encounter with demons and demon-possessed people. It certainly wasn't my last, and boy, have I ever used that revelation since then. I found out, it doesn't make any difference how strong a demon is. It's not more powerful than the name of Jesus.

21
The Hundredfold Principle

Brother Copeland had been invited to speak at the Full Gospel Businessmen's Convention in Birmingham, Alabama, in 1972. Before the meeting started, Brother Copeland said, "Let's you and I fly to Birmingham and spend a couple of days in prayer together before that meeting gets underway. God's been dealing with me about going on television, and I need the mind of Christ; I need the wisdom of God concerning this. Not only that, but God's been dealing with me about this ministry needing a bigger and faster airplane, and I need to get the wisdom of God about that as well. So let's you and I go early. We'll spend a couple of days in prayer together."

So we flew to Birmingham in Brother Copeland's little Cessna 310. We checked in the hotel in Birmingham, and the first night he said, "I want you to meet me in my room at 6:00 in the morning, and we're going to pray together and just see what we hear from God regarding these things."

I was really excited because it was the first time that he had actually invited me to participate in his prayer time. I had seen him pray publicly in meetings, but I had never been invited to be in the same room with him during his private prayer time. Usually, he isolated himself during his prayer time.

I thought, *Well, this is going to be a great opportunity because I'm going to watch him pray. Jesus said, "Watch and pray." I'll let Brother Copeland pray, and I'll watch.*

Brother Copeland had said, "We're going to get the wisdom of God," and I thought, *Yes. You'll get it, and I'll find out how to get it.* I thought, *If God's going to talk to anybody in that room, it will probably be Brother Copeland, not me.*

Prayer Time with Kenneth Copeland

The next morning we met at 6:00, and he said, "Let's just begin praying in the Spirit. If you get anything from God, you just go ahead and speak it out."

We started praying in the Spirit. I was sitting there kind of in a corner in that hotel room, and I noticed Brother Copeland knelt down by his bed and had his notebook and his Bible out. He prayed in the Spirit, and then he flipped through pages of the Bible every once in a while. So I thought, *That looks good.* So I got down on my knees in front of the chair and prayed in the Spirit and flipped through my Bible like he was doing.

He would pray in the Spirit a little while and then he'd quote a verse that he saw in the Word that pertained to the wisdom of God. For instance, in Corinthians where it says, "Jesus has been made unto us Wisdom." Then, he went to James where it said, "If any man lacks wisdom, let him ask in faith nothing wavering, because God gives liberally."

He started off finding verses that pertained to what he was believing God for, and then he quoted them. As he spoke them out, I would turn to those verses and read them as well. Not out loud, but I would follow along and read them as he spoke them out loud.

Then there were quiet times. I noticed he would get real quiet and listen. We did that for about two hours that first morning. Then he said, "Well, let's go ahead and clean up and go have some breakfast."

After we had breakfast, that was the last time I saw him that day until we had dinner that night. I assumed he was still praying in his room, so I went through the same process of what I saw him do and just prayed in the Spirit most of the day. If I heard anything, I wrote it down. The next morning, we did the same thing. We met at 6:00 a.m. and went through basically the same process.

After breakfast that morning, he called me in my room and said, "Come on back over here. I believe I've got something from God, and I want to share it with you."

I went back to his room, and he said, "I believe I've got the mind of Christ on how we're going to start this television ministry. I've got the basic format."

And he shared it with me. He said, "We're going to do what you and I are doing right now. We're going to teach people how to pray. We're going to have an informal setting, you and Carolyn and Gloria and me. We might invite another minister and his wife, and we're just going to have an informal living room setting with a sofa and chairs, and then I'm going to teach on prayer. We're going to invite the television audience to send in their prayer requests, and then each week we'll pray over their requests, and we'll show them how we pray. The name of the program will be *The Prayer Group.*"

Then he said, "I'm believing God to pay cash for this. It's going to take a lot of money for us to go to the television studio in Dallas. But I believe I've got the mind of God on this. But first, we've got to plant a seed in order to get a harvest to pay for this."

Of course, I was agreeing to everything, but I was really listening to how he planned to do this more than anything else. I was learning how to tap into the wisdom of God, and I was learning how to appropriate that wisdom once I received it.

He said, "Now, we've got to have the money for the television programs, and we've got to have the money for a new airplane. You know I don't borrow money. We pay cash for everything we do. Obviously, there's no way to do this except that we first plant seed. I've got to plant my best seed. The best seed I've got is my airplane. I'm going to give my airplane away."

How Are We Gonna Get Home?

The first thought that came in my mind was, *How are we gonna get home?*

I'm glad I didn't say it! I had never heard of anything like that - giving an airplane away! You don't give away airplanes. I had seen him give clothes away; I had seen him give money away; I had even seen him give cars away. But now we're talking airplanes! I couldn't imagine anybody giving an airplane away. My first reaction was, "How are we gonna get home?" I could just see us riding the Greyhound Bus.

And usually when he said he was going to give something away, he did it right then. So, I was concerned about my ride home. I didn't say, "Praise God!" I just kept quiet and acted like I was in total agreement. Sometimes people won't know you're ignorant if you'll just be quiet.

He said, "God told me the name of the preacher he wants me to give it to. I'm going to call him right now, and I'm going to tell him what God told me."

He called a preacher friend of ours who lived in Arlington. I heard him say, "Joe Nay, this is Kenneth."

I was sitting in the room listening to this conversation, but obviously, I couldn't hear Joe's response. He said, "Joe, this is Kenneth. Jerry and I are here in Birmingham," (it amazed me how he included me in everything as if to say, "Jerry and I both heard this from God.") He said, "Jerry and I have been praying over the television ministry and over the next airplane we need in this ministry, and God spoke to me and told me that I was to give my airplane to you."

I knew Joe was believing for an airplane. I couldn't hear Joe's response until Brother Copeland told him that. In fact, Brother Copeland held the phone away from his ear because you could hear Joe screaming. He was shouting. I could just picture him dancing and running around in circles.

Then Brother Copeland said, "Now, Joe, we're going to fly it back home, and then we'll make all the necessary arrangements to get it to you. But before I give it to you, I'm going to redo the engines first. It will be a few weeks before you actually take possession. But it's yours now. I've given it to you. In my heart, it's yours. It belongs to you now, but I want to do this work on it before I actually bring it to you."

And then he hung up.

I was sitting there speechless. My next thought was, *If you're going to give it away, why spend any more money on it? Let Joe repair the engines.* Brother Copeland perceived my thoughts. He said, "I know what you're thinking."

I said, "What?"

He said, "You're thinking, if I'm going to give it away, why spend any more money on it."

I said, "Well, that's exactly what I'm thinking. I have never heard of anything like this before." He didn't just *preach* prosperity; he didn't just *preach* sowing and reaping; he *lived* it – everyday of his life. Not just from the pulpit, but in every area of his life.

You've got to understand, I wasn't on Brother Copeland's level financially. I was still believing for food on my table, and I was believing for a suit to wear. I was believing for money to give Carolyn and the babies while I was gone. I was believing for rent money, and he's giving airplanes away. I said, "Well, why would you spend more money on the airplane if you're going to give it away?"

The Hundredfold Principle

He said, "Because I believe in the hundredfold principle."

I knew what he was talking about because I had read Mark 10:29-30 about the hundredfold. I said, "What do you mean by that?"

He said, "I don't want to give an airplane away with bad engines because if I do, I'll receive a hundredfold return on that seed, and I'll wind up with a bigger, faster airplane that needs the engines rebuilt. I want to give one away that's first class. I'm going to do everything I can to make that airplane first class when I give it away so that the one that I get in return will be first class."

Give God Your Best

I thought, *How many preachers do I know that think like that?* He was the only one on the planet I knew that thought like that. I didn't see most preachers live that way. I didn't see Christians live that way. But his attitude was, I'm not giving some old worn out airplane away. His attitude was, *You always give God your best seed.* That really went down into my spirit.

We flew home after that meeting, and Brother Copeland started the process of rebuilding the engines. I think, at that time, it was going to cost him somewhere around $10,000. In 1972, $10,000 was like $100,000 now. So, for me to think he was going to give an airplane away and then before he does it, he's going to put another $10,000 into it, it almost boggled my mind!

Approximately eleven days after he sowed the airplane into Joe Nay's ministry, I received a phone call around 10:30 one night. It was Brother Copeland, and he said, "Do you and Carolyn and the girls want to see a miracle?"

I said, "We'd love to see a miracle."

He said, "Then meet me at Oak Grove Airport. You're going to see a miracle."

I hung up and told Carolyn, "Brother Copeland said if we'll meet him at Oak Grove Airport, we'll see a miracle."

She said, "What kind of miracle?"

I said, "I don't know, but I want to see a miracle. Let's get dressed and go."

We drove out to the airport and saw Brother Copeland, Gloria, Kellie and John standing around the taxi area, just looking down the runway. We walked up behind them and said, "What are you doing?"

He said, "I'm watching for my miracle. Just keep your eyes on the end of that runway down there. You're going to see a miracle."

We just stood there and looked with the rest of them. In a little while, I saw some lights in the distance, and I could tell it was an airplane making its final approach. We stood there as we watched this airplane touch down, go down the runway, and then pull right up in front of us. It was the most beautiful airplane I had ever seen at that time. It was a Cessna 414. The man got out of it, walked up to Brother Copeland, handed him the keys and said, "Here's your airplane."

Eleven days after he sowed that seed, he received a bigger, faster airplane completely paid for! We all sat in it and praised God over it. It was quite a miracle.

Faith vs. Foolishness

Of course, I took notes on that experience. When you don't have anything and you need everything, and you see something like that work, your first reaction is, *I'm going to give everything I've got away!*

Immediately you think, *Let's just give everything away!* I was impressed. I just wanted to give something away – anything. I had been giving but not to that level. I thought, *I'm going home and find something I can give away. I need a new car – I'll give the car away.*

The Lord always protected me. He knew when I was about to make a mistake. He knew I was sincere, but sincerely wrong. The Lord told me, "Now before you jump out here and do this, let's make sure that this is a revelation to you like it is to Brother Copeland. You're not ready for this, but I'll get you ready if you'll listen to Me."

He led me to the Book of Acts where the Apostle Paul had cast out devils, and the sons of Sceva decided that they could do the same thing. So they found a demon-possessed man and said, "In the name of Jesus Christ of Nazareth whom Paul preacheth, come out of him." Remember what the demons said? "Jesus we know and Paul we know. Who are you?"

Then those devils jumped on those boys, beat them up and tore their clothes off of them. As I was reading that, I heard this in my spirit: *The moral of this story is, If you try to live on somebody else's revelation, you could lose your britches!*

You can't live on someone else's revelation; it's got to be a revelation to you. I can't live on Kenneth Copeland's revelation. It's got to be a revelation to me.

I had seen people try to do what Brother Copeland did, and it didn't work for them the same way. They would wind up blaming the message or the messenger. There's nothing wrong with the message, and there's nothing wrong with the messenger – it simply was not a revelation to them. You don't give your car away because I gave mine away. You give because it's a revelation to you, and you're inspired by the Holy Ghost.

A Revelation to Jerry

I learned not to just jump up and give everything away just because I saw this miracle in Brother Copeland's life. Faith comes by hearing and hearing by the Word of God. So I kept feeding my spirit, listening to Brother Copeland's tapes on the laws of prosperity, sowing and reaping, and watching him demonstrate it through his life. And after a while, it *did* become my revelation.

I began to see God bless Carolyn and me. And now, everything in our ministry has come that way. Every airplane I've ever owned in this ministry came that way. I've given several airplanes away in this ministry, and God blesses me with better ones. It's just the way my family and I operate. It became a revelation to Jerry many years ago, and it's still working in my life today. I learned the laws of sowing and reaping watching Brother Copeland live it and demonstrate it.

I encourage you right now to feed your spirit the Word of God, study the outlines in this book on the Laws of Prosperity until they really become a revelation to you. And then put them to work in your life. God will meet your every need. He is faithful!

22
Seven Steps to Prayer that Brings Results

Brother Copeland often taught on the subject of prayer in his morning services. He would tell the people that he learned these principles from the ministry of Kenneth Hagin.

I watched him get results, and of course, I was after results. The following is the outline that I wrote in my notebook after hearing him teach on the Seven Steps to Prayer that Brings Results.

> Matthew 21:22 says, *And all things, whatsoever ye shall ask in prayer, believing, ye shall receive.*
>
> Mark 11:24 says, *Therefore I say unto you, What things soever ye desire, when ye pray, believe that ye receive them, and ye shall have them.*

1. **Prayer that brings results must be based on God's Word.**

Brother Copeland always found out what the Bible said about the situation he was facing, and then he based his prayer on the Word of God.

a. **1 John 5:14-15** — *And this is the confidence that we have in him, that, if we ask any thing according to his will, he heareth us: And if we know that he hear us, whatsoever we ask, we know that we have the petitions that we desired of him.*

b. **1 John 3:22** — *And whatsoever we ask, we receive of him, because we keep his commandments, and do those things that are pleasing in his sight.*

c. **Romans 12:2** — *And be not conformed to this world: but be ye transformed by the renewing of your mind, that ye may prove what is that good, and acceptable, and perfect, will of God.*

If you base your prayer on the Word of God, then you'll always pray the will of God. God will never say something in His Word that is not His will. His Word and His will are one in the same.

d. **Start with the answer – the Word of God.**

When most people pray, they're looking for an answer. That's the religious kind of praying. They say I'm asking God to *answer my prayer.* When you learn how to pray the Word, then you can start with the answer.

For instance, if you need healing, then go to the Word of God and find out what the Bible says about healing, and start your prayer with the **answer**.

2. **Begin the application of faith.**

a. **Start your confession before you have the manifestation. Believe you receive the moment you pray. Confess the truth. God's Word is truth.**

James 3:11-17 — *Doth a fountain send forth at the same place sweet water and bitter? Can* *the fig tree, my brethren, bear olive berries? either a vine, figs? so can no fountain both yield salt water and fresh. Who is a wise man and endued with knowledge among you? let him show out of a good conversation his works with meekness of wisdom.*

But if ye have bitter envying and strife in your hearts, glory not, and lie not against the truth. This wisdom descendeth not from above, but is earthly, sensual, devilish. For where envying and strife is, there is confusion and every evil work. But the wisdom that is from above is first pure, then peaceable, gentle, and easy to be entreated, full of mercy and good fruits, without partiality, and without hypocrisy.

Hold fast to your confession.

Hebrews 4:11-16 – *Let us labour therefore to enter into that rest, lest any man fall after the same example of unbelief. For the word of God is quick, and powerful, and sharper than any twoedged sword, piercing even to the dividing asunder of soul and spirit, and of the joints and marrow, and is a discerner of the thoughts and intents of the heart.*

Neither is there any creature that is not manifest in his sight: but all things are naked and opened unto the eyes of him with whom we have to do. Seeing then that we have a great high priest, that is passed into the heavens, Jesus the Son of God, let us hold fast our profession.

For we have not an high priest which cannot be touched with the feeling of our infirmities; but was in all points tempted like as we are, yet without sin. Let us therefore come boldly unto the throne of grace, that we may obtain mercy, and find grace to help in time of need.

b. **Act as though it is already done.**

James 2:14-24 – *What doth it profit, my brethren, though a man say he hath faith, and have not works? can faith save him? If a brother or sister be naked, and destitute of daily food, And one of you say unto them, Depart in peace, be ye warmed and filled; notwithstanding ye give them not those things which are needful to the body; what doth it profit? Even so faith, if it hath not works, is dead, being alone.*

Yea, a man may say, Thou hast faith, and I have works: Show me thy faith without thy works, and I will show thee my faith by my works. Thou believest that there is one God; thou doest well: the devils also believe, and tremble. But wilt thou know, O vain man, that faith without works is dead? Was not Abraham our father justified by works, when he had offered Isaac his son upon the altar? Seest thou how faith wrought with his works, and by works was faith made perfect?

And the scripture was fulfilled which saith, Abraham believed God, and it was imputed unto him for righteousness: and he was called the Friend of God. Ye see then how that by works a man is justified, and not by faith only.

Faith demands action. If you truly believe, then you'll act as though it has already manifested.

c. **To be afraid to confess or to act on God's Word before you have it is to doubt God's Word.**

In other words, if you're afraid to confess what God's Word says, then you don't truly believe it. If you're afraid to act on God's Word, then you are doubting that what He's saying is true.

3. **Refuse to allow doubts and fear to enter your consciousness.**

   a. Satan works in the area of suggestions, dreams, and thoughts.

   b. **You are the establishing witness.** Control your mind with the Word of God. Dwell on the answer instead of the problem.

      2 Corinthians 10:5 – *Casting down imaginations, and every high thing that exalteth itself against the knowledge of God, and bringing into captivity every thought to the obedience of Christ.*

      Philippians 4:6-8 – *Be careful for nothing; but in every thing by prayer and supplication with thanksgiving let your requests be made known unto God. And the peace of God, which passeth all understanding, shall keep your hearts and minds through Christ Jesus. Finally, brethren, whatsoever things are true, whatsoever things are honest, whatsoever things are just, whatsoever things are pure, whatsoever things are lovely, whatsoever things are of good report; if there be any virtue, and if there be any praise, think on these things.*

      1 Peter 5:6-7 – *Humble yourselves therefore under the mighty hand of God, that he may exalt you in due time: Casting all your care upon him; for he careth for you.*

4. **See yourself succeeding and not failing.**

   Proverbs 4:20-24 – *My son, attend to my words; incline thine ear unto my sayings. Let them not depart from thine eyes; keep them in the midst of thine heart. For they are life unto those that find them, and health to all their flesh.*

   Keep thy heart with all diligence; for out of it are the

issues of life. Put away from thee a froward mouth, and perverse lips put far from thee.

Keep the Word in front of your eyes. This helps you to become single-minded.

Matthew 6:22-23 – *The light of the body is the eye: if therefore thine eye be single, thy whole body shall be full of light. But if thine eye be evil, thy whole body shall be full of darkness. If therefore the light that is in thee be darkness, how great is that darkness!*

5. **Testify to what you believe.**

   Revelation 12:11 – *And they overcame him by the blood of the Lamb, and by the word of their testimony; and they loved not their lives unto the death.*

   Your testimony establishes what you believe.

   a. ***Say it, do it, receive it, and tell it.*** Mark 5 shares the illustrations about Jairus and his daughter and also the little woman with the issue of blood. In these illustrations you will find that they both *said* what they believed even before it had manifested.

   Brother Copeland would often say that this is the formula for releasing the God kind of faith. Say it, do it, receive it, and tell it.

6. **Get involved in praying for someone else.**

   1 Timothy 2:1-2 – *I exhort therefore, that, first of all, supplications, prayers, intercessions, and giving of thanks, be made for all men; For kings, and for all that are in authority; that we may lead a quiet and peaceable life in all godliness and honesty.*

   Faith works by love.

   Galatians 5:6 – *For in Jesus Christ neither circumcision* *availeth any thing, nor uncircumcision; but faith which worketh by love.*

(In other words, don't spend all your prayer time on yourself. Get involved in praying for someone else.)

7. **Get on the giving end**.

   Luke 6:38 – *Give, and it shall be given unto you; good measure, pressed down, and shaken together, and running over, shall men give into your bosom. For with the same measure that ye mete withal it shall be measured to you again.*

   If you need healing, give the message of healing to someone else. If you need money, give money to someone who also has a need. It's God's law: you will reap what you sow.

Those are the Seven Steps to Prayer that Brings Results. I still use these principles today. Again, I urge you to review this outline and apply these steps when you pray. It's worked for me and produced outstanding results in my life. I'm convinced that it can and will work for you too!

23
How to Transmit the Anointing

The next meeting that made a major impact in my life was in Shonto, Arizona, in 1972 on the Navajo Indian Reservation. God had just blessed Brother Copeland with his Cessna 414 airplane. I had watched him believe God for it, and I was looking forward to flying in it with him for my first time.

Walk in Love

Brother Copeland, Joe Nay and I were to go on this meeting. I arrived early with the sound system (amplifier, recorder, speakers, tapes, etc.) and all the materials that he had planned to give the Navajo ministers. When Brother Copeland arrived, he pulled the airplane out of the hangar, and we began loading everything.

Then Joe Nay and his wife arrived. They unloaded Joe's luggage, and as she was leaving, she accidentally ran over the speakers. She backed over them and just crushed them. I was sitting there thinking, *Oh, God, I'm glad I didn't do that.*

She felt terrible. Joe felt terrible. I was standing there watching to see how Brother Copeland was going to react to this. He just walked up to them, put his arms around them, and he said, "Don't worry about it. God gave us those, and He'll give us some more."

I saw him walk in love and minister to them because he knew how terrible they felt. He just ministered in love and told them, "Don't have a second thought about it."

They said, "We'll buy you another set of speakers."

He said, "No, don't you worry about it. God'll take care of it."

In the natural, I know that was hard to do. But he made a decision to walk the love walk. I had heard him preach a sermon that he called, "Walking the Love Walk." Now I was watching him do it. That really impressed me. It impressed Joe Nay too, because when we were flying to Arizona, Joe asked me, "Do you think he really meant it?"

I said, "He meant it. Don't worry about it. He's a man of his word. He told you not to worry about it, so don't worry about it."

We arrived at the Navajo Indian Reservation. We didn't have hotel accommodations; we stayed in two little trailers. I had never seen so much sand in all my life. It was like being in a Third World country, and it was in Arizona.

All we had to eat while we were there was commodity peanut butter, cheese, and prunes. Dear Jesus!

Joe and I were in one little camping trailer, and Brother Copeland was in a mobile home with the Pastor and his family. Our trailer had a bent frame right in the middle. It was quite a sight!

During the day, Brother Copeland would walk over to our trailer. I can still picture him in his cowboy boots, his Levis and a T-shirt carrying his Bible and his notebook. He would say, "What have y'all got to eat?"

I said, "Prunes, cheese, and peanut butter. How do you want me to fix it today?"

He said, "Stew me some prunes."

I said, "Stew you some prunes?"

He said, "Yes. Do you know how to stew prunes?"

I said, "Just put them in a pan with water and heat them up, I guess."

He said, "Yes, do it."

So, I put those prunes in a pan and filled it full of water and heated them up, and I stewed the prunes. When they were ready, Brother Copeland sat there and ate them. Then he noticed that the screen door on the trailer had a little hole in it. Brother Copeland turned toward that screen door, and went, "Puhh!" and spit that prune seed right through that hole. It was a small hole. But it went clean through!

Joe Nay said, "I don't believe that!"

Brother Copeland said, "I can do it again."

Joe said, "You can't do that again! That was nothing but luck!"

He said, "I don't believe in luck. I walk by faith, not by luck."

He said, "Do it again!"

Brother Copeland chewed on that prune, and by then we had him tickled because he was going to try it again. He spit that thing, and it went right through that hole again. We couldn't believe it. He got up and walked off. He knew if you got two out of two, then you need to quit.

Joe and I spit seeds the rest of the afternoon and never did get one through that hole! We had a pile of seeds in front of the screen door. Brother Copeland came back later and saw all those seeds piled up, and almost passed out laughing. We were desperate for entertainment out there in the dessert!

How to Transmit the Anointing

Once the meetings got underway, we noticed right off that there was a lot of demon activity. Every night, we saw demonic activity. Brother Copeland was casting out devils and ministering deliverance to people. It was awesome. I learned so much just watching him follow the leadership of the Holy Ghost.

The last night that we were there, Brother Copeland called all the Navajo ministers up to the front. We were under a tent with a little makeshift platform, and Brother Copeland sat on that platform and started ministering to them about the anointing of God. It was so powerful that I wrote it all down.

He was teaching them how to transmit the anointing of God. He was endeavoring to instruct those young Navajo ministers in how to properly lay hands on people, minister deliverance, and how to get results. I wrote at the top of my notes, *Transmitting the Anointing of God.*

Here's what he said to them:

#1. *When you lay hands on someone to administer God's anointing, don't make physical contact with them until you are ready to release your faith.*

In other words, don't just go up there and lay your hands on somebody. The moment you put your hands on them, that's your point of contact. That's when you want all the faith that is in you to be channeled toward that person.

#2. *When you're ministering to little children, be cautious about releasing your faith when you touch them because you are releasing so much power that they don't know how to react to it.*

The reason he brought that up was because he had ministered to a lot of Navajo children, and many times when he would get ready to lay his hands on them, some of them would just scream. It was mostly because of the demonic activity that was going on in that meeting.

He said, "Sometimes they'll try to fight back, but just lay your hands on them when you're ready to release your faith, and don't react to their reactions. Just stay conscious of the fact that the anointing of God is leaving your hand and going into them."

> #3. *Don't ever lay your hands on someone before you pray. While you're praying, you will sense your faith reach its highest peak. That's the moment you lay your hands on the people.*
>
> #4. *Sometimes the anointing will feel like electricity flowing through you. The anointing works very similar to electricity. Your hand is the conductor for that anointing just like a cable is for electricity.*
>
> #5. *When the anointing of God comes on you and is operating in you, be very cautious because you tend to want to yield to it by shouting, laughing, running, or leaping. Don't absorb it. Channel it toward those who need it.*

He explained that the main purpose for the anointing is to channel it into somebody else so that it will remove their burdens and destroy their yokes.

> #6. *You can run the anointing off, you can jump the anointing off, you can shout the anointing off, but don't waste it; get your hands on somebody. The anointing can be transmitted into those who need healing and deliverance.*
>
> #7. *Watch your words, and watch your actions. Don't do anything that would drain that anointing. Channel it into the lives of others.*
>
> #8. *Your hands are the vehicles that the Spirit of God will use to channel that anointing. There are two primary ways in which the anointing can be channeled: Your words and your hands. Therefore, don't waste words, and don't waste motions. Put your words and your motions in a direct line and use them to bring deliverance to the people. It's similar to shooting a rifle. You have to aim it in*

order to hit the target. When you waste words and you waste motions, you'll miss the target.

#9. *One of the things you need to learn about the anointing, is if you want it to operate strongly in your life, then discipline yourself to spend much time with God before every service. Don't run around with people just before the service, and then run into the church, get behind the pulpit, and expect the anointing to be strong.*

#10. *The anointing flows out of your innermost being. It's like rivers of water in the very core of your spirit. Protect it, and it will be there when you need it.*

#11. *You can't give someone something that you don't have. You can't expect the anointing to go into someone if you haven't prepared yourself properly to operate in the anointing. If you don't have it, you certainly can't give it to someone else. This is the reason it is so important that you never allow anyone or anything to rob you of your prayer time before a meeting.*

Brother Oral Roberts taught Brother Copeland that. He knew that after 3:00 in the afternoon, you didn't talk to Oral Roberts. After 3:00 in the afternoon, you didn't talk to Kenneth Copeland. After 3:00 in the afternoon, you don't talk to me when I'm in a meeting. I lock myself away and prepare for that meeting, and I don't engage in conversation with others. I could see the results in Brother Copeland's life, and that's what I wanted. A lot of people see results, but they're not willing to do what it takes to get them.

Brother Copeland went on to say: *This is the reason that it's so important that you don't allow anyone or anything to rob you of your prayer time. Get alone with God. He is the only One who can do anything for the people in whom you are ministering. If you get alone with God, then His anointing will come on you, and then you will have something to transmit into the people. Without the anointing, you have nothing to offer them.*

Everyone wants to be anointed, but few people know how to get in position to receive. To get in position to receive the anointing, you must fel-

Jerry Savelle   *Don Burton*

KEN COPELAND SENDS TWO MEN FROM SHREVEPORT, LOUISIANA

Don Burton and Jerry Savelle arrived by air for the Pismo Beach outreach. Their ten day trip lacked nothing. It was like another exciting chapter in the Book of Acts. People getting born again, Baptized in the Holy Spirit and in water, healed, and then moving out for God in almost supernatural ways. They said we can't wait to get back to our young people who are sitting on a "powder keg" just waiting for direction. Now we know. It's make Jesus Lord, get out and scatter the seed everywhere, all the time, and to everyone.

Trained to share Christ gave them vision to reach the world

Like thousands of people in the world today, I was an addict. For twelve years I was ad___ to the "bench" in my church. Six months ___ delivered me from "bench warming" and ___ Lord of my life. Since this time, my fa___ been living a beautiful life; depending ___ Jesus for our healing, finances and all o___ love Jesus and I'm proud to serve Him.

Ken Copeland sent Don and I to California ___ we certainly received valuable training on how ___

Los Angeles airport ___ alkin, Director of Action Life Ministries ___ Pismo Beach over the 4th of July ___ perienced miracles. Over 2000 people ___ th about the Lord Jesus Christ. Hun___ ceive Christ. Lives were transformed ___ in the streets, and ___ the beaches. ___ saw a ___ dn't stand up, receive ___ for Jesus. Saw a ___ or his healing

Newspaper clip about Brother Copeland sending me to Pismo Beach to learn how to share Jesus.

Preaching to anyone who would listen. I just had to tell somebody what I knew.

The man who taught me how to win souls for Jesus, Dave Malkin.

The Savelle family moves to Fort Worth, in 1971. (left to right: me, Carolyn, Terri and Jerri)

Our first house in Fort Worth with very little furniture and a small refrigerator from a camping trailer.

Gloria and Kenneth Copeland in the early 70's . . . haven't the styles changed!

While flying in Brother Copeland's airplane, I learned many lessons about living by faith.

Brother Copeland praying for people's legs to be lengthened.

Taking notes, absorbing every word while working for Kenneth Copeland Evangelistic Association.

Jerry Savelle (on right) an Associate Minister for Kenneth Copeland Ministries, 1973.

KEYS TO OVERCOMING FAITH

VOLUME 2   SEPTEMBER, 1975

"That Your Joy Ma...

by: Jerry Savelle

Dr. Fred Price, myself, and Brother Copeland during one of our seminars in the 70's. (We've all changed.)

One of our first newsletters and tape brochures.

**Jerry Savelle Evangelistic Association,
early publicity photo, 1974.**

Preaching at an outdoor rally in El Paso, TX, in the early 70's.

A sign advertising our meeting in Levelland, TX, in the early 70's.

Ministering one-on-one (what I learned from Dave Malkin).

Preaching with Brother Copeland (behind me) ... still a team.

Preaching in front yards, laundromats, and hotel ballrooms.

Making some appearances on television, 1980.

Preaching in Nigeria to over 50,000 people, 1984.

The "fiery young preacher" with a burning desire to teach people how to live a victorious life through faith in God's Word.

lowship with God. Sometimes it's a lonely life. Sometimes you feel like you're the loneliest person in the world when you're shut away. But when you come out, and you operate in that anointing, you feel like the most blessed person in the world because God has used you to bring deliverance to others.

In order to become strong in the anointing, you must become single-minded. Your primary purpose in ministry: meet the needs of the people. Bring deliverance everywhere you go.

These are very valuable points that you should take very seriously. You never just lay your hands on somebody unless you're ready to release your faith. Learn how to properly release your faith, and you'll see the anointing of God transmitted into those who need deliverance, healing and miracles.

The Trip Back Home - Put Your Oxygen Mask On

After the meeting was over that night, Brother Copeland said, "How do you feel?"

I said, "I feel good."

He said, "Do you want to stay here another night, or do you want to fly home?"

I said, "I'm ready, if you are."

He said, "Let's go!"

It was late at night, and we were going to take off from this runway that was rough, it looked too short, and it was right up next to a mountain. I just kept praying in tongues. I knew Brother Copeland knew what he was doing. I was sitting in the cockpit with him in the right seat, and we then took off down that runway. I could see mountains everywhere. It was the roughest ol' runway I'd ever been on. We got airborne and we we're flying along, and it looked like those mountains were getting closer and closer, and I was praying in tongues – under my breath. I didn't want to disturb Brother Copeland. Then, Brother Copeland said, "That mountain range up ahead is 13,000 feet. We've got to climb over 13,000 feet to top those mountains." At this time, I hadn't flown a lot, so everything was still new to me. He said, "Something has happened, and I can't pressurize the cabin, so you'll have to put on your oxygen mask, but I'll tell you when to do it."

When he said, "oxygen mask," all I could think of was, *We're gonna die! Why do we need oxygen?*

Inside, I was in a panic stage. I'm thinking, *I'm never gonna see Carolyn and the girls again. They're going to find us out here somewhere dead with an oxygen mask on.*

(By the way, this is Brother Copeland's favorite story about me.)

So, we got over those mountains, and he said, "Put your mask on."

I said, "Where is it?"

He said, "Under your seat."

So, I reached under my seat, and I found a container. By the time I got to it, Brother Copeland already had his mask on.

I was sitting there trying to figure out how to put the thing on. It was in pieces. I think John Copeland had been playing with the oxygen mask – he was always into something.

Brother Copeland raised his mask up and said, "Get it on!"

I said, "I'm trying!"

Finally, I put it on. I had never had an oxygen mask on before, so I didn't know what to expect. He said, "Just breathe normal."

There's Not Enough for Both of Us

I didn't know what to expect. I'll never forget this as long as I live. All of a sudden, Brother Copeland raised his mask, and he said, "There's not enough oxygen for both of us; take your mask off!"

Then he put his back on. I looked over at him with the saddest look you have ever seen in your life. I couldn't believe it. "There's not enough oxygen for both of us; take your mask off!"

I took my mask off, and this pale look came on me, and then I looked over at him again. I didn't say anything; I was in shock! He was getting us over this mountain range, and I didn't want to disturb him. I noticed he looked back at me, but then he focused back on the instruments. I sat there thinking, *I can't believe it. I have been faithful to him, I have carried his coat, I have driven him to the meetings, I've given him 100 percent service since I joined this ministry. And now, when there's not enough oxygen, we can replace Jerry!*

Then I thought, *He will get another servant after I'm gone. There's not enough oxygen for both of us. Big faith man! If there's not enough oxygen for both of us, why doesn't he just believe God, and let me breathe! He's the faith man! I can't believe the prophet wants the servant to remove his mask!*

I took my mask off, and I really thought that at any moment, I was going to take my last breath. I considered writing a letter to Carolyn and the girls and ask Brother Copeland to give it to them when he gets home. One of us was going to make it home. The man with the mask on is going to make it home!

I couldn't believe it. I just sat there thinking, *Any minute it will all be over.*

Finally, Brother Copeland landed in Albuquerque. When he landed, he got out of the airplane, and I was sitting there pinching myself in disbelief that I was still alive. Brother Copeland went outside, and fell to his knees laughing. He laughed from way down deep. He threw his head back, his mouth was wide open, and he just kept laughing. I came walking out of the airplane with this sheepish look on my face, and I said, "What are you laughing at?"

He said, "You! I knew what you were thinking, but I didn't have time to explain. I had to get us over that mountain range. I know you were thinking, the big faith man! He gets the oxygen and the servant gets none!"

It's still his favorite story to this day.

24

The Laws of Prosperity, Part I:
Wisdom for Prosperity

The latter part of 1972, Brother Copeland conducted his very first "Laws of Prosperity Seminar" in Oklahoma City. It was a very special meeting.

Brother Copeland had been learning how to apply God's laws of prosperity, and then he felt it was time to teach them in his meetings. He had mentioned them occasionally, but he had never actually done a "Prosperity Seminar." So he was very excited about it.

My job when we arrived was to go in and set up the little hotel ballroom. I set up the sound system and the chairs and platform. Brother Copeland wanted this meeting to be very special. He wanted to make sure that we were able to get good recordings because these tapes were going to be our "masters" for our new tape series entitled, "The Laws of Prosperity."

"Turn Me On, Jerry"

The opening night, we had a good crowd, and the people were excited. I lead the praise and worship, and then I introduced Brother Copeland. I went to the back of the platform and put my headset on and waited for my cue, "Turn me on, Jerry." As soon as he said that, then I turned the tape recorder on and made sure that I was getting a good signal. Then I took the headset off and started taking notes. I still have those notes from Brother Copeland's first series on "God's Laws of Prosperity" Parts I-V. What I learned in those five services changed my financial future.

The first four services went well. The people seemed to be receiving the message, and Brother Copeland was really excited and the anointing was so strong on him.

However, during the last service, something happened. You might say that the last service was the most important service because he had been teaching us all week about how to make deposits in our heavenly bank account and this final message was to be, "How to Make Withdrawals." Everybody wants to know how to make withdrawals.

I was sitting there ready to learn how to make withdrawals from my heavenly bank account. I got a good signal on the recorder, and everything was going great. About fifteen to twenty minutes into the message, all of a sudden, there was a loud pop, and smoke started coming up out of the tape recorder. When Brother Copeland heard it, and then saw the smoke, he turned around, and the first thing he said was, "What did you do?"

I said, "I didn't do anything! I didn't touch it!"

He said, "Well, what's wrong with it?"

I said, "I don't know. The thing just blew up."

There we were listening to the most important part of this entire series, and the recorder blew up. We still had sound, but we couldn't get a recording. I couldn't do anything. I didn't know how to repair it. And you could just see the disgust on Brother Copeland's face.

I felt like a dog. It wasn't my fault, but I felt so badly for him because I knew how desperately he wanted those masters for the tape series. The good thing about it was, there was a guy who came to every service with his tape recorder. So, we had him set his recorder in front of the speaker with a microphone pointed toward it, and we were able to get a recording. It wasn't a direct recording, but it worked, praise God!

When you listened to those series of tapes, the first four messages were very clear, good copies, but the last message sounded like Brother Copeland was in a tunnel. But at least we did get it recorded. It became our most requested set of tapes. Even though he preached it and recorded it again later, he never felt like it was quite the same as that very first time. It was an attack of the devil because he didn't want those powerful, life-changing messages to get out to the Body of Christ.

The following are my personal notes from those five services. I hope that they will bless you as much as they have blessed my life.

The Laws of Prosperity — Part I

A. God's wisdom produces prosperity.

  1.   Proverbs 3:13-16 – *Happy is the man that findeth wisdom, and the man that getteth understanding. For the merchandise of it is better than the merchandise of silver, and the gain thereof than fine gold. She is more precious than rubies: and all the things thou canst desire are not to be compared unto her. Length of days is in her right hand; and in her left hand riches and honour.*

   It stands to reason if you want to know about prosperity, then ask a prosperous man.

  2.   There is none more prosperous than God.

  3.   ==Dealing wisely in every situation will bring prosperity.==

  4.   God's wisdom has been made available to you.

   Colossians 2:1-3 – *For I would that ye knew what great conflict I have for you, and for them at Laodicea, and for* as many as have not seen my face in the flesh; That their hearts might be comforted, being knit together in love, and unto all riches of the full assurance of understanding, to the acknowledgement of the mystery of God, and of the Father, and of Christ; In whom are hid all the treasures of wisdom and knowledge.*

1 Corinthians 1:30 – *But of him are ye in Christ Jesus, who of God is made unto us wisdom, and righteousness, and sanctification, and redemption.*

James 1:8 – *A double minded man is unstable in all his ways.*

5. Meditation in God's Word is the key to receiving God's wisdom.

Joshua 1:8 – *This book of the law shall not depart out of thy mouth; but thou shalt meditate therein day and night, that thou mayest observe to do according to all that is written therein: for then thou shalt make thy way prosperous, and then thou shalt have good success.*

B. The world's prosperity vs. God's prosperity.

1. The world's definition of prosperity is gold, silver, political power, social prestige, and comfort.

2. Don't ever look at prosperity from a carnal viewpoint. If you do, you'll only see the world's definition.

3. True prosperity is to be loved by God and His Son and to have them manifest themselves in your life.

John 14:23 – *Jesus answered and said unto him, If a man love me, he will keep my words: and my Father will love him, and we will come unto him, and make our abode with him.*

4. When God manifests Himself in your life, He will teach you how to be free from poverty, lack, and want.

5. Matthew 6:33 – *But seek ye first the kingdom of God, and his righteousness; and all these things shall be added unto you.*

   Seek first the kingdom of God, and everything you need will be added.

C. **God's definition of prosperity.**

   1. **The ability to use God's power in order to meet the needs of humanity.**

   2. We are partners with God in carrying out His plan for the world.

      2 Corinthians 6:1 – *We then, as workers together with him, beseech you also that ye receive not the grace of God in vain.*

   3. When you go in business with God, you will learn how to do things His way. This is true prosperity.

   4. Failures are not God-made.

      John 15:5 – *I am the vine, ye are the branches: He that abideth in me, and I in him, the same bringeth forth much fruit: for without me ye can do nothing.*

      He's the vine; you're the branch.

   5. **You cannot fail when God's wisdom is at work in your life.**

   6. Begin to declare and confess frequently, "I have the mind of Christ."

D. **Prosperity is governed by spiritual law.**

   1. **Spiritual laws override natural laws.**

      Romans 8:2 – *For the law of the Spirit of life in Christ Jesus hath made me free from the law of sin and death.*

2. Faith is the force that causes the laws of the spirit to function.

3. There are only two systems in operation in the earth: (a) the world's system; (b) God's system.

4. Learning God's system of operation makes you dangerous to Satan. He will do everything in his power to keep you from learning this system.

5. Putting God's system to work in your life, in every area of your life, will cause failure to be a thing of the past.

25
The Laws of Prosperity, Part II:
God's Covenant with You

A. **Become established in God's covenant.**

    1. Ephesians 2:12 – *That at that time ye were without Christ, being aliens from the commonwealth of Israel, and strangers from the covenants of promise, having no hope, and without God in the world.*

        Spiritual bankruptcy is to be without God or to be without a covenant.

    2. To be without God and to be without a covenant is to be hopeless.

    3. As a believer, you are not hopeless.

    4. ==Your covenant with God provides prosperity.==

        Deuteronomy 8:18 – *But thou shalt remember the Lord thy God: for it is he that giveth thee power to get wealth, that he may establish his covenant which he sware unto thy fathers, as it is this day.*

Deuteronomy 9:5-6 – *Not for thy righteousness, or for the uprightness of thine heart, dost thou go to possess their land: but for the wickedness of these nations the Lord thy God doth drive them out from before thee, and that he may perform the word which the Lord sware unto thy fathers, Abraham, Isaac, and Jacob. Understand therefore, that the Lord thy God giveth thee not this good land to possess it for thy righteousness; for thou art a stiffnecked people.*

5. It's not only your covenant right to prosper, but it's also God's oath to you.

6. Become highly developed in your covenant rights.

   Deuteronomy 28:1-2 – *And it shall come to pass, if thou shalt hearken diligently unto the voice of the Lord thy God, to observe and to do all his commandments which I command thee this day, that the Lord thy God will set thee on high above all nations of the earth: And all these blessings shall come on thee, and overtake thee, if thou shalt hearken unto the voice of the Lord thy God.*

B. You have a better covenant than those in the Old Testament.

1. Hebrews 8:6 – *But now hath he obtained a more excellent ministry, by how much also he is the mediator of a better covenant, which was established upon better promises.* A better covenant with better promises.

2. You are redeemed from poverty.

   Galatians 3:13 – *Christ hath redeemed us from the curse of the law, being made a curse for us: for it is written, Cursed is every one that hangeth on a tree.*

3. God has promised to supply your every need.

   Philippians 4:19 – *But my God shall supply all your need according to his riches in glory by Christ Jesus.*

4. God's greatest desire is that you prosper and be in health. 3 John 2.

   a. ==God wants you to prosper spiritually, mentally, physically, financially and socially.==

   b. ==You must have your heart established in what belongs to you.==

   > Psalm 112:1-10 – *Praise ye the Lord. Blessed is the man that feareth the Lord, that delighteth greatly in his commandments. His seed shall be mighty upon earth: the generation of the upright shall be blessed. Wealth and riches shall be in his house: and his righteousness endureth for ever. Unto the upright there ariseth light in the darkness: he is gracious, and full of compassion, and righteous.*
   >
   > *A good man showeth favour, and lendeth: he will guide his affairs with discretion. Surely he shall not be moved for ever: the righteous shall be in everlasting remembrance. He shall not be afraid of evil tidings: his heart is fixed, trusting in the Lord. His heart is established, he shall not be afraid, until he see his desire upon his enemies.*
   >
   > *He hath dispersed, he hath given to the poor; his rightousness endureth for ever; his horn shall be exalted with honour. The wicked shall see it, and be grieved; he shall gnash with his teeth, and melt away: the desire of the wicked shall perish.*

   c. Don't be afraid to prosper. Money is not evil; only the love of it is.

C. **Ignorance of your covenant rights prevents you from prospering.**

   1. ==Satan's most powerful weapon is deception.==

2. ==Satan's greatest act of deception is to keep you ignorant of what belongs to you.==

3. ==If Satan can't deceive you, he can't defeat you.==

4. Examples: Luke 15:11-32 – *And he said, A certain man had two sons: And the younger of them said to his father, Father, give me the portion of goods that falleth to me. And he divided unto them his living. And not many days after the younger son gathered all together, and took his journey into a far country, and there wasted his substance with riotous living. And when he had spent all, there arose a mighty famine in that land; and he began to be in want. And he went and joined himself to a citizen of that country; and he sent him into his fields to feed swine.*

   And he would fain to have filled his belly with the husks that the swine did eat: and no man gave unto him. And when he came to himself, he said, How many hired servants of my father's have bread enough and to spare, and I perish with hunger! I will arise and go to my father, and will say unto him, Father, I have sinned against heaven, and before thee, And am no more worthy to be called thy son: make me as one of thy hired servants. And he arose, and came to his father.

   But when he was yet a great way off, his father saw him, and had compassion, and ran, and fell on his neck, and kissed him. And the son said unto him, Father, I have sinned against heaven, and in thy sight, and am no more worthy to be called thy son.

   But the father said to his servants, Bring forth the best robe, and put it on him; and put a ring on his hand, and shoes on his feet: And bring hither the fatted calf, and kill it; and let us eat, and be merry: For this my son was dead, and is alive again; he was lost, and is found. And they began to be merry.

   Now his elder son was in the field: and as he came and drew nigh to the house, he heard music and dancing. And he called one of the servants, and asked what these things meant. And he said unto him, Thy brother is come; and thy father hath killed the fatted calf, because he hath received him safe and sound.

And he was angry, and would not go in: therefore came his father out, and entreated him. And he answering said to his father, Lo, these many years do I serve thee, neither transgressed I at any time thy commandment: and yet thou never gavest me a kid, that I might make merry with my friends: But as soon as this thy son was come, which hath devoured thy living with harlots, thou hast killed for him the fatted calf.

And he said unto him, Son, thou art ever with me, and all that I have is thine. It was meet that we should make merry, and be glad: for this thy brother was dead, and is alive again; and was lost, and is found.

a. The older brother could have had the fatted calf and anything else that he wanted, ==but he didn't know what belonged to him.==

> Mark 10:17-30 – *And when he was gone forth into the way, there came one running, and kneeled to him, and asked him, Good Master, what shall I do that I may inherit eternal life? And Jesus said unto him, Why callest thou me good? there is none good but one, that is, God.*
>
> *Thou knowest the commandments, Do not commit adultery, Do not kill, Do not steal, Do not bear false witness, Defraud not, Honour thy father and mother. And he answered and said unto him, Master, all these have I observed from my youth. Then Jesus beholding him loved him, and said unto him, One thing thou lackest: go thy way, sell whatsoever thou hast, and give to the poor, and thou shalt have treasure in heaven: and come, take up the cross, and follow me.*
>
> *And he was sad at that saying, and went away grieved: for he had great possessions. And Jesus looked round about, and saith unto his disciples,*

How hardly shall they that have riches enter into the kingdom of God!

And the disciples were astonished at his words. But Jesus answereth again, and saith unto them, Children, how hard is it for them that trust in riches to enter into the kingdom of God! It is easier for a camel to go through the eye of a needle, than for a rich man to enter into the kingdom of God.

And they were astonished out of measure, saying among themselves, Who then can be saved? And Jesus looking upon them saith, With men it is impossible, but not with God: for with God all things are possible.

Then Peter began to say unto him, Lo, we have left all, and have followed thee. And Jesus answered and said, Verily I say unto you, There is no man that hath left house, or brethren, or sisters, or father, or mother, or wife, or children, or lands, for my sake, and the gospel's, But he shall receive an hundredfold now in this time, houses, and brethren, and sisters, and mothers, and children, and lands, with persecutions; and in the world to come eternal life.

    b.   ==The hundredfold blessing belongs to you but if you are not aware of it, then Satan will keep it from you.==

D.   **Laying up treasures in heaven.**

    1.   Matthew 6:19-21 — *Lay not up for yourselves treasures upon earth, where moth and rust doth corrupt, and where thieves break through and steal: But lay up for yourselves treasures in heaven, where neither moth nor rust doth corrupt, and where thieves do not break through nor steal: For where your treasure is, there will your heart be also.*

        a.   Jesus is telling us to establish a heavenly bank account.

- b. Your treasure in heaven is as much yours now as eternal life is.

- c. Jesus is telling us to let heaven be our treasury; then regardless of what happens on the earth, we have a supply that is not subject to theft, ruin, inflation, or depression.

    Philippians 4:19 – *But my God shall supply all your need according to his riches in glory by Christ Jesus.*

2. 1 Timothy 6:17-19 – *Charge them that are rich in this world, that they be not highminded, nor trust in uncertain riches, but in the living God, who giveth us richly all things to enjoy; That they do good, that they be rich in good works, ready to distribute, willing to communicate; Laying up in store for themselves a good foundation against the time to come, that they may lay hold on eternal life.*

3. God gives us richly all things to enjoy while we're on the earth.

4. ==Giving is what produces a heavenly bank account.==

5. ==When you give to others, you are laying up treasures in heaven.==

6. If you don't have any treasures in heaven, then you can't make a withdrawal.

26
The Laws of Prosperity, Part III:
Laying up Treasures in Heaven

It's important that you understand that you can make deposits in your **heavenly bank account.** When Jesus said, "Lay not up for yourself treasures in earth," He was not saying that you can't have earthly bank accounts. What He's saying is, don't put your trust in them. Don't make that your source of supply.

Jesus isn't saying that you can't have money in savings or that you can't have money set aside. I have a savings account, I have a retirement fund, and I have a trust fund for my children, and for my children's children. But that's not where my trust is. The world calls it a "trust fund," but my trust is in God. My trust is in His ability to supply all my needs even when the world's system of finance fails.

My trust is in the fact that I am a tither, and I am a sower. It doesn't make any difference what happens to the economy, I will be taken care of. If not, then God's Word isn't true. But He's not a Man that He should lie. Heaven and earth might pass away, but not one jot or one tittle of God's Word will pass away.

Let's look now at my next outline from Brother Copeland's first Laws of Prosperity Seminar.

A. **Laying up Treasures in Heaven.**

1. Matthew 6:19, 20. 1 Timothy 6:17-19. Philippians 4:17.

    Matthew 6:19,20 — *Lay not up for yourselves treasures upon earth, where moth and rust doth corrupt, and where thieves break through and steal: But lay up for yourselves treasures in heaven, where neither moth nor rust doth corrupt, and where thieves do not break through nor steal.*

2. In other words, Jesus is telling us that we can establish a heavenly bank account.

3. This heavenly bank account is not subject to rust, corruption, or theft. In other words, it doesn't make any difference what's happening on planet Earth, inflation, or depression, your heavenly bank account is not affected by that.

4. 1 Timothy 6:17-19 — *Charge them that are rich in this world, that they be not highminded, nor trust in uncertain riches, but in the living God, who giveth us richly all things to enjoy; That they do good, that they be rich in good works, ready to distribute, willing to **communicate**; Laying up in store for themselves a good foundation against the time to come, that they may lay hold on eternal life.*

5. "Communicate," in the Amplified is translated "giving." In other words, people with the ability to do so, should be quick to give, to invest in and bless other people.

6. Jesus said in Matthew 6 that we are to lay up treasures in heaven. So once again, people that bless other people, people that distribute, people that "communicate" with others, invest in them financially, are laying something up in store. Every time you bless somebody, your heavenly bank account is accumulating. Every time you sow seed into someone else's life, you get credit for that in heaven. Your heavenly bank account is increasing in assets.

7. Philippians 4:15-17 – *Now ye Philippians know also, that in the beginning of the gospel, when I departed from Macedonia, no church communicated* (Now there's that word "communicate" again. In other words, no church supported me in giving and receiving) *with me as concerning giving and receiving, but ye only. For even in Thessalonica ye sent once and again unto my necessity. Not because I desire a gift: but I desire fruit that may abound to your account.*

8. Notice every time they invested in Apostle Paul's ministry, funds were accumulating in their heavenly bank account. That doesn't mean that there's money in heaven, and God's going to rain it down. He's keeping an account of every deed that you do, every blessing that you bestow on someone else, and every seed that you sow.

9. Four major ways that we discover from the Word of God in which you can lay up treasures in heaven.

    a. Tithing.

    b. Giving to the poor.

    c. Investing in the Gospel.

    d. Giving as a praise to God.

B. Scriptural rules for giving.

1. Matthew 6:1 – *Take heed that ye do not your alms before men, to be seen of them: otherwise ye have no reward of your Father which is in heaven.*

    Don't give just to be seen of men. This will stop your return. (Motivation for giving is everything.) What's your motivation for giving? Is it so you can be seen of men? If that's your motivation, then the only reward you will get is men will think that you are charitable and that's all.

2. 2 Corinthians 8:11-14 — *Now therefore perform the doing of it; that as there was a readiness to will, so there may be a performance also out of that which ye have. For if there be first a willing mind, it is accepted according to that a man hath, and not according to that he hath not. For I mean not that other men be eased, and ye burdened: But by an equality, that now at this time your abundance may be a supply for their want, that their abundance also may be a supply for your want: that there may be equality.*

Once you have become willing to give, be quick to perform it. Don't hesitate.

There are times when you have an impression in your spirit to give to someone, and if you don't respond immediately, Satan will try to talk you out of it. This is why you must learn to be quick to perform it.

I have this little rule about my obedience to God: "Obey quickly and quietly." In other words, don't hesitate. Because if you hesitate, you can talk yourself out of it or Satan will talk you out of it.

The moment you have that impression in your spirit, do it. Many times, God has a difficult time getting people to obey. When you hesitate, all you're doing is delaying your blessing. I don't know about you, but I need mine now. So don't hesitate. The moment you sense that you are to sow into someone's life, then do it.

After a service one night, a pastor took several of us out to dinner. I noticed that our waitress had such a pleasant and sweet personality. She acted like she loved what she was doing. She was just a tremendous blessing to all of us. So, the Pastor paid for the meal, and he gave her a tip. And then I called her over, and I said, "What is your name?"

She said, "My name is Betsy."

I said, "I don't know if your employer knows it or not, but you are an asset to this restaurant. You make people want to come back here. I don't know what's going on in your life, but I just sense in my spirit that I'm supposed to give you this." I just reached out and placed a $100 bill in her hand. She was just overwhelmed. In fact, tears came to her eyes. She said, "Who are you?"

The Laws of Prosperity, Part III:
Laying up Treasures in Heaven

I said, "Well, I'm just a person who likes to bless people when they do a good job. You do a good job, and I just want you to know it. So be blessed."

She started crying. She said, "I don't know who you are, but I can tell you this, you're an answer to my prayer. I prayed this morning because I needed an extra $100."

So you see, if I had not been quick to obey, I would have missed God. I believe when you're quick to obey, it makes God smile. That's the way we need to live. I want God smiling at me all the time, nudging Jesus, and saying "That's My boy! Isn't he something? I can tell him to do something and before I even finish the sentence, he's already doing it." That's the way God wants us to live.

3. 2 Corinthians 9:6-7 — *But this I say, He which soweth sparingly shall reap also sparingly; and he which soweth bountifully shall reap also bountifully. Every man according as he purposeth in his heart, so let him give; not grudgingly, or of necessity: for God loveth a cheerful giver.*

Don't give reluctantly or sorrowfully, but learn to become a cheerful giver.

These are rules for giving. Don't give reluctantly. If you're attitude is "Oh, man, I have to give again?" You might as well keep it. There's no return on that. You gave it reluctantly. You weren't cheerful in it. There are rules for giving, and a lot of people are missing out on their return because they're not giving properly.

a. You purpose in your heart what you will give.

If you purpose in your heart what you will give, then you also establish the amount of the return. In other words, God wants us to become mature in our giving. God's not looking for a people that He has to tell to give all the time. He wants them to grow up. I don't have to wait until God tells me. I live to give. I'm a sower. I look for opportunities to give.

C. Tithing.

1. Deuteronomy 26:1-2 — *And it shall be, when thou*

art come in unto the land which the Lord thy God giveth thee for an inheritance, and possessest it, and dwellest therein; That thou shalt take of the first of all the fruit of the earth, which thou shalt bring of thy land that the Lord thy God giveth thee, and shalt put it in a basket, and shalt go unto the place which the Lord thy God shall choose to place his name there.

2. Tithing is not just an Old Testament practice; it is a principle for believers today. Hebrews 7:8 – *And here men that die receive tithes; but there he receiveth them, of whom it is witnessed that he liveth.*

3. Tithing is the first fruit of your income. "Tithe" means "10 percent."

4. Bring the tithe to God. It's His. It's holy. It belongs to Him. Leviticus 27:30 –*And all the tithe of the land, whether of the seed of the land, or of the fruit of the tree, is the Lord's: it is holy unto the Lord.*

5. Jesus is the Priest of our day. Hebrews 3:1– *Wherefore, holy brethren, partakers of the heavenly calling, consider the Apostle and High Priest of our profession, Christ Jesus.*

6. Make a confession of faith over your tithe. If you'll read Deuteronomy 26, you can discover what God says we are to say over our tithe. So, when you bring your tithe to God, don't just throw it in the bucket, say something over it. Speak God's Word over it.

7. Don't give your tithe into a dead work. Put it in a church or a ministry that is alive.

8. Malachi 3:9-10 – *Ye are cursed with a curse: for ye have robbed me, even this whole nation. Bring ye all the tithes into the storehouse, that there may be meat in mine house, and prove me now herewith, saith the Lord of hosts, if I will not open you the windows of heaven, and pour you out a blessing, that there shall not be room enough to receive it.* Tithing is a very serious matter with God.

9. Tithing is the only thing in God's Word in which God said you have the right to prove Him. Put God to the test.
10. Tithing is the only thing in God's Word in which God says He will rebuke the devil for you.
11. Tithing guarantees a return that you will not be able to contain. (Malachi 3:10 Lamsa Translation). In this translation it says that God will open the windows of heaven for you, pour out blessings for you until you shall surely shout, "It's enough."

Your first responsibility in applying these laws of prosperity is to become a tither. Then you must learn to give over and above the tithe.

When you learn these principles, then you'll be in position to receive from God in ways you've never dreamed possible before.

God wants to be your source of supply. He will become your source when you become a tither and a giver.

The first day that I went to work for Kenneth Copeland, he told me that if I ever got paid, it would be because I used my faith. After my first two weeks, there wasn't enough money to pay the staff. My first thought was, *Well, I must not have used my faith.*

So, I went back to my office (which was a hallway) and it became my "wailing wall." I prayed in tongues and shouted and bound the devil and loosed the angels and did everything I knew to do.

Later, Brother Copeland came in about 2:00 that afternoon and told us that he had sown seed for the payroll and gave us the report that enough money had come in to pay the salaries.

We never missed payroll. God always brought the money in. There were a few times when Brother Copeland would call my hotel room when we were on the road, and he'd say, "Are you believing God?"

I'd say, "For what?"

He'd say, "Your salary."

I'd say, "Yes, Sir."

He'd say, "Well, I just talked to the office, and we still need some more money to cover all the salaries, so keep believing God."

And I would continue to pray and believe God.

One morning we were told that there was not enough money to cover payroll because they had just paid all the bills. So, I went to my "office" and started praying! I needed my paycheck badly!

At 12:00 noon, we still hadn't been paid. So I kept praying all through the afternoon. Well, I later found out that the money had come in, but Brother Copeland told the bookkeeper, "Don't tell Jerry yet because he'll pray in next month's salaries too."

27
The Laws of Prosperity, Part IV:
Give Your Best

If you remember the story that I shared about Brother Copeland giving his airplane away, that represented his best seed, and God honored it. He received a bigger, better airplane.

If you're believing God for something, then don't give away something that you don't even like anymore. Give your best.

For instance, if you're believing for new clothes, then don't go through your closet and give away some old worn out suit or dress that you never wear. Give something you really like. Give your best seed. God will honor that. Your harvest will come back to you in the same measure that you measured out. In other words, you'll get back something that you'll really like. Let's take a look at my next outline on the Laws of Prosperity.

A. **Giving to the poor.**

    1. Matthew 25:35 – *For I was an hungered, and ye gave me meat: I was thirsty, and ye gave me drink: I was a stranger, and ye took me in.*

==Jesus takes giving to the poor very personally. When you give to the poor, Jesus considers that as though you had given it to Him personally.==

2. ==Jesus had a reputation of giving to the poor.==

> *John 13:27-29 – And after the sop Satan entered into him. Then said Jesus unto him, That thou doest, do quickly. Now no man at the table knew for what intent he spake this unto him. For some of them thought, because Judas had the bag, that Jesus had said unto him, Buy those things that we have need of against the feast; or, that he should give something to the poor.*

Do you remember at the Last Supper when Jesus called Judas over and said, "That which you have to do, do it quickly"? He was talking about his betrayal. Judas got up and left the room. When he left the room, the other disciples said, "He must be going to give to the poor." They had no idea he was about to betray Jesus. That tells me that Jesus must have had a reputation of giving to the poor because every time the treasurer leaves the room, they automatically thought he was going to give to the poor again.

3. ==Everything you set your hand to do will be blessed by God when you give to the poor.==

> *Deuteronomy 15:7-10 – If there be among you a poor man of one of thy brethren within any of thy gates in thy land which the Lord thy God giveth thee, thou shalt not harden thine heart, nor shut thine hand from thy poor brother:*
>
> *But thou shalt open thine hand wide unto him, and shalt surely lend him sufficient for his need, in that which he wanteth.*
>
> *Beware that there be not a thought in thy wicked heart, saying, The seventh year, the year of release, is at hand; and thine eye be evil against thy poor brother, and thou givest him nought; and he cry unto the Lord against thee, and it be sin unto thee.*

Thou shalt surely give him, and thine heart shall not be grieved when thou givest unto him: because that for this thing the Lord thy God shall bless thee in all thy works, and in all that thou puttest thine hand unto.

God says when you're impressed to give to the poor, then don't hold back. Give graciously, and God will bless everything you set your hand to do.

4. Giving to the poor causes you to have no lack in your life.

   Proverbs 28:27 – *He that giveth unto the poor shall not lack: but he that hideth his eyes shall have many a curse.*

5. To fail to invest in the poor could cause you to miss the greatest financial blessing you have ever been offered.

   Mark 10:17-22 – *And when he was gone forth into the way, there came one running, and kneeled to him, and asked him, Good Master, what shall I do that I may inherit eternal life?*

   And Jesus said unto him, Why callest thou me good? there is none good but one, that is, God.

   Thou knowest the commandments, Do not commit adultery, Do not kill, Do not steal, Do not bear false witness, Defraud not, Honour thy father and mother.

   And he answered and said unto him, Master, all these have I observed from my youth.

   Then Jesus beholding him loved him, and said unto him, One thing thou lackest: go thy way, sell whatsoever thou hast, and give to the poor, and thou shalt have treasure in heaven: and come, take up the cross, and follow me.

   And he was sad at that saying, and went away grieved: for he had great possessions.

Jesus said, "Sell what you have and give to the poor," and the man walked away grieved because he had great possessions. Jesus said, "If you give to the poor, then God will repay what you gave and you shall receive a hundredfold because you gave it for Jesus' sake." That rich young ruler walked away from the greatest financial blessing he'd ever been offered.

    6.   Proverbs 19:17 – *He that hath pity upon the poor lendeth unto the Lord; and that which he hath given will he pay him again.*

        When you give to the poor, God considers that as a loan to Him, and He will repay.

B. Investing in the Gospel.

    1.   You can expect one hundredfold return.

        Mark 10:29-30 – *And Jesus answered and said, Verily I say unto you, There is no man that hath left house, or brethren, or sisters, or father, or mother, or wife, or children, or lands, for my sake, and the gospel's, But he shall receive an hundredfold now in this time, houses, and brethren, and sisters, and mothers, and children, and lands, with persecutions; and in the world to come eternal life.*

    2.   Philippians 4:10-19 – *But I rejoiced in the Lord greatly, that now at the last your care of me hath flourished again; wherein ye were also careful, but ye lacked opportunity.*

        Not that I speak in respect of want: for I have learned, in whatsoever state I am, therewith to be content.

        I know both how to be abased, and I know how to abound: every where and in all things I am instructed both to be full and to be hungry, both to abound and to suffer need.

        I can do all things through Christ which strengtheneth me.

        Notwithstanding ye have well done, that ye did communicate with my affliction.

> *Now ye Philippians know also, that in the beginning of the gospel, when I departed from Macedonia, no church communicated with me as concerning giving and receiving, but ye only.*
>
> *For even in Thessalonica ye sent once and again unto my necessity.*
>
> *Not because I desire a gift: but I desire fruit that may abound to your account.*
>
> *But I have all, and abound: I am full, having received of Epaphroditus the things which were sent from you, an odour of a sweet smell, a sacrifice acceptable, wellpleasing to God.*
>
> *But my God shall supply all your need according to his riches in glory by Christ Jesus.*
>
> In these verses the Apostle Paul talks about partnership. God promises that when people give, He will supply their every need according to His riches in glory by Christ Jesus.

3. ==Investing in the Gospel will cause you to become self-sufficient and furnished in abundance.==

> 2 Corinthians 9:8 – *And God is able to make all grace abound toward you; that ye, always having all sufficiency in all things, may abound to every good work.*

C. Giving as a praise to God.

1. Luke 8:1-3 – *And it came to pass afterward, that he went throughout every city and village, preaching and showing the glad tidings of the kingdom of God: and the twelve were with him,*

   And certain women, which had been healed of evil spirits and infirmities, Mary called Magdalene, out of whom went seven devils,

> *And Joanna the wife of Chuza Herod's steward, and Susanna, and many others, which ministered unto him of their substance.*

In these verses, several women ministered unto Jesus of their substance. They blessed Him. They gave to Him as a praise. They had been healed and delivered. They're not trying to pay for their healing or for their deliverance. They ministered to Jesus of their substance simply because they wanted to show Him how thankful they were for what He had done for them.

So, there are times when you can give as an investment into the poor. There may be times when you just want to give as a praise to God for what He has done in your life. You may want to say to Him, "God, I just want to worship You. I want to praise You. I want to thank You for healing my body, saving my marriage, delivering my children. This offering is just a praise unto You."

2. When you give as a praise to God, you give your best.

Think about all the wonderful things that He has done for you. Isn't He worthy of your best seed? Of course He is, so why don't you show Him next Sunday when the tithes and offerings are received. Give Him your tithe, and then give over and above as a praise offering.

Now get ready, because He's going to bless your life abundantly.

28

The Laws of Prosperity, Part V:
How to Make Heavenly Withdrawals

This is the final outline from the Laws of Prosperity Seminar that Brother Copeland conducted in Oklahoma City in 1972. Carolyn and I learned many life-changing truths, and we immediately put them to work in our lives. Acting upon them took us to a new level of prosperity and shaped our future.

As you read each point in this outline, determine in yourself to apply them to your life and watch what God will do for you.

A. **God delights in a cheerful giver.**

    1.   2 Corinthians 9:5-11 – *Therefore I thought it necessary to exhort the brethren, that they would go before unto you, and make up beforehand your bounty, whereof ye had notice before, that the same might be ready, as a matter of bounty, and not as of covetousness.*

            But this I say, He which soweth sparingly shall reap also sparingly; and he which soweth bountifully shall reap also bountifully.

Every man according as he purposeth in his heart, so let him give; not grudgingly, or of necessity: for God loveth a cheerful giver.

And God is able to make all grace abound toward you; that ye, always having all sufficiency in all things, may abound to every good work:

(As it is written, He hath dispersed abroad; he hath given to the poor: his righteousness remaineth for ever.

Now he that ministereth seed to the sower both minister bread for your food, and multiply your seed sown, and increase the fruits of your righteousness;)

Being enriched in every thing to all bountifulness, which causeth through us thanksgiving to God.

    2.   God is unwilling to do without a cheerful giver, and He will never abandon them.

    3.   God provides daily bread for the cheerful giver.

    4.   God provides seed for the cheerful giver and multiplies (or increases) their resources for sowing.

B.   **How to make heavenly withdrawals.**

    1.   Decide on the amount that you need. Be specific.

        a.   Don't cut yourself short. God's not broke!

    2.   Declare (out loud) the amount that you need.

        a.   Mark 11:23-24 – *For verily I say unto you, That whosoever shall say unto this mountain, Be thou removed, and be thou cast into the sea; and shall not doubt in his heart, but shall believe that those things which he saith shall come to pass; he shall have whatsoever he saith.*

> *Therefore I say unto you, What things soever ye desire, when ye pray, believe that ye receive them, and ye shall have them.*

3. Find someone, a person of faith, who will agree with you (preferably your spouse).

   a. Matthew 18:19-20 – *Again I say unto you, That if two of you shall agree on earth as touching any thing that they shall ask, it shall be done for them of my Father which is in heaven.*

   > *For where two or three are gathered together in my name, there am I in the midst of them.*

   b. Refuse to relent. Stay in agreement.

4. Receive it by faith and lay hold upon it when you pray.

   a. Matthew 21:22 – *And all things, whatsoever ye shall ask in prayer, believing, ye shall receive.*

   b. ==Look through the eyes of your faith, and not with the natural eye.== 2 Corinthians 4:13-18 – *We having the same spirit of faith, according as it is written, I believed, and therefore have I spoken; we also believe, and therefore speak;*

   > *Knowing that he which raised up the Lord Jesus shall raise up us also by Jesus, and shall present us with you.*

   > *For all things are for your sakes, that the abundant grace might through the thanksgiving of many redound to the glory of God.*

   > *For which cause we faint not; but though our outward man perish, yet the inward man is renewed day by day.*

> *For our light affliction, which is but for a moment, worketh for us a far more exceeding and eternal weight of glory;*
>
> *While we look not at the things which are seen, but at the things which are not seen: **for the things which are seen are temporal**; but the things which are not seen are eternal.*

5. **Bind the devil.**

    a. Matthew 18:18 – *Verily I say unto you, Whatsoever ye shall bind on earth shall be bound in heaven: and whatsoever ye shall loose on earth shall be loosed in heaven.*

6. **Loose the ministering spirits.**

    a. Hebrews 1:13 – *But to which of the angels said he at any time, Sit on my right hand, until I make thine enemies thy footstool?* The Bible says that the angels are ministering spirits sent forth to minister for those who are heirs of salvation.

7. **Continually praise God.**

    a. Psalm 8:2 – *Out of the mouth of babes and sucklings hast thou ordained strength because of thine enemies, that thou mightest still the enemy and the avenger.*

    b. **Praise keeps the door of abundance wide open.**

8. **Avoid strife and unforgiveness.**

    a. Mark 11:25 – *And when ye stand praying, forgive, if ye have aught against any: that your Father also which is in heaven may forgive you your trespasses.*

I encourage you to write on a sheet of paper your needs and the Scriptures that you are standing upon and hang it on your refrigerator or mirror so that every time you walk by it, you are reminded that God is supplying your needs. Remember that He is working behind the scenes to bring your breakthrough to pass in your life. Now if you truly believe this, then praise Him continually for doing it.

29
How to Petition God for Your Needs

After Carolyn and I began to learn the laws of prosperity, we heard Brother Copeland make a reference to the way that he and Gloria prayed. We understood how to make deposits in our heavenly account, and we were learning how to make heavenly withdrawals. Everyone needs additional funds from time to time, and at this time in our lives, we needed them all the time.

We had a lot of needs. I still had some business debts back in Shreveport, Louisiana. We needed furniture, clothes, food, a better car . . . we needed money badly! So, when Brother Copeland started teaching us about how to make heavenly withdrawals, he had my undivided attention.

Have you ever been in need of everything? Well, I was and I needed to know how to make withdrawals *now*. I had pressing needs, *now*.

Heavenly Grants

I remember Brother Copeland sharing how that when he

and Gloria had a need, they would go to God and ask for a grant.

He referred to John 16:23 — *And in that day ye shall ask me nothing. Verily, verily, I say unto you, Whatsoever ye shall ask the Father in my name, he will give it you.*

Brother Copeland got the word "grant" from the Amplified version. It says, *And when that time comes, you will ask nothing of Me [you will need to ask Me no questions]. I assure you, most solemnly I tell you, that My Father will **grant** you whatever you ask in My Name.*

Brother Copeland said that the first time he read this verse and he saw the word "grant," it just seemed to jump out of the pages into his spirit. He said that he understood the word "grant." When he enrolled at Oral Roberts University, there were a lot of students there that could only go as a result of a "grant," a Government grant.

That word got his attention. He began saying, "Well, Father, I need a heavenly grant. I have certain needs in my life, and I'm asking You for a heavenly grant according to John 16:23."

He said that as he began meditating and studying this, he was impressed of the Lord to write it out and make it official. Grants are usually written out in contract form. He decided that he would write it out, and it would be a point of contact for his faith. It would also enable him to stay single-minded and focused on what he was believing God for.

The Prayer of Petition

He began teaching us about how to write out a heavenly grant or petition. This became a real foundation for our faith. I could see the results that Brother Copeland experienced, and I was desperate to see results in my life too. I was determined that if it would work for Brother Copeland, and if I did what he did, then it should work for me. God is no respecter of persons.

We began learning how to ask God for heavenly grants and petitions. I want to share with you one of the first "Petitions for a Heavenly Grant" that Carolyn and I ever wrote back in 1972.

Petition for a Heavenly Grant

Be it known this day, May 15, 1972, 11:25 p.m., I receive a heavenly grant in the amount of $900. Father, in the Name of Jesus, I come boldly to the Throne of Grace, and present Your Word.

According to John 16:23 (Amplified), Jesus said, "I assure you most solemnly I tell you, that My Father will grant you whatever you ask in My Name."

Jesus, You said in Mark 11:24, "Whatever you ask for in prayer, believe, trust, and be confident that it is granted you, and you will get it."

Your Word states in Luke 6:38, "Give and it shall be given unto you; good measure, pressed down, and shaken together, and running over, shall men give unto your bosom." In accordance to Your Word, I give, I sow seed, in order to set this Spiritual Law to work in my behalf.

According to Matthew 18:18, I bind Satan and all his forces, and I render them helpless and unable to operate. They will not hinder my grant.

According to Hebrews 1:13 and 14, I loose the ministering spirits, and I charge them to go forth and cause my grant to come into my hands.

The amount of this grant is for the following: (And then I wrote what the grant was for.)

Jesus, You said in Matthew 18:19, "Again I say unto you, that if two of you shall agree on earth as touching any thing that they shall ask, it shall be done for them of My Father which is in heaven."

Therefore, Carolyn and I set ourselves in agreement, and we believe we receive now, and we praise You for it.

And we signed it.

I made a copy for Carolyn, and she carried that around with her everywhere she went. I carried my copy around with me everywhere I went, and it came to pass eventually. In fact, we were surprised at just how quickly we got results. I've got notebooks full of grants that we wrote out from 1972 to the present, and they have all come to pass. That was a real milestone in our lives when we learned how to petition God for heavenly grants.

Believing for Our First House in Ft. Worth, Texas

As I mentioned earlier, when Carolyn and I first moved to Fort Worth back in 1971, the first house that we rented wasn't much, but it was all that we could afford at the time.

We were paying $100 each month, and that was stretching our faith to pay that much. About six months later, we were able to lease a nicer house. After several months there, we felt like it was time for us to buy a home.

I was on my way home from work one day, and when I got to the intersection where I normally turned left, for some reason I turned right, knowing that wasn't the way to my house. I went one block and turned left. I had never been in that area before. I drove down this street, and just about five houses down the street there was a cute little two-story Cape Cod style home that had a "For Sale" sign on it. When I saw it, it just felt like it was my house!

I went home and I said, "Carolyn, I want you to come with me to look at this house."

She and the girls jumped in the car with me, and we drove over to that house. When Carolyn saw it, she fell in love with it. She said, "I can already tell you what it looks like inside. That's the house I've seen in my spirit and been praying for."

We called the Realtor, and he came and showed us the house. It was exactly the way Carolyn described what she saw in her spirit. He told us how much he was asking for the house, so we made an offer on it. There were already two other people who had made offers on it, and the realtor said, "One of the applications has already gone through for approval, everything looks great, and it's probably already sold."

I told him, "Well, it's my house, and it's not going to sell."

He said, "What do you mean?"

I said, " I don't know if you'll understand this or not, but we believe this is the house God wants us to have. If it is, then it will not sell."

He didn't understand that, but he just kind of nodded his head and said, "Thank you. We'll let you know."

We went ahead and made an offer on it, and we started making arrangements to sell our house that we had rented out in Shreveport. We only had a short time to get all that done. I was concerned about selling the house in Shreveport. I didn't know how long it would take. In the natural, you don't just put it on the market one day and sell it the next day.

So, I called my father-in-law who had built our house in Shreveport and I said, "Would you help me put my house up for sale because we're going to buy a house here. I need to sell it very quickly. If you know anybody who wants to buy it, then tell them it's for sale."

He said, "Well, consider it sold. I want it."

And he bought it from me. Praise God, I got the money that I needed for the new house. The only thing, there was another party that already had a contract, and they were eager to buy. I had the money, but they had the approval.

So, we were standing on the Word of God believing that it was our house. And right at the last minute, those people decided that they didn't want the house. It was a real testimony to the Realtor. He called us and said, "I can't believe this. This has never happened to me. These people were ready to move in. It was sold, it was a 'done deal.' I don't know who you people are or what you do, but whatever you did, it worked!"

So we got the house we believed for, but now we needed furniture. We had very little and needed everything. I sent Carolyn shopping (with no money) to decide what she wanted. I said, "Carolyn, this is what I want you to do. I want you to go find all the furniture that you think you will need for this house, price it, and then bring back an itemized list of everything you need. When you have finished, I'll write our petition for our furniture."

She did as I requested, and then I wrote a petition titled, "Request for New Furniture." I typed all my Scriptures out, listed all the things that we needed along with the total price. And just in case, I added this clause: *Father, You do realize that these prices are subject to change.* I didn't know how long it might take to bring in the money. I wanted to be sure that I covered myself.

We dated it, we signed our names, we sowed seed towards it, and we believed God for it. And every piece of that furniture came in. It's exciting when you believe God for the things you need, and then you get to watch God bring it all in. It really builds your faith. It is a great confidence builder, a faith energizer. You never forget how you did it, and so you repeat it. You just keep doing it over and over again. We've done this for thirty years now, and it works every time.

There's a basic outline that I use every time I write a heavenly petition, but I endeavor to listen to the Holy Spirit to inspire me to write some specific things about each particular need.

There will always be those basic components in your petition. You decide on the amount; you declare how much you need; you get someone (preferably your spouse if you're married) to get in agreement with you; offer praise and thanksgiving to God; and remove all unforgiveness or strife from your heart.

I always go through those basic points. Then, as I'm preparing it, the Spirit of God may bring to my attention another Scripture that inspires my faith in that area, and I'm always listening to the Holy Spirit for that. It establishes a much stronger point of contact for my faith.

I present it to the Lord, and I include the time in which I prayed it, I date it, and then Carolyn and I sign it. I read it many times to myself, just to keep me focused and single-minded. I believe I receive **when I pray**, and I thank God continually for it.

The greatest expression of my faith is praise and thanksgiving. So **I don't ask God for it again**, I've already made my petition. But I do read it again. I do keep it before me just so I'll stay single-minded and have a reference point. But I'm praising God for it all the time. I may hold it up and say, "Father, I just want to thank You for my heavenly grant. Thank You that my petitions have been granted according to Your Word, in Jesus' Name."

I don't go back and say, "Oh, God, I've got this need." No, I've already presented to Him my need. I'm thanking Him for supplying it. In my opinion, writing a heavenly petition is the quickest way to get results when you are facing impossible situations.

When Brother Copeland taught us the Laws of Prosperity, particularly how to make withdrawals, how to write out a petition and how to ask God for a heavenly grant, it was life changing for us. I still use those very same principles today. The only difference is the amount of money that I need has changed considerably.

I want to encourage you to read these outlines, and keep them fresh in your spirit. Meditate on them. If you're not already doing it, then I challenge you right now to do so. The beautiful thing is, once you get results, you will never forget how you got them.

Never Let Go of the Basics

Kenneth Copeland taught me the basics of living by faith thirty years ago, and I have applied those principles ever since. Why? They work! Never let go of the basics. You can't build a house without first laying a foundation.

In reality, if you need $500, and you have no way of producing it, then the pressure that is on you to get that money is no different from the guy who needs $500,000. The only difference is a few more zeroes. The pressure is exactly the same.

You'll find that whatever level you are on right now, your faith will produce as much as is needed no matter how many zeroes you add to it because you're applying the same principles. You don't have to learn some new concept when the figure is higher. You never let go of the basics. God may give you greater insight into them, but you never let go of those basic principles.

30
Three Steps to Success

As I mentioned before, one of my jobs was to pick Brother Copeland up at the hotel and drive him to the meeting hall, and I did not speak unless spoken to. I didn't want to distract him from what the Spirit of God was sharing with him in preparation for the service. Just out of respect, I kept quiet!

So, one evening back in 1972, I picked Brother Copeland up at the hotel, and we were driving to the meeting. I was sitting there being real quiet just driving, and all of a sudden, Brother Copeland hit me on the shoulder and said, "I'm going to give you the three steps to success. If you will act on these three principles, you will succeed in every area of your life."

I had already gotten into the habit of writing everything down that he said so I wouldn't forget it later. But I was driving, and I couldn't write. So, I was confessing under my breath, "I have the mind of Christ; I will remember everything he says." I was desperate for success. I wanted God's anointing, I wanted God working in my life like I saw him work in Brother Copeland's life. So when we got to the meeting, I wrote everything down. Here is what Brother Copeland shared with me that night.

Three Steps to Success by Kenneth Copeland

1. **Find out the will of God.**

2. **Once you find out the will of God, confer no more with flesh and blood.**

He said, "Many times after you find out God's will, if you tell a lot of people, some will not believe, some will doubt, and some will try to talk you out of it. Sometimes, it's best to keep it between you and God. Of course, if you're married, share it with your spouse, but if you go out and tell just anybody the vision God has given you, they might say, 'Well, I don't believe God will do that for you.' And then you will begin hearing their unbelief instead of faith."

3. **Get the job done at any cost.**

I've applied those three steps in every area of my life since 1972. I endeavor to find out the will of God first. Once I know the will of God in a particular situation, I'm selective about who I share it with. I don't tell just anybody. I pray and listen for God's timing, and then, once I know that God has told me, "It's time," then I get the job done at any cost.

Let me encourage you to apply these three steps in your life. Find out first the will of God. Don't do anything because somebody else is doing it. Even if what they're doing works. Find out if it's the will of God **for you** to do it. It may not be what God wants you to do at all. So find out God's will for **your** life. Success begins where the will of God is known.

I define success as "fulfilling what God has told you to do; not what God told somebody else to do." And once you find out the will of God, be very selective about who you tell it to, and then get the job done at any cost.

Don't give up, and refuse to give in when it looks as though it will never come to pass. Diligence and perseverance are a must!

Ask yourself, "How desperate am I for success?" When you are truly desperate, and you want success more than anything else, then you will find that God will honor your uncompromising stand.

Always remember that it is God's will for you to succeed in every endeavor of your life. Don't ever accept anything less than God's best for you.

31
Always be Prepared

he Lord spoke to me in the latter part of 1972 and said, "I want you to start preparing yourself as if you're going to preach in every meeting."

At that time, I had not started preaching in Brother Copeland's meetings. I did soulwinning seminars between his services. I would invite anyone who would like to learn how to witness one-on-one to remain in the auditorium after Brother Copeland finished his morning session. I would spend from 30 to 45 minutes teaching soul-winning, and then we would go to the streets and apply what we had learned.

But the Lord was saying to me that I should prepare myself as though I was going to preach in every meeting. He said, "There may be times when the anointing of God is so strong on Brother Copeland, that he may not be able to finish the service, and I want you to be able to take up where he leaves off."

I knew all of Brother Copeland's messages. He normally taught on "Prayer" in the morning sessions and "Faith" in the evening services. I had listened to those messages hundreds of times, and I studied them all of the time. As I said before, traveling with him was my Bible school.

I knew when he started his message by saying, "Open your Bibles" to such-and-such verse, I could jump in and finish that message although not as good as he could. I knew all of his illustrations. I knew the next Scripture reference. I knew I could finish his message if, for some reason, Brother Copeland couldn't finish.

In obedience to the Lord, I began preparing as if I was going to preach. The Lord told me to just "Be ready!" I noticed when I started doing that, it took me to another level of being sensitive to what Brother Copeland was going to do next. Particularly when it came time to pray for the sick. It seemed to bring me up to another level to where he didn't catch me off guard like he used to. I began to move up to the same level of faith with him, particularly in ministering to the sick.

But one day, the Lord said to me, "I want you to get up this morning, and I want you to prepare yourself like you're preaching tonight." I began praying and studying my outline. I was ready. If he ever called on me, I wouldn't have to say, "Well, you've caught me off guard. I'm not ready." I had a sermon. All I needed was an opportunity.

I saw myself preaching. The Lord said, "Now, you've got that part of the image perfected, let's add this to it. Start interceding for all the people who will hear you preach." Every morning, I'd get up and start praying just like I had a whole congregation to preach to. I started interceding that people would receive the Word, and that God would give me utterance in the Holy Ghost. I prayed that people would be healed and delivered. I was prepared if the opportunity ever came.

I was creating a God-given image on the inside of my spirit. I was seeing myself fulfilling the dream that God had put in my heart. There wasn't anything happening on the outside. But on the inside, I was seeing my dream become a reality. If he ever called, I was ready.

Jerry, Are You Ready?

One day, I was driving to Jacksonville, Florida, for a meeting with Brother Copeland, and I was listening to reel-to-reel tapes on a battery operated tape player in my car. I kept a sack full of batteries because I had a long way to drive, and the batteries would run down. (We didn't have tape decks in the cars back then.)

While I was driving, the Spirit of God simply said this to me, "Are you ready?"

I said, "For what?"

He said, "This meeting will be a turning point in your life. Stay ready."

That's all He told me.

I didn't know what that meant, but I was doing my best to stay ready.

I arrived in Jacksonville, and I went to the auditorium to set up the speakers and chairs and get everything ready for the opening service. I went back to my hotel room, and I studied and meditated on the Word and prepared myself as if I was going to preach that night. We went to the meeting, and Brother Copeland preached an awesome message. But if Brother Copeland had said to me, "Jerry, I believe God would have you preach tonight," I could have taken the service. I was prepared. However, he didn't do that.

The next morning, I woke up, got in the Word, and prepared myself just like I was going to do the preaching. I had never said a word about any of this to Brother Copeland. I was standing in my room praying, and the telephone rang about fifteen minutes before I was to go pick up Brother Copeland. It was Brother Copeland on the phone. His opening line was, "Are you ready?"

I said, "Yes, Sir. I'm ready."

He said, "What are you ready for?"

I said, "Anything! God told me to get ready, and I've been ready for whatever."

He said, "Well, we're going to change some things, and today you're going to do the morning service."

I said, "I am?"

He said, "Yes, you're going to do the morning service. From now on, you're going to do the morning services in our meetings. It's time for you to launch out into your teaching ministry as an associate minister of this ministry."

I said, "Well, fine. I'm ready."

He said, "All right. Come get me, and we'll go to the service."

Now that surprised me.

I thought if I was going to do the morning service, he would stay in his room. It never crossed my mind that he would be going.

I said, "You're going?"

He said, "Yes, I'm going, and I'll introduce you."

I said, "I don't need any introduction."

He said, "Well, I'm going, and I'm going to tell them who you are and introduce you, and then you'll take the service."

I got nervous. I had never preached in his presence. He didn't stay around for those soulwinning seminars, so he had never heard me preach. I thought, *Dear God, he's going to be there!*

Then I thought, *Well, maybe he's just going to introduce me, and then he'll leave. He'll get somebody to take him back to the hotel. But I'm the one who takes him to the hotel. Oh no! He's going to stay!*

I got really nervous then. I thought, *I'm actually going to preach, and Brother Copeland is going to be present. What could I possibly say that he doesn't already know? I'm going to preach his messages.*

So we drove to the auditorium, and of course, I didn't talk unless he started the conversation, so it was silent. We got to the meeting, and he said, "Now I'm going to open the service this morning with prayer, and then I'm going to introduce you, and you do whatever God tells you to do."

I said, "Well, where will you be afterwards?"

He said, "I'll be here with you."

At that point, I was beginning to sweat!

Let's Welcome Jerry Savelle

He walked up to the podium, had everybody stand, opened in prayer, and then said, "Now, most of you folks have noticed this young man who works with me. You've seen him running around doing everything. Well, his name is Jerry Savelle. He's my associate minister. Today, God is going to launch him into his teaching ministry. He will be doing the service this morning. So I want you to welcome my associate minister, Jerry Savelle."

They clapped, and then they sat down, and I thought, *Well, maybe he'll go out in the audience or something.* I was still concerned about where he was going to be. He didn't go into the audience. He walked over and got one of the chairs that was on the platform, pulled it right up next to the podium, sat down, crossed his legs and looked at me with those piercing eyes.

I said, "You're going to sit right there?"

He said, "I'm going to sit right here."

I couldn't remember my name, my address, much less my sermon. I fumbled around, it seemed like for an eternity, but it was actually just a few seconds. Finally, Brother Copeland said, "Well, what are you going to preach?"

I said, "Your sermon, 'The Greatest Faith.' That's my favorite sermon."

He said, "Well, preach her, boy."

So, I started preaching on *The Greatest Faith.* I was standing there thinking, *This is his message word-for-word, right off the tape. I did not change the title, I didn't change the Scriptures, I didn't change the illustrations.* And then I thought, *I don't even have any illustrations of my own! I'm just preaching word-for-word what I've learned from him.*

But then as I got into it, God began to give me some insight. I had been taking all that Word in for years, and now it was flowing out of me. As I began to give out what I had learned, more was being given to me. And it surprised me! I was actually getting revelation knowledge as I was preaching.

Afterwards, Brother Copeland got up and said, "You said some things this morning that I've never thought of. Praise God, I'm glad I came."

I thought, *Dear God! I said something Kenneth Copeland didn't know?*

That was a monumental time in my life because it launched the teaching gift in me. When Brother Copeland recognized the teaching gift in me, it opened the door to a greater anointing on my gift as a teacher. From that moment on, I began preaching all the morning services.

I remember having thoughts like, *Will I have enough to say for an hour?* I thought I would probably finish my sermon in about twenty minutes, but as I became more comfortable, they almost had to make me stop preaching. I wanted to preach everything I knew in one sermon.

Gloria came up to me one time and said, "Jerry, I've waited for one preacher to get through half of my life, and I'm not waiting on you the second half! Shorten your sermon, boy!"

I might add, a few years later, when Gloria began preaching, Brother Copeland and I both told her, "Shorten your sermons, girl!" She can preach longer than both of us!

Not a Competition — A Completion

One of the things that impressed me the most about Brother Copeland was the fact that he wasn't, and still isn't, competitive. He wasn't afraid that turning his ministry over to one of his associates might cause people to think less of him and more of me. A lot of preachers wouldn't be able to do that. Brother Copeland was not threatened. He was more interested in getting the Word out regardless of who was doing the preaching.

Eventually, he stopped going to those morning services. He stayed in his room and prepared for the afternoon service. Apparently, he trusted me to represent his ministry, and he had confidence in me that I would not do anything that wasn't appropriate. That really impressed me. That spoke volumes to me of his security in who he was in Christ.

If you believe that God has called you to preach, then I want to encourage you right now to always be prepared. You just never know when God may want to use you to minister to someone. You could get a phone call tonight. You need to stay full of the Word so it will flow out of you in abundance whenever the need arises.

32

Jerry Savelle – Associate Minister

In early 1973, Brother Copeland had gone on television with a program called, "The Prayer Group." One of the stations that he was on was in my home town of Shreveport, Louisiana. So Brother Copeland said, "I think you need to start doing some meetings as the associate minister of Kenneth Copeland Ministries. When you're not with me, I'm going to set up meetings in the cities where we're on television for you to go preach as my representative."

My First Seminar

So, February 1973 was the first time I went out under the banner of Kenneth Copeland Evangelistic Association, and I held a meeting in his place. And this is what the announcement card said that we sent out:

Jerry Savelle of the television series, The Prayer Group, will be ministering in Shreveport, Louisiana, February 16 and 17, 1973.

Few people in my home town had ever heard me preach. When I left Shreveport to move to Fort Worth, there wasn't but four people there who believed I was called, and two of them were wavering!

So I went back to the Shreveport area to the Holiday Inn and conducted four services on Friday and Saturday at 2:00 and 7:30 p.m.

I had my first budget for a meeting, and I was responsible for believing God to meet it. So, I remembered the teachings on "Heavenly Grants," and I wrote on the back of the announcement card:

Father, in the name of Jesus, I make this covenant with You this day, February 16, 1973. I believe every need involved in this seminar in Shreveport, Louisiana, is met according to Your riches in glory by Christ Jesus. I receive, by faith, my budget of $750 met, in Jesus' name. Amen.

I was going to preach for two days, and my budget was $750. It might as well have been $750,000 because $750 in 1973 for a two-day meeting was a lot of money. I was by myself, Brother Copeland was not around; he couldn't do my believing for me; and I didn't know if two people would show up or two hundred. Seven hundred and fifty dollars looked like a fortune to me. I wrote out my petition, and I carried it around with me as my point of contact to believe I received.

I had four sermons that I preached in those meetings:

1. The Blood Covenant.

2. What Happened From the Cross to the Throne?

3. Redeemed From the Curse.

4. The Reality of Righteousness.

Those messages were straight out of Kenneth Copeland's faith library. He had tapes by those same titles. I knew right from the beginning that I didn't have to wait for my own personal revelation or my very own "sermon" from God; I preached what was real on the inside of me and what I had been studying for months.

Those messages didn't start with Kenneth Copeland. They didn't start with Kenneth Hagin. They didn't even start with E. W. Kenyon. They started with Jesus. One time Brother Copeland said, "I've never had an original thought in my life." Don't be afraid to share with others what you've learned from someone else. Don't wait for your very own sermon. Preach what is real on the inside of you.

If It Has Ministered to You, Then Preach It

If a particular message has really ministered to your spirit, don't be afraid to take that tape and outline it, dissect it, break it down, and share it with others. Don't be afraid of using the same illustrations. Eventually, as you continue to act on it, it will become **your** sermon.

So, whatever has ministered to you, don't be afraid to share it with someone else.

The way you can truly tell when something has become a revelation to you is when you are capable of communicating it to someone else. When you can communicate it to someone else clearly, articulately, and accurately, then it's your revelation.

My first meeting was another life-changing experience for me, and we did meet our budget. It was very successful and people were greatly blessed, as well as me.

It was thrilling to me that people from my home town came to hear me preach, and many of them recognized the anointing of God on me. Some still thought, *Well, one of these days, he'll make a fine, little preacher.*

My Pastor from Shreveport, Pastor Nolan Logan, was a little concerned that I had gone too far out on this "faith stuff," but he did believe in me. I'll never forget when he walked up to me after that last service, put his arm around me and told me how proud he was of me. He said, "I appreciate your boldness. You're going to make it. You're young, but you're bold. And God will use that."

That really ministered to me.

33
Time to Launch Out

There were some things that happened that indicated to me that there might be a possibility that God would have me launch out into my own ministry. I went to the Lord about it and really argued with Him saying, "Lord, if this is You, I don't understand. This contradicts what You said in that prophecy. You said we'd be a team. If I leave this organization to start my own ministry, it will split up the team. Now, didn't You say we'd be a team, and we'd preach all over the world together? I don't see how we can do that if I leave."

I had noticed in some other ministries that once somebody left, it severed the relationship. I didn't want that to happen. So, I went to Brother Copeland and talked to him about it.

What About the Team?

We were in El Paso, Texas, in the middle of 1973, and I had an opportunity to talk to Brother Copeland. I said, "Brother Copeland, I need to ask you how you feel about this. You know how I feel. I've told you before, and I'm just as serious about it today as I've ever been. I am here to serve you; I am prepared to serve you and work as an employee of this ministry for the rest of my life. That's all I want to do. I have no ambitions of starting my own ministry. But I keep hearing in my spirit that there might be the possibility of that. Now, if I'm wrong, correct me so I don't have to deal with this anymore. What do you think?"

He dropped his head, looked at me and said, "I know it's coming. I don't want it to happen, but I know it's coming."

I said, "What?"

He said, "God's going to have you launch out into your own ministry. I don't want to lose you, but I'm not going to stand in God's way. So we'll just pray for the perfect timing. You let me know what you get from God, and I'll let you know what I get. But, it's inevitable. You know too much, and God's going to use you in a greater way than what you could be used here working for me."

So we prayed over that, and believed God for the perfect timing.

The Turning Point

In October of 1973, I was holding a meeting in Hot Springs, Arkansas, and I was staying with an elderly couple who had a large pond at the back of their home. Everyday between services I would go sit under their big oak tree and pray before the next service. While I was sitting under that big oak tree one day, I heard the Spirit of God say, "You will launch out into your own ministry January 1, 1974."

I was still arguing with God. I said, "God, I don't want to do this. I want to keep working with Brother Copeland. I want to serve him."

He said, "You will always serve Brother Copeland, and you'll always be a team." But then He said, "The way it is now, you are limited. But by you launching out into your ministry, the team will be able to cover twice as much territory with the same message."

In the past, we were almost always together preaching in the same meeting. The Lord said, "But now, the team will broaden its boarders. You'll be able to cover twice as much territory with the same message."

I said, "All right. Then You reveal this to Brother Copeland."

I concluded my services in Hot Springs and flew to Long Beach, California, to meet Brother Copeland for a week of meetings. I had asked the Lord to give me an opportunity to talk to Brother Copeland about this, but it just never seemed appropriate. So as we were flying home from Long Beach, I was sitting in the cockpit with Brother Copeland, and when he reached his cruising altitude and set the auto pilot, he folded his hands, looked over at me, and he said, "When are you leaving?"

I said, "Well, let me tell you what I've heard in my spirit, and then I want you to judge it and see if it bears witness with your spirit. Because if it doesn't, I'm not making a move."

Don't Pay Me

I told him that the Lord told me that we would be able to cover twice as much territory with the same message if I left his organization and started my own. He said, "That's God. I know this is God. So, you've got my blessings on this. When are you leaving?"

I said, "Well, I'm going to work for you the rest of this year, but starting December 1, don't pay me. My last paycheck in November will be the last paycheck I'll receive. I don't want you to pay me during the month of December, but I'm going to work for you just like I have been. January 1, 1974, I will launch out into my own ministry, and I might as well have a one-month jump start on believing God to sustain me financially and not be able to look to Kenneth Copeland Evangelistic Association for a paycheck."

He said, "You don't want me to pay you the last month you're here?"

I said, "No. I'll do whatever you want me to do; I'll give you 110 percent, but don't pay me during the month of December because that's the month that I'm going to learn how to believe God a month in advance for whatever I need for my ministry starting January 1, 1974."

He said, "Are you sure that's the way you want it?"

I said, "That's the way I want it."

He said, "Then consider it done, and I'll stand in agreement with you for the best month financially that you've ever had."

So December 1973, I worked for Brother Copeland just like I had the two and a half years before. I didn't receive a paycheck, and God supernaturally blessed me financially. I even made more money that month. God brought in almost more in December than I'd made the whole year working for Brother Copeland. When God launched me out in my ministry on January 1st, He launched me out with money in the bank. I believe the reason why is because of my faithfulness to Brother Copeland.

So, December 31, 1973, was my last day as a full-time employee of Kenneth Copeland Evangelistic Association. When I walked out of his office that last day, I walked out with money in the bank, ready to start Jerry Savelle Evangelistic Association.

A Man Named Charles Capps

My very first meeting when I launched into my ministry was in England, Arkansas. A man named Charles Capps had invited me to come. Charles was a farmer, and he was beginning his teaching ministry. We had met back in October 1973, and we discovered that we "talked the same language."

In that meeting in 1973, Charles' oldest daughter came up to me and said, "You sound like my daddy!"

I said, "Who's your daddy?"

She said, "Charles Capps."

I said, "Well, I've never heard of Charles Capps."

She said, "Not many people have, but they will. And you sound like him. And you and my daddy would get along really well. In fact, I'm going to call him and invite him and Mamma to come hear you tomorrow night."

I said, "Well, great. I'd like to meet them."

So, she did. After the service, we had dinner together, and Charles and I hit it off. We preached to each other all night long at the dinner table. So Charles invited me to come preach in his home church in Arkansas and stay with him and his wife, Peggy, in their home.

I preached about five nights there, and we had revival. It was an outstanding meeting. After the service, the pastor gave me a check, and I was very thankful.

The next morning as I was packing my car, Charles said, "Have you got a tape deck in your car?"

I said, "No, sir."

I had a 1973 Ford station wagon.

He said, "Well, would you follow me to Little Rock? I'd like to buy you one. I've got some tapes I want you to listen to on the way home."

So we went to a shop, and he had a tape deck installed in my car, and he gave me some tapes of his sermons. After they installed the tape deck, I thanked him and prepared to leave, but Charles said, "Wait a minute. Peggy and I want to invest into your ministry."

And he handed me a check for $5,000. I had never seen $5,000 all at one time. Charles Capps had become the largest contributor to my ministry! Hallelujah!

God Supplies Our Needs

I shouted the entire way home from Arkansas to Texas. I had $5,000 plus the offering that the church had given me in addition to the money God had blessed us with during that month of December.

When I got home, I met with a businessman named Ted Mutto, who had some offices he was leasing. He came to me and said, "Where are you going to house your ministry?"

I said, "Well, right here in my home until I need offices."

He said, "I've got some offices, four rooms, fully equipped, furniture, typewriters, copier, everything. I've got a complete office set up. I'll leave the pencils, the erasers, the staples, the paper clips and the pads. You can walk right into it. You'll be helping me, and at the same time, I believe I'll be helping you because I've got a lease on this office that doesn't end until the end of this year. I don't want to have to pay this money out on something that I'm not going to use anymore."

He said, "I'll give you everything in there for $2,500, and you can take up the lease for the same amount that I've been paying until the lease expires."

I paid him $2,500, and I moved into that office fully equipped.

I walked into *my* office within the first two weeks of January 1974. Every morning, I would go to my office, all by myself, no secretary, and I'd change desks every hour just to see which office I liked the best.

Later, I received a call from Brother Copeland. He said, "Well, how are you doing? How was your first meeting?"

I said, "It was a landslide, praise God. God's just blessing me."

He said, "You're going to record what you preach, aren't you?"

It had never dawned on me to record what I preach. I had always recorded what he preached, but I thought, *Who would want to listen to what I have to say twice?* I knew they'd want to hear what he said twice, but me?

He said, "You're going to start your tape ministry right away, aren't you?"

I said, "Well, you know, I hadn't thought of that."

He said, "Well, you need to. I've just been blessed with some brand new equipment, and I want to sow into your ministry the equipment that you used while you were here since you're already familiar with it. I want to sow the duplicators, the recorders, the amplifiers, sound system, everything, into your ministry."

I drove my station wagon over to his office and loaded it up. I started out with money in the bank, a complete office, tape duplicators, sound system, everything! All I needed was an invitation! And they came.

I hit the ground running. I never had to ask for a place to preach. I was booked up with invitations. And now the same message was being carried to twice as much territory.

==When you move in God's perfect timing, He will supply all of your needs.==

34
How Desperate are You for Success?

Brother Copeland's father, A.W. Copeland, called me one day and said, "I want to come see your offices and talk to you for a while." So he came, and he sat down in front of my desk, and he asked me a question. He said, "Do you intend for this ministry to be successful?"

I said, "Well, of course."

He said, "Are you desperate for success?"

I said, "I'm desperate."

He said, "What are you willing to do to be successful?"

I said, "Whatever it takes."

And then he related a story to me. He said, "I want to tell you how desperate you've got to be if you're going to be successful. I used to share this story with young men that would come into my insurance business, and I want to share it with you."

He said, "There was a young man who had decided to go fishing one day. He noticed sitting on the dock was a very rich, prominent, successful man. He knew who he was, but he had never met him before. He was just sitting there alone on the dock, fishing. He thought, *What an opportunity! I believe I'll go and ask this man if I can sit next to him and just ask him some questions about how he became successful.*"

"So he walked up to him and said, 'May I sit down?'

"The older gentleman said, 'Yes.'

"The young man sat down, and then he said, 'I know who you are. I hope I'm not intruding, but people don't get an opportunity like this but maybe once in a lifetime. I'd just like to ask you something. Could you please tell me the secret to your success?'"

"The older man got up and pushed the younger man into the water. Then he jumped in behind him, and he held the man under water. Then he raised him up by the hair of his head. The man was trying to get his breath. And then he shoved him down again and held him down a little longer this time. Then he raised him up. The man was gasping for air, and he shoved him down one more time. When he raised him up this time, the man, struggling and gasping for air, finally got his breath. He calmed down, looked at the older man, and he said, 'Why did you do that?'"

"He said, 'When you want success as desperately as you wanted that next breath, then you'll succeed.'"

Then Brother A.W. Copeland got up, said, "Goodbye," and then walked out and left me with that. I thought, *You're just like your son! Leaving me with these things, and then walking out!*

I thought about that, and then I realized the point he was endeavoring to make. Some people talk about wanting success, some people talk about how they would like to be successful, but not everybody is desperate enough for it. But if you're as desperate as that guy was to get his next breath, then there's no devil in hell that can defeat you.

God's Formula For Success

In 1973, Gloria Copeland wrote her first book entitled, *God's*

Will for Your Life. While she was writing it, every once in a while she would hand me a chapter to read before it was published. It is such a powerful book, containing such tremendous revelation and insight that it became a handbook for me. I carried my Bible and her book, *God's Will for Your Life*, everywhere I went.

She had done some extensive studying endeavoring to reveal to people that God's will for their life was healing and prosperity. Sometimes Brother Copeland would be preaching, and he would say, "If you're wondering where I got all this revelation, it's because of Gloria."

The outline I want to share with you is called, *God's Formula for Success*. It's an outline that I made from what I learned from Gloria's book. I still use these principles today.

A. **It is God's will for you to be successful.**

   Joshua 1:8 says, *This book of the law shall not depart out of thy mouth; but thou shalt meditate therein day and night, that thou mayest observe to do according to all that is written therein: for then thou shalt make thy way prosperous, and then thou shalt have good success.*

   1. The Bible was written for your benefit, not God's. He's already successful.

   2. The Bible is God's wisdom made available to you.

   3. Read God's Word with a positive attitude, not only as a set of rules, but also as the open door to your success.

B. **Keep the Word in your mouth.**

   1. Talk God's Word constantly. Joshua 1:8.

      Deuteronomy 6:6-7 says, *And these words, which I command thee this day, shall be in thine heart:*

      And thou shalt teach them diligently unto thy children, and shalt talk of them when thou sittest in thine house, and when thou walkest by the way, and when thou liest down, and when thou risest up.

2. When your heart is full of God's Word, your mouth will speak God's Word.

   Matthew 12:34 says, *O generation of vipers, how can ye, being evil, speak good things? for out of the abundance of the heart the mouth speaketh.*

3. What you put in your heart in abundance is what you will speak.

4. Listen to yourself talk, and you can determine what is in your heart in abundance.

5. We live in a negative world. Unless you take action against the world's order, you will be negative, too.

6. You receive in this life what you believe in your heart and what you speak with your mouth.

   Mark 11:23 says, *For verily I say unto you, That whosoever shall say unto this mountain, Be thou removed, and be thou cast into the sea; and shall not doubt in his heart, but shall believe that those things which he saith shall come to pass; he shall have whatsoever he saith.*

7. Your words will bring sickness or health, lack or abundance, defeat or victory, and failure or success.

8. God's Word in your mouth will cause good things to come to pass in your life.

   Matthew 12:35 says, *A good man out of the good treasure of the heart bringeth forth good things: and an evil man out of the evil treasure bringeth forth evil things.*

C. **Meditate God's Word day and night. Joshua 1:8.**

   1. Meditating God's Word is God's method of getting His Word in your heart.

2. Meditation is more than just reading. It is fixing your mind on the Word so that you will learn to do all that is written therein.

3. You must set time aside daily to meditate the Word of God.

4. Meditation causes God's Word to come alive in your spirit.

5. Seven objectives to meditating God's Word.

   a. Apply the Word to yourself personally.

   b. Allow the Holy Spirit to make the Word a reality in your heart.

   c. Carefully ponder how the Word applies to your life.

   d. Dwell on how the Word changes your situation.

   e. Place yourself in agreement with what the Word says about you.

   f. See yourself as the Word sees you.

   g. Realize the integrity of God's Word. God is not a Man that He should lie.

Make It Personal

Now, let's take a closer look at these seven objectives to meditating God's Word.

#1. **Apply that Word to yourself personally.**

Philippians 4:19 – *But my God shall supply all your need according to his riches in glory by Christ Jesus.*
How would I apply Philippians 4:19 to myself per-

sonally? "My God shall supply Jerry's needs according to His riches in glory."

Now, that's personal, isn't it?

#2. **Allow the Holy Spirit to make the Word a reality in your heart.**

How would that be done?

As you continually confess God's Word, it suddenly becomes more than just words in a book. It becomes more real than your problem.

#3. **Carefully ponder how this Word applies to your life.**

If you've got a need of $10,000 and God's Word says, "My God shall supply all your need according to His riches in glory by Christ Jesus," then you're going to apply this word to your need by declaring, "I believe my need is met, and I call things that are not as though they are in Jesus' name."

#4. **Dwell on how this Word changes your situation.**

Before anything can happen outwardly, it's got to take place inwardly first. You've got to see it happening on the inside before it ever happens on the outside.

So, now you've meditated Philippians 4:19, you've applied it to yourself personally, it's become a reality in your heart, you're pondering on how it applies to your life. Now you're dwelling on how it changes your situation. You no longer see yourself with a $10,000 need, you now see yourself with a need met.

#5. **Place yourself in agreement with what God says about you.**

How do you do that? With your mouth. Affirm it. Confirm it. Say it. Confess it. That's how you place yourself in agreement. Now you're declaring, "God says He will supply all my need according to His riches in glory by Christ Jesus. I place myself in agreement with that, and I call my need met."

#6.   See yourself as God sees you.

You can't go around talking "lack" after meditating Philippians 4:19. You can't go around talking your "need" after meditating Philippians 4:19. If you're still talking "lack" and "need," then you didn't allow the Holy Spirit to make it a reality in your heart.

#7.   Realize the integrity of God's Word.

When you truly understand the integrity of God's Word, then you don't walk around with a sad look. When you truly understand the integrity of God's Word, you walk around with your head up high, a smile on your face, a dance in your step, joy in your heart, and confidence in God's ability to meet your need. If the devil brings up your need, just say, "You'll have to go talk to God about that. I've cast that care over on Him."

Now, back to our outline on God's Formula for Success.

D.   Act on God's Word.

1.   Be a doer of the Word and not a hearer only.

Matthew 7:24-27 says, *Therefore whosoever heareth these sayings of mine, and doeth them, I will liken him unto a wise man, which built his house upon a rock:*

And the rain descended, and the floods came, and the winds blew, and beat upon that house; and it fell not: for it was founded upon a rock.

And every one that heareth these sayings of mine, and

> *doeth them not, shall be likened unto a foolish man, which built his house upon the sand:*
>
> *And the rain descended, and the floods came, and the winds blew, and beat upon that house; and it fell: and great was the fall of it.*

2. It's not enough to only know what the Word says; you must do it in order to get results.

3. Once you meditate the Word, the Holy Spirit will next teach you how to apply the Word.

E. **Mental assent, one of the greatest enemies of faith.**

1. Mental assent agrees that the Word is true, but never acts on the Word.

2. Mental assent is usually moved by what it sees and feels.

3. Mental assent can usually be detected by these words: "But you don't understand," and "what if."

Have you ever heard a person say, "I know the Word says that, but what if?" That's mental assent. What they're actually saying is, "My circumstances are greater than the Word."

F. **Putting this formula into action.**

1. Find out what the Word says about every situation in your life.

2. Keep that Word in your mouth. Talk it all the time.

3. Do the Word. Apply what God's Word says about your situation immediately.

4. To be afraid to act on God's Word is to be faithless.

5. To be afraid to act on God's Word is to doubt God's Word.

6. Hold fast to the Word of God. Refuse to give up.

7. Constantly praise God for the manifestation.

You can apply the principles in this outline to every situation in your life and experience great success. Go back and read it again and then "do it." You'll find that God is faithful to His Word, and He will uphold your non-compromising stand.

Preaching with Kenneth Copeland in his Believers' Conventions for three decades.

(1981)

(1994)

(1986)

One of our first petitions to God after learning how to believe for a "heavenly grant." What a life-changing revelation!

REQUEST FOR NEW FURNITURE

Father, in the Name of Jesus, I come boldly to the throne of grace according to Heb. 4:16; as your very own child; as the righteousness of God, with a sense of reverence but also a sense of belonging.

John 16:23 states: "And in that day ye shall ask me nothing. Verily, verily, I say unto you, Whatsoever ye shall <u>ask the Father in my name, he will give it you.</u>"

Mark 11:24 states: "Therefore I say unto you, <u>What things soever ye desire</u>, when ye pray, <u>believe that ye receive</u> them, and <u>ye shall have them.</u>"

Psalm 37:4 states: "Delight thyself also in the Lord; and <u>he shall give thee the desires of thine heart.</u>"

John 10:10 states: "...I am come that they might have life, and that they might have it more <u>abundantly.</u>"

... states: "Christ hath re-
... rse of the law,...."
... I know that it is your
... me to live an abund-
... should prosper; and have
... rt. We base our request
... ct Jesus to act as our

The following is a list of the new furniture we desire. We believe the sum of 1500.00 will cover the cost of the items. (The prices per item are subject to change).

ITEM:	APPROX. PRICE:
2--square lamp tables	$ 74.95 ea.
1--oblong coctail table	104.95
1--bookcase	127.95
1--stereo component set	68.95
1--early-American dining table (two leaves, six chairs)	400.00
4--bar stools	24.00
2--mirrors	12.00
2--ocassional round tables	10.00
1--bedroom chair	50.00
2--two-drawer chest	21.95 e
2--twin head boards	22.00
1--double head board	100.00
2--twin bedspreads	50.00
2--twin pillow shams	6.00
2--pairs bedroom drapes	24.00
2--pairs living room drapes	30.00
2--pairs bedroom drapes	24.00
2--living room chairs	238.00
2--living room lamps	60.00
1--bedroom lamp	15.0

1 John 5:14-15 says: "And this is the confidence we have in him, that, if we ask any ... to his will, he heareth us: ... whatsoever we

Carolyn and me, 1973.

Publicity photos through the years. I think we get better with age.

The two men who have impacted my life the most, Kenneth Copeland and Oral Roberts.

Preaching with Dr. Roberts at my annual Revival Fires Conference in Fort Worth, TX.

Carolyn, me, Oral and Evelyn Roberts.

My "spiritual grandfather," Oral Roberts, will forever be honored in the Savelle house.

The Savelle family, 1997 (backrow left to right: Michael Everage, me, Carolyn, Rodney Foy, front row: Mark James Everage, Preston Everage, Jerriann Savelle Everage, Kassidi Foy, and Terri Savelle Foy).

Carolyn and me with our wonderful grandchildren in Denver, CO, (me holding Kassidi, Carolyn holding baby Madison Everage, and Mark James and Preston standing).

My younger daughter, Terri, with her daughter, Kassidi, and husband, Rodney.

My older daughter, Jerriann, with her husband, Michael, and children, Mark James, Preston and Madison.

A covenant relationship with Kenneth and Gloria Copeland. Thank God for his obedience to come to my hometown and preach the message that took me from a failure to victorious living.

35
Things Which are Seen are Temporal

he ministry began to grow, and it finally got to the point where I could not do everything by myself, and it was now time to hire someone to assist me.

My first secretary was a young lady named June Stocks. Carolyn and I had become friends with her parents. Their daughter, June, had just graduated from high school, and she came to work for me. She wore many hats. She was my personal secretary, she did the duplicating of the tapes, she wrote the articles for a little newsletter that we sent out (to a handful of people) called, *The Overcomer*. She answered the phone, and she typed my letters. The office staff of Jerry Savelle Evangelistic Association in early 1974 consisted of June and me.

Eventually, it got to the point where June couldn't do it all, and the demand on my ministry was increasing. There were more and more invitations, and I was doing everything on the road myself. I was the "Road Crew" and the preacher for Jerry Savelle Evangelistic Association.

Back then, not many churches believed in the message of faith and God's will to prosper you, so I was not invited to many churches. People who would invite me to come speak in their city would say, "We don't have a church; we just want to know if you'll come to our city. If you will, we'll find a building." I preached in everything you can imagine: front yards, abandoned laundromats, open fields, living rooms, anywhere people wanted to hear the Word of Faith.

I would drive to a city carrying all my equipment, and then I would set it up before the service. I would set up my own sound system, set up the tapes on the table, set up books that I sold by Kenneth Copeland and Kenneth Hagin. I only had a few tape series myself, but I didn't have any books yet. However, I wanted people to have faith-building materials, so we kept a good supply of material from Kenneth Copeland, Kenneth Hagin and E.W. Kenyon on our tape tables.

As soon as I would finish preaching and praying for people, I would take my microphone off and run back to the tape tables to sell the tapes. When the meeting was over, I would take everything down, load up my car, and drive to the next meeting.

Finally, it got to where the demand was such that I needed someone to travel with me to do those things like I had done for Brother Copeland. But it didn't happen immediately; it didn't happen overnight. I wasn't hiring somebody just so I could create a "staff." We endeavored to use wisdom and do it at the proper time when there was a demand because it also meant that I would have to believe God for another salary.

Recently, I looked back at my Board of Directors' Minutes for 1974 just to see what it took for us to operate every month. I found that we were believing God for $1,500 a month in 1974. That paid office rent, my salary, June's salary, and got me out of town and back. I can't even open my doors for $1,500 a day now. But I'm telling you, my faith was stretched to believe God for $1,500 a month back then.

So I was at the point where I needed someone to travel with me, and we starting believing God for the right person as well as the finances to pay him.

Imparting Into Others

While I was working for Brother Copeland, we went to El

Paso, Texas, several times for meetings. During one of these meetings, I met a man named Charles Nieman, who would always volunteer to help me at Brother Copeland's tape tables. He helped me take down the sound system and load the car and anything else that I might need him to do.

So later when I went back to El Paso to conduct my own meeting, he and his wife, Rochelle, volunteered to assist me. He helped me with everything. So we began to develop a friendship, and one day he told me that he believed he was called to preach. So I asked him, "Would you pray about coming to work for me? I need someone to travel with me, and I need someone to do what you've helped me do here in this meeting. Would you pray about moving to Fort Worth and coming to work for me?"

He said God had laid that on his heart, and he was praying that I would ask. It's amazing how God has divine appointments for you if you just follow where He leads you. Charles worked with me for about a year, and he did exactly what I had done for Brother Copeland. Today, Charles Nieman is the pastor of one of the finest churches in America there in El Paso, Texas. It's a joy to know that I had a part in his ministry and had an opportunity to impart into his life.

Shortly after Charles Neiman left, I met another young man in Arkansas. This young man had one of the most powerful singing voices that I had ever heard. I had been invited to preach on the Arkansas Tech Campus to the University students. They were having what they called a "Jesus Rally."

People were singing and giving testimonies, and then at the end, they had me preach. The young man who sang just before I preached was about 20 years old, and had one of the most powerful voices that I'd ever heard.

So we got acquainted after the rally. Later, I went to Hot Springs, Arkansas, to preach again, and found out that this young man lived in Hot Springs. He actually lived with the family that had invited me to come and preach. So once again, we were united there. I asked him to sing before I preached every night that week, and he did.

A few months later, I went back to Hot Springs to preach again, and he was there. The Lord had spoken to me and said, "This man will come to work for you." I didn't say anything, I just listened to the Lord and said, "Well, Lord, You talk to this young man."

He came to me one day and said, "I feel like I'm supposed to work for you."

I said, "Well, I do, too. I believe it's God."

He said, "But, I'm fighting it."

I said, "Why?"

He said, "You're so disciplined, and I think you would create demands on my life that I'm not ready for."

I said, "What do you mean?"

He said, "Well, I've never met anybody that is as disciplined as you are. I just don't think I'm ready for that. But I know I'm supposed to work for you."

I said, "When the time is right, you call me and let me know."

Well, at the time, he was traveling with a singing group called "The Sounds of Joy." They were nearly starving trying to get started.

One night, just before I was to go to North Carolina on a tour, I got a call at about 10:00 p.m., and it was this young man. He was in Temple, Texas, with his singing group. He said, "Can I come to work? I'm tired of starving!"

I said, "Where are you?" He told me and I said, "How soon can you be here?"

He said, "I can be there whenever you want me there."

I said, "I'm leaving on a tour in the morning, be here by 10:00 a.m., and I'll expect you to go with me."

He arrived just in time for us to leave. I knew he was wiped out, so I said, "I'll start driving. You lie on the back seat and sleep. As soon as you wake up, we're going to talk."

After a few hours, he woke up, and I told him what I expected of him. I said, "You are a highly anointed singer, but you have absolutely no discipline in your life. But you are about to get some! I've got a set of tapes by Brother Copeland that you're going to start listening to right now, and you're going to listen to these tapes all day long. When you're in your hotel room, you will listen to tapes, and I will quiz you afterwards to make sure you're listening to them. You're going to be in every meeting that I preach. You'll sing and assist me in the meeting, and before you go to bed, you will listen to another tape."

This young man's name was Russ Taff. After about a year and a half of working with me, he got the Word in his heart and the fire of God in his eyes. Russ went on to become a Grammy Award winning Christian recording artist.

Russ would often write songs after hearing me preach. Later, he recorded some of them, and they became very well-known songs.

One day, he received a phone call from a man named Armond Morales of the Imperials. Armond had heard Russ sing before and wanted him to join the Imperials and become their lead singer.

Well, that was Russ' dream. He had always wanted to sing with the Imperials. So, he asked me about it. I said, "Well, Russ, if this had happened to you about a year and a half ago, I'd say no because you weren't ready. But now you've got the Word in you. You know who you are in Christ. I believe you can handle this, so you go tour with them for about a month. Then come back and let me know if this is really what you want to do. If it is, then I'll send you out with my blessing."

After about a month, he decided that this was what God wanted him to do, and he joined the Imperials. Later, he branched out into his own music career and became extremely well-known in Gospel Music. Russ was a blessing to our ministry.

It's a joy to look back and see that I've had the privilege of helping launch some people into the ministry just like Brother Copeland did with me.

Things Which are Seen are Temporal

My ministry continued to grow. We outgrew our offices within the first year, and it was time to move on. In the area in which I lived, there were a few offices, but they were all taken. But I really felt in my spirit that God wanted me in that area of town. So I was driving around one day, and I kept hearing in my spirit, 2 Corinthians 4.

2 Corinthians 4:18 says, *While we look not at the things which are seen, but at the things which are not seen: for the things which are seen are temporal; but the things which are not seen are eternal.*

I said, "Lord, what are You trying to say to me?"

He said, "Things which are seen are temporal."

I said, "That's what it says. But what are You trying to get across to me?"

He said, "Everywhere you've gone asking about office space, you've been told there is none. Things which are seen are temporal. If you can see it, then it's temporal."

Then He gave me this phrase, and I'll never forget it, "Another meaning for the word *temporal* is *subject to change*. Son, just because they say there is no office space available doesn't mean that it's final. It's subject to change. Didn't I say if you delight yourself in Me, I'll give you the desires of your heart?"

I said, "Yes."

He said, "Is it the desire of your heart to have an office near your home?"

I said, "It is."

He said, "Then don't be moved by what you see or what you feel or what you hear, because what 'they' say is subject to change. Where do you want an office?"

There was a particular office building that I had looked at and thought it would be perfect, but it was occupied. He said, "Go talk to them again, but this time talk to the owner."

I went back to that building, and I asked to see the owner who was a man named Clinton Wright. The receptionist said, "He's here today, but do you have an appointment?"

I said, "No, I don't. I'd just like to know if I could talk to him."

So she went back and asked him if I could speak to him. He came out to the lobby. There were secretaries sitting at their desks so everybody could hear my conversation. We didn't go to his private office.

I said, "My name is Jerry Savelle. I'm a minister, and I've driven by your building, and I really like this area. I need office space, and I would really like to lease some from you."

He said, "Are you talking about where my office is occupied?"

I said, "No, you have another office that's connected to this one, and I understand that it's occupied too. But that's where I'd like to have my office."

He said, "Well, Sir, the man that's leasing that office from me has been here for over five years, and he has a three-year lease left on that building."

I said, "That's what they told me earlier. Sir, I don't know if you understand what I'm about to say, but I'm going to tell you anyway. I really believe God wants me here."

He said, "Oh, really?"

I said, "Yes, and I hear what you're saying, but I'd like to read a Scripture to you." I had a little New Testament in my pocket, and I pulled it out, and I said, "I don't know if you've ever heard this before, but I want you to listen to what this says: 'Things which are seen are temporal.' That means subject to change. Now, I realize the man's been here five years; he's been a good tenant; you don't want him to leave; and he's got three more years on his lease. But a remaining three-year lease with this man is subject to change.

And when it happens, would you call me? I want that office."

He said, "Well, it's unlikely that will happen."

I said, "I know it's unlikely. But the Bible says, 'Things that are unlikely to change are subject to change.'"

He said, "I've never heard anything like that before."

I said, "All I'm asking is, when this man decides to leave, would you call me? I want first choice on that office."

He said, "Well, that's probably not going to happen, but if it does, yes, I'll call you."

So I gave him my number and said, "I'll be leaving on a trip, and if you call while I'm gone, you can just leave the message with my wife, and I'll call you when I get back."

He said, "Sir, nothing's going to happen in three days."

I said, "Well, if it does, would you call and leave the message? Because everything you're saying is subject to change."

He just shook his head, and he said, "I've never heard anything like this."

I was gone for three days, and I came back, and there was no message. So I went back to see him. I said, "Sir, I noticed there was no message while I was gone. Did you just fail to call?"

He said, "No. Nothing's changed."

I said, "Well, that's subject to change."

And he said, "Well, I heard what you said, and I've thought about that a lot. I've never heard anything like that. But, no. Nothing's changed."

I said, "I'm leaving town again, and I'll be gone for about three days, and if anything happens, call my wife, leave the message, and I'll get back with you when I get back."

He said, "Sir, nothing's going to happen in the next three days. You might as well go look for another office."

I said, "No, Sir. This is where I'm going to have my ministry. Every time I drive by here, I see a 'Jerry Savelle Evangelistic Association,' sign out front. I will be in this office."

He said, "You're very sure of yourself, aren't you?"

I said, "My confidence is in the Word of God."

So, I was gone another three days. When I came back, there was no message, so I went back to his office again. I said, "I'd like to see Mr. Clinton Wright."

By this time, they knew me. I didn't have an appointment but the receptionist said, "He's been expecting you!"

I said, "Would you tell him I'm here?"

So she called him, and he came into the lobby, but this time, he brought all of his employees with him. There were about twelve people with him, and he said, "Now, I know what you're going to say, and I want all of my employees to hear it. Go through that whole thing with me again."

I got my New Testament out, and I said, "Well, the Bible says, 'Things which are seen are temporal,' and temporal means subject to change. That means that whatever people say is impossible is subject to change. Now, I believe God wants me to have an office in this building. I have been telling Mr. Wright that I know that the man who is leasing from him next door has three years left on his lease, but that's subject to change. And I believe my ministry will be housed in that office."

He looked at them and said, "Have you ever heard anything like this before?"

They're all looking at me like, *Poor nut*. But Mr. Wright was not looking at me like that. He said, "I've never heard anything like this in my life. And I want to tell you what happened yesterday."

I said, "What?"

He said, "Have you talked to the man next door?"

I said, "I've never met him. I just know he's in my office."

He said, "This man has been here for five years, and he's got three years left on his lease, but he came to me yesterday wanting to know if he could get out of his lease. And I think you had something to do with that!"

I said, "Well, I think God had something to do with that."

He said, "If you want this office, it's yours. In fact, I want you here. I want a man like you around me, and I want to be able to come talk to you from time to time."

I said, "How soon can I move in?"

He said, "It'll take him about two weeks to move out, and then you can move in."

I said, "Well, now, we've never talked about this. How much is the lease payment each month?"

When he told me, I said, "Well, that's subject to change!"

He looked around at his people, and he just grinned. He said, "I'm not going to argue with you because I know this will change. What do you want to pay?"

I told him what I wanted to pay. He said, "I'll take it! I want you here."

I offered him what I believed I could pay, and it was not much more than what I had been paying at my other office. But this office had more space.

He said, "Come in tomorrow, and we'll have the contract drawn up."

So, I went in to sign the contract, and I noticed it was for a five-year lease. I said, "Sir, I can't sign for five years."

He said, "Why not? That's our normal policy here."

I said, "Well, that's subject to change."

He just grinned at me, and he said, "How long can you lease?"

I said, "Sir, I don't have any idea how long I'll be here. I may outgrow this place in a month. I may outgrow it in a year, and I don't want to be bound to a five-year contract. So, if you don't mind, a five-year contract is subject to change."

He said, "Whatever you want, I want you here. I'll put a clause in the contract that states the office is yours for however long you want to stay."

So we moved in, and Mr. Wright was in my office often to talk about the Bible. I began to develop a wonderful relationship with one of the most successful realtors in our city.

I learned how to listen and know the voice of God in my own spirit. I depend on that "rhema" from God every day. I don't do anything without a rhema from God.

I keep a notebook with me all the time. I keep one on my bed stand just in case I hear something before I go to sleep, then I can write it down. I endeavor to stay in a listening mode. Once I hear it, and I know it's God, then I'm going to do it no matter what anybody else thinks or says. I'm prepared to do whatever I have to do until the manifestation of what I'm believing for comes to pass.

That one little phrase, "subject to change," became the theme of my ministry. I preached it almost everywhere I went.

Preaching with Brother Copeland Once Again

Brother Copeland called me one day in 1975 and asked me to go to Gadston, Alabama, to preach in a meeting with him. He said, "I want to talk to you about some things that God's dealing with me about. I want you to preach in one of the morning services like you used to do when you worked for me."

I said, "I'd be happy to."

We arrived in Gadston, and Brother Copeland preached that night. The next morning I preached on *Subject to Change*, and I'll never forget what happened next. Brother Copeland jumped up and shouted: "My Lord, boy, why didn't you tell me that five years ago?" It affected him the same way that it had affected me.

I experienced some of the greatest miracles that I had ever seen and received testimonies from many people who had experienced extraordinary things in their lives as well. You see, nothing is final. The only thing that is final is the Word of God. No matter what men say; no matter what your body says; no matter what your mind says; that's not final. That's subject to change.

If it can be perceived by the five physical senses, then it's not permanent. Not having enough money is subject to change. Incurable diseases are subject to change. Jesus said mountains are subject to change. Fig trees are subject to change. Dead bodies are subject to change. You can see it throughout the Bible. When you get a revelation of that, it will change your life forever.

Blow the Horn of Jubilee

While we were in that meeting in Gadston, Brother Copeland said that God had been dealing with him about him and me doing some meetings together, and we were going to call them, "Jubilee Meetings."

He said, "I want you to study Luke 4 and Leviticus 25. You and I are going to the various cities that God told me to go to and hold 'Jubilee Meetings.' We're both going to preach on Jesus, our Jubilee. I'm going to start it off, and where I leave off, you'll take up, and where you leave off, I'll take up. We won't compare notes. God's going to do this supernaturally."

It was one of the most supernatural things that we had ever experienced. Brother Copeland would start off, and the very Scripture that he would end with, would be my first Scripture on my outline, and I'd take up where he left off. And the last Scripture I talked about would be his first Scripture on his second outline.

In fact, one time we were preaching in Arrowhead Springs, California, at the Campus Crusade Headquarters. Brother Copeland said, "You want to go first?"

I said, "I don't care. You can go first."

He said, "Well, you go first."

We hadn't talked to each other about what we were going to preach. We hadn't seen each other's notes or anything like that. So, I started off, and when I read my last verse, I said, "Now Brother Copeland's coming to explain this."

He leaned over to the man who was the host of the meeting, and he said, "I want you to look at this. I want you to verify this." The opening Scripture on his outline was the last one I had read.

Believers' Conventions

Those "Jubilee Meetings" launched the next phase of our ministry together: The Kenneth Copeland Believers' Conventions. His very first Believers' Convention was in Long Beach, California, in 1978. The speakers were Brother Copeland, Gloria, myself, Charles Capps, and Kenneth Hagin.

That was over twenty years ago, and I haven't missed one Believers' Convention. That began a whole new dimension of "the team." Since that time, the team has added Jesse Duplantis and Creflo A. Dollar, Jr.

Many people are amazed at the relationship that I share with Kenneth Copeland. They ask, "How can you both have your own ministries, preach together, never become competitive and never have any strife?" I just simply tell them that God put this together thirty years ago, and we've held fast to what He said.

36
Preparation for Ministry

now want to share with you the key principles that I learned from Brother Copeland regarding preparation for ministry.

1. **You must set time aside for prayer and meditation that is not to be interrupted.**

If you study the ministry of Jesus, He was a Man of prayer, and a Man of deep meditation in the things of God. Many times you read about Jesus being alone early in the morning and late at night in preparation for ministry. Many times you read that while the disciples were off doing something else, Jesus was in a deserted place seeking God . . . praying. He was listening to His father for instructions. This is vitally important if you are going to be successful in ministering to people.

Everything Starts in the Prayer Closet

If you're going to be effective in ministry, you have to set time aside for prayer and meditation. I believe it was E. M. Bounds who said, "The real sermons are made in the prayer closet."

He also said, "Before you can talk well to men about God, you have to first of all be able to talk well to God about men."

Everything starts in the prayer closet. It's not a matter of having eloquent speech or being able to memorize a lot of Scripture. Effective ministry to people is determined by how effective you are in the prayer closet.

In my observing Brother Copeland, there was time set aside for prayer. In fact, one of the quickest ways for you to lose your job while working with him back when I did was to interrupt his prayer time. Never interrupt his time with God.

When I launched out into my own ministry, I developed the same attitude in my life. For instance, when someone picks me up at the airport and I'm scheduled to preach that evening, I don't go play golf all afternoon or sight see. That's not what I'm there for. I want to be sensitive to what God wants me to do and say in that service.

When I walk in the auditorium that night, I want to know that I've heard from God. I'm not relying on some sermon that worked in Chicago last year. I want the people to know that I have heard from God for them today.

You have to ask yourself: How desperate am I for results? How desperate am I to be used by God? How desperate am I for the anointing of God to flow in my life? If that's not important to you, then go play golf right up until service time. Go fellowship with everybody in town, eat until you can't breathe, and then when you go to the platform, you're not going to have anything to say. You may get away with it a few times, but eventually, the people will know you haven't properly prepared.

Does Your Family Recognize Your Calling?

It is very important that your family recognizes the calling on your life, especially if you're married and have children. Carolyn realized how important the anointing of God was to me and how desperate I was for results, and she honored that in me. And she taught our children to honor that.

My daughters were very small when we started our own ministry, but Carolyn taught them to respect the anointing; respect Daddy's preparation time for each service. My first study was in my garage. I didn't have a spare room to study in, so I built a study out in the garage. My girls knew that if Daddy was out in the garage, then don't interrupt him. Later, when I did have a study in the house, they knew that if the door was shut to Daddy's study, then don't interrupt him. Carolyn taught the girls how to respect my prayer time.

It's important that you set aside time to spend with God and let Him give you a word for that congregation. The last thing you want to hear is the voice of God before you go to that platform.

You have to ask yourself: Am I just going to fit in the category of "average," or am I going to be anointed? Average preachers are a dime a dozen. But then there are anointed ministers, praise God. And that only comes when you spend quality time with God.

2. **Never lose sight of the fact that it is God Who is the Healer.** *It is God Who is the Deliverer. It is God Who is the Savior. You are only an instrument that He has chosen to use. In other words, don't be high-minded.*

If you properly prepare yourself, then God is going to use you. If you properly prepare, people are going to be healed. People are going to be delivered. People are going to be set free. It's not going to happen occasionally; it's going to happen frequently. And when it starts happening, people are going to look at you as if you're *somebody*. And you're not . . . you're just the instrument.

Never forget that God is the Source. He's the Source of the power. He's the Source of the anointing. He's the Source of the healing, the deliverance, the salvation. All we are, are instruments that God has chosen.

T. L. Osborne told me years ago, "There's only two kinds of people in the Body of Christ: those that jeer you and those that cheer you." Those that love you and those that hate you. There's no middle ground. They'll either love you or hate you. Some of them, because of what they see God doing in your life, will worship the ground you walk on. And others will hate the mention of your name. But you can't be moved by either one. The ones that are really the worst are the folks who cheer you because if you listen to it, then it can create pride, and pride comes before a fall.

If you prepare yourself properly by setting time aside for prayer and meditation, then God is going to use you, and He's going to do it in a powerful way. People will be healed, and some will think that you're the healer. You have to be bold to tell them: "I am nothing. I am nothing but an instrument." Brother Copeland used to say, "I'm just a delivery boy."

3. **You must become tireless in your zeal to help people.**

Once again, it all goes back to preparation time. There were times when the disciples would go to Jesus and find that He had set Himself apart from the crowd to pray and fellowship with His Father. One particular reference in Mark says that when they found Him, they said, "All men seek Thee."

Notice Jesus didn't have a PR man? Jesus didn't have somebody to run ahead of Him and publicize the meeting. He prayed, and all men sought Him. Men will seek men and women of God **who are anointed**.

When Jesus went down to the crowd, there would be thousands of people, and the Bible says, "He was moved with compassion, and He healed them all."

You've got to be tireless. How long do you suppose it would take to heal them all? It could have been one mass miracle. But it doesn't say that.

In fact, in Mark 4 where Jesus had just completed teaching on the sower sows the Word, it says that afterwards He told the disciples to get into the ship. It says that He got them in the boat, and then He finished His ministry to the people. Then, He Himself got in the boat, and they launched off. That makes me think that perhaps there were still some who hadn't been healed yet, and Jesus wouldn't leave until He had prayed for them all.

The idea is to become tireless in your zeal to help needy people.

Once I was in a service where the anointing of God was just absolutely so strong that we didn't get out until almost 2:00 in the morning. It was so powerful. People didn't want to leave.

I said, "Pastor, do you want me to minister to them all?"

He said, "We're here for as long as you are."

I ministered to every person in the building. In ministry, you've got to be willing to stay and obey God in whatever He instructs you to do.

4. Be moved with compassion. Your heart should be filled with the love of God for hurting people.

If you're not compassionate about hurting people, then it's unlikely you're going to get results. If the only reason you're praying for somebody is so you can build a ministry, then you're not going to get very far. Compassion is loving what God loves and hating what God hates. God hates sickness. God hates disease. God hates cancer. Why? Because it takes life from people.

Sympathy vs. Compassion

Carolyn and I have some friends in New York City named Dan and Ann Stratton who are extremely zealous about God. I have never met anyone like Ann. She has to preach everywhere she goes. One time we spent a day with them just walking around the city, and everywhere we went, we would see a homeless person, and Ann would just have to stop. She'd have Dan stop the car in the middle of the street, and she would get out and go minister to them. She brings them all to church and loves on them. She just sees them the way Jesus sees them. They're human beings, they need Jesus, and if somebody doesn't reach out to them, then they may never be reached. That's compassion.

God loves the sinner, but He hates the sin. He loves the sick man, but He hates the disease that's trying to take that man's life.

That's what compassion is.

You may have some people come into your meetings that will absolutely break your heart. But you have to be careful that you don't move over into sympathy. Because sympathy and compassion are not the same.

Sympathy identifies with the problem and says, "Oh, I wish there was something I could do." You can't get anything done with sympathy alone.

There are times when I sense sympathy coming on me, and I have to pray in the Spirit so that I can move into the compassion of God. The compassion of God says there is something we can do. As long as I have breath in my lungs, the ability to pray and use of the name of Jesus, then there's something we can do. Compassion moves. Compassion acts. Compassion gets results!

5. **Pray in the Spirit. There is no substitute for tapping into the anointing of God like praying in the Spirit.**

1 Corinthians 14:2 says, *For he that speaketh in an unknown tongue speaketh not unto men, but unto God: for no man understandeth him; howbeit in the spirit he speaketh mysteries.*

The Amplified says, *For one who speaks in an [unknown] tongue speaks not to men but to God, for no one understands or catches his meaning, because in the [Holy] Spirit he utters secret truths and hidden things [not obvious to the understanding].*

1 Corinthians 2:6-7 says, *Howbeit we speak wisdom among them that are perfect: yet not the wisdom of this world, nor of the princes of this world, that come to nought:*

But we speak the wisdom of God in a mystery, even the hidden wisdom, which God ordained before the world unto our glory.

The Bible teaches us that when we pray in the Spirit, we are praying or speaking mysteries and hidden things. That's why it is so important that you pray in the Spirit in preparation for ministry. That's what I do the majority of my time in those several hours that I spend before a service. It's not only reading the Bible; it's not only jotting down notes or creating my outline to preach from; but most of it is praying in the Spirit. In fact, I start my time praying in the Spirit, then I go into my study time, my meditation time, and then I end that time praying in the Spirit.

Praying in the Spirit enables me to shut my mind down. I don't want to hear what my mind has to say; I want to hear what the Holy Ghost has to say, and He's not speaking to my mind; He's speaking to my spirit. My spirit will then relay that information to my mind.

Praying in the Spirit, as we saw in the Word, enables us to tap into the mysteries of God. This has happened to me frequently. You may go into a meeting and hear things come out of you that you did not know you knew. What happened is, you prayed mysteries in the Spirit. But then when you went out and preached in your known language, you were actually interpreting what you had said in the Spirit.

There's no substitute for praying in the Spirit. Praying in the Spirit creates a greater sensitivity to the direction of the Holy Spirit.

6. Confess that you are sensitive to the Holy Ghost. Make that a confession before you go into a service.

I enjoy reading from 1 Corinthians 12:11 – *But all these worketh that one and the selfsame Spirit, dividing to every man severally as he will.*

I read that before I go into a service. Notice it says that the Holy Spirit gives these gifts to every man liberally, *as He wills.*

I believe it's the will of God that I flow in those gifts. I believe it's the will of God that those gifts operate in me. These gifts of the Holy Spirit are designed to flow through you in behalf of the person who needs them.

If someone needs healing and the Gift of Healing is flowing, then it's for their benefit. If there's someone who is struggling with some issues in their life and God gives you a Word of Knowledge about that person, then who was that gift for, you or them? It was for them.

I confess 1 Corinthians 12 before I go into every meeting, and I put my name in those verses. I say, "Father, tonight as I minister to these people, I confess Your Word and declare that these Gifts are given liberally to every man as the Spirit wills. I believe it's Your will that I flow in these Gifts because there will be people in that meeting tonight who need these Gifts. So I confess I'm sensitive to the Holy Spirit. I'm sensitive to the Word of Wisdom. I'm sensitive to the Word of Knowledge. I'm sensitive to the Gifts of Healing, the Gift of Faith, the Working of Miracles and the Discerning of Spirits."

When I confess these verses, then my expectations are high. I expect it. I believe I'm going to flow in a prophetic word, and I believe that the Gifts of the Spirit are going to be in operation.

If you're going to tap into God's Wisdom, if you're going to speak prophetically, if you're going to speak the mysteries of God, then you've got to spend much time praying in the Spirit.

37
Ministry Standards

Now I'd like to share with you some of the ministry standards that I learned while working for Brother Copeland.

These standards should not only be observed and carried out in ministry but also in your every day life no matter what your profession may be. Not only will your lifestyle be pleasing to God, but you will also experience success in every area of your life. You just can't help but to achieve success when you develop integrity and demand excellence from yourself.

1. **Demand excellence. "Good enough" is never good enough. Don't ever have a "that's- good-enough mentality" about your ministry**.

When I was in college, one summer I worked as a draftsman for an engineering firm. We were working on government projects. A large engineering firm from Chicago was hired to design Interstate 20 through the state of Louisiana. My job was to draw maps of the entire Shreveport area where I lived.

We drew maps from aerial photos that had been taken of the city to determine what the best route would be before this Interstate would be constructed. We had to place everything we saw on those aerial photos onto these maps.

My boss came in one time to look at one of the maps that one of my co-workers had drawn. He said, "This is not accurate. You haven't put everything from the photo on this map."

He scolded him because it was very important. They were about to make some major decisions, and it demanded accuracy.

When the boss left, my co-worker made a comment that I have never forgotten. He said, "It's close enough for government work." And then he laughed about it.

He said that all the time. He didn't demand excellence in his work. If you're not careful, you can develop a "that's-good-enough" mentality to the point that you never stretch yourself and you'll never excel in anything.

- Demand excellence. Represent Jesus first-class. You're going to have to make rules for yourself, and you're going to have to draw some boundaries in your life that you refuse to cross. Demand excellence in everything.

One thing that I personally believe that Brother Copeland has done more than any other preacher in the world today is bring excellence in the ministry. He absolutely demands it. Even when he didn't have very much, he demanded excellence. Whatever he did, he did it with excellence.

2. The ministry must always maintain a high standard of ethics and integrity.

1 Thessalonians 2:1-3 says, *For yourselves, brethren, know our entrance in unto you, that it was not in vain:*

But even after we had suffered before, and were shamefully entreated, as ye know, at Philippi, we were bold in our God to speak unto you the gospel of God with much contention. For our exhortation was not of deceit, nor of uncleanness, nor in guile.

The Amplified says, *For our appeal [in preaching] does not [originate] from delusion or error or impure purpose or motive, nor in fraud or deceit.*

The Ben Campbell Johnson's Paraphrase says it this way:

But in persuading you to believe the Good News, I was not deceptive nor did I manipulate, nor was I game playing. God trusted me with the Good News, and I have faithfully passed it on. Not primarily for your or any person's approval, but to please God Who examines our inner selves.

Verse 10 in the King James says, *Ye are witnesses, and God also, how holily and justly and unblameably we behaved ourselves among you that believe.* In the Amplified it says, *You are witnesses, [yes] and God [also], how unworldly and upright and blameless was our behavior toward you believers [who adhered to and trusted in and relied on our Lord Jesus Christ].*

The Ben Campbell Johnson's Paraphrase states verse 10 like this:

You witnessed my behavior as God did. I was completely absorbed in God's will, full of integrity and beyond criticism.

This is how every minister should conduct himself.

    a.   *Be completely absorbed in God's will.*

    b.   *Be full of integrity.*

    c.   *Be beyond criticism.*

3. **When your methods are misunderstood and your motives misinterpreted, you must persevere. Have a single-mindedness toward God and a sincerity toward the people.**

What do I mean by that? Many times, even though you have determined that you're going to be honest, upright, and full of integrity, there will be some people that will misunderstand your methods and misinterpret your motives. But you have to persevere even when you are falsely accused.

Jesus is the only preacher that has ever lived Who was *without sin.* He perfectly expressed the character of God, but the religious people misunderstood His motives and misinterpreted His methods.

I'm not perfect, and neither are you! We're working on it. We're striving for it. But if Jesus was perfect, and yet He was misunderstood and misinterpreted, then you can count on it, you will be too. People will misunderstand your motives and your methods. They may say things about you that are untrue.

Don't ever defend yourself from the pulpit. That's not what the pulpit is for. Truth will prevail, and God will vindicate. He'll work those things out. You don't have to do that from the pulpit. Unfortunately, some of the meanest people in the world are Christians. Don't let them distract you.

"You're a Kenneth Copeland Clone"

When I was a young preacher just starting out, one pastor said to me, "Well, you need to go find out what God wants you to do. All you are is a Kenneth Copeland clone. You're just mimicking him."

When I got back home from that meeting, I remember thinking, *Well, is that all I am? Do I not have anything to say? Am I just copying Brother Copeland?* It really bothered me.

Not too long after that, I was visiting with Brother Copeland, and he asked me how the meeting was. I said, "I had a good meeting, but do you mind if I ask you a question?"

He said, "What?"

I said, "That pastor told me that all I was doing was copying you."

He said, "What's wrong with that?"

I said, "Well, I just want to be sure that I do have a ministry, and I do have something to say."

He said, "Who was that guy?"

I told him, and he said, "I preached for him years ago

myself, and he told me the same thing! He said I'm just copying Kenneth Hagin."

Well, Paul said, "Follow me as I follow the Lord." In fact, the literal Greek says, "Imitate me as I imitate Jesus."

Those words from that pastor could have wounded me and held me back, but I didn't allow it.

Brother Copeland said, "Don't worry about that. People tell me all the time that I'm just copying Kenneth Hagin. That's all right. Preach what gets results. If it's working in your life, then preach it and let them say what they want."

I did exactly that, and eventually, my own personality began to come out in those messages. I had my own style. I encourage you to do the same thing. You'll find that God will start incorporating the way you think and the way you present things into a message you may have heard from somebody else. It may sound like the same message, but it will come out with your personality in it.

Once again, when people misunderstand your methods and your motives, don't let it distract you. Just persevere, keep on going, fulfill what God's called you to do.

4. Never doubt God's call on your ministry. Keep it ever present in your thinking.

Do you really believe that God has called you? If so, then don't ever doubt it. If you're called of God, then there's room for you in this world as a preacher. There are a lot of preachers in the world today, and a lot of people going into the ministry, and sometimes the devil would love to try to tell you, "Who do you think you are? What makes you think you'll ever have a ministry? What makes you so special? Why would anybody want to hear what you have to say?"

Don't ever doubt the call of God on your life. In reality, God has called all of us to preach. In the eyes of God, every member of the Body of Christ is a proclaimer of the Gospel. We are Ambassadors for Christ. So don't ever doubt the call of God on your life. And because there is a call of God on your life, then there is room for your ministry.

5. **The success of your ministry is not dependent upon your ability, but upon God's ability in you.**

It's not about you. It's not about what you can do. It's about what God does in you and through you. Your sufficiency is not of yourself but of God.

6. **If you deeply believe that God has called you, then you will never have to take advantage of people.**

It's not people who are going to make your ministry; it's God. If you deeply believe you're called, then you'll never have to take advantage of people. You won't have to play "religious politics."

Some preachers try to get around someone who can help them climb that "religious ladder." If you really believe you're called, then you won't have to be self-promoting or self-exalting.

If you're called, and you really believe it, then God will promote your ministry. Promotion begins in the prayer closet. There are people who will seek you out. People will want to hear what you have to say, but it all begins in that prayer closet. If you seek God, then people will seek you, and you'll always have a place to preach.

7. **Overcoming opposition in your ministry only comes by being single-minded. <u>The things you compromise to get, you will ultimately lose.</u>**

A double-minded man can't expect to receive anything from God. Double-mindedness will cause you to compromise. And once again, whatever you compromise to get, you will ultimately lose. (Brother Copeland learned this principle from Oral Roberts, and then he passed it down to me.)

8. **You must become engulfed with the fact that God cannot fail, and He will not fail you.**

You must develop a deep conviction that God cannot lie. That is the primary basis for faith. Until you are totally convinced that God cannot lie, then you're always going to struggle with your faith. The Scriptures tell us that God is not a man that He should lie.

Not one word of God shall pass away. No word from God is void of power. When it becomes a reality in you that God cannot lie, then the next revelation that you'll receive is, "I cannot be defeated."

As in the story about my daughter's fingers, I believed first that God could not lie. And if He couldn't lie, then He couldn't fail. After we experienced that major miracle with the restoration of Terri's fingers, it marked me for the rest of my life. I became convinced that God's never going to fail me. To this day, every time I look at the little scars under Terri's fingernails, it reminds me of my covenant with God. It reminds me that God cannot fail.

9. **Pattern your ministry after Jesus. You are literally an extension of His ministry.**

When approaching the sick, look upon them as Jesus did. He was moved with compassion. See them as people who are being attacked by evil forces attempting to reduce them to nothing. Begin to literally hate the powers that have come against them until you have an irresistible urge to pray for them and lay your hands upon them.

If you apply these standards to your life and ministry, God will promote, exalt and bless you. Your Heavenly Father will be very pleased with you. What could be more rewarding than that?

38
The Power of Commitment

Commitment is a powerful word. We should be deeply committed in every area of our lives. We should be committed to God, to our spouse, to our family, and to our jobs.

The word *commitment* is defined as a pledge, promise, guarantee; to obligate oneself. When you commit to something, you are promising or guaranteeing that you will follow through with your word.

There are certain commitments that must be made if we want to fulfill the call that God has placed on our lives. Study the following outline and become committed to each one of these key principles.

1. *You must develop a deep commitment to the supernatural power of God and its ability to meet the needs of humanity.*

2. *To minister freedom and deliverance to humanity as Jesus did, you must be consumed with compassion.*

3. *You must become dependable and faithful to the call of God on your life. God is depending on you.*

4. *You must become deeply committed to be against sin, disease, fear, and demonic activity and strive to become an instrument of action and power.*

5. *You must become totally dedicated to the ministry of deliverance for all human suffering.*

6. *Develop a strong desire to see all of humanity set free.*

7. *Fasting often is a must if you're going to become a powerful instrument of God.*

   a. The definition of *fasting* means deliberately abstaining from food for spiritual purposes.

   b. Fasting disciplines the soul and it opens the door to the heavenly.

   c. You fast in order to shut your physical senses down so that your spirit can ascend to a level that enables you to hear the voice of God more clearly.

There are four kinds of fasting:

1. **Supernatural fast.** *Which means no food or water.*

An example of this is found in Exodus 34:27-28 talking about Moses. Exodus 34:28 – *And he was there with the Lord forty days and forty nights; he did neither eat bread, nor drink water.*

That is a supernatural fast. That is not the normal fast that you would go on. This one was called by God. Moses was directly in the presence of God, and that's the reason he could be sustained for that length of time. In the natural, your body can go without food for forty days but not without water.

So keep in mind that the only reason he was able to be sustained on a forty-day supernatural fast was because he was directly in the presence of God, and the glory of God sustained him.

2. ***Total fast.*** *This is a fast without food but you do drink water.*

Water is an important element in the body because it contains no calories nor will it stop you from entering into a true state of fasting. The body is 80 percent water, and it may lose several quarts daily by evaporation, so it must be replenished.

Matthew 4:2 says, *And when he had fasted forty days and forty nights, he was afterward an hungered.*

Jesus was hungry when He came off this fast. Now it's possible that He did drink water during that fast because normally if He had fasted forty days without food and water, the first thing it would have said was, "He thirsted." But it said, "He hungered." There's a strong possibility that on this forty-day fast Jesus did drink water.

3. ***Non-total fast.*** *This is a fast in which you don't eat food, but you are consuming water and possibly juices.*

You could consume juices, such as orange juice or tomato juice, which have only a few calories, but will still permit your system to get into a true state of fasting.

Many times when people go on an extended fast with no food, only water, they get nauseated. Juices help to keep you from getting nauseated so that you can continue your fast. It also provides you with sufficient strength so that you can go about your duties and activities for the day.

4. ***No pleasant bread fast.*** *You are drinking water and you are eating little portions of food, but it's not the things that you crave or desire. It's not stimulating or appealing.*

In other words, you can still enter into a state of fasting by eating little portions of food, but not the things you crave. It's not your favorite dishes. You're not going to get into a true state of fasting if you love ice cream and that's all you're eating on your fast.

A no pleasant bread fast is found in Daniel 10:3. *I ate no pleasant bread, neither came flesh nor wine in my mouth, neither did I anoint myself at all, till three whole weeks were fulfilled.*

Daniel was on a twenty-one day fast. He did eat, but he didn't eat anything that was pleasant to him. You can still enter into a true state of fasting by just eating small portions, and not necessarily something that you crave or desire. It could be something like just eating an orange or an apple; but not dozens of them.

There are two general categories of fasting:

1.   Proclaimed fast.

2.   Personal fast.

A *proclaimed fast* is found in Joel 1:14. It says, *Sanctify ye a fast, call a solemn assembly, gather the elders and all the inhabitants of the land into the house of the Lord your God, and cry unto the Lord.*

A *proclaimed fast* is one that has been directed by God. God has specifically instructed you to fast for specific purposes.

A *personal fast* is found in Matthew 6:16. Jesus said, *Moreover when ye fast, be not, as the hypocrites, of a sad countenance: for they disfigure their faces, that they may appear unto men to fast. Verily I say unto you, They have their reward.*

This is a fast that you directed. It was your choice to do this. Now notice the phrase, *when ye fast.* Jesus didn't say, *if ye fast,* He said *when* you do it. So this would indicate that He expects you to fast.

The longest fast I've ever been on has been about twenty-one days. Most of the time when I fast, I'll do it for about three days. The purpose of my fasting is when I know there are some things that God's dealing with me about, and I want my spirit to ascend so it can hear the voice of God more clearly.

Jesus expects us to fast. Notice He said, *When ye fast, be not, as the hypocrites.* In other words, don't go around letting everybody know you're fasting. He says the hypocrites have a sad look. They come into the crowds with this sad look trying to get sympathy from people and trying to get people to talk about how spiritual they are. You don't have to tell everybody. Jesus said, *they have their reward.*

If the reward you're after is for people to say, "Oh, aren't they spiritual? Look! They're fasting." Then that's all the reward you'll get.

You won't get any spiritual benefits, you'll get the praise of men.

When you fast, don't have a sad countenance. Your appearance is important both physically and spiritually. Put your clothes on, comb your hair, wash your face, look sharp. Nobody has to know that you're fasting. But you will know, and God will know. There is a fast that pleases God:

Isaiah 58:6-14 tell us the rewards of fasting. *Is not this the fast that I have chosen? to loose the bands of wickedness, to undo the heavy burdens, and to let the oppressed go free, and that ye break every yoke?*

Is it not to deal thy bread to the hungry, and that thou bring the poor that are cast out to thy house? when thou seest the naked, that thou cover him; and that thou hide not thyself from thine own flesh?

Then shall thy light break forth as the morning, and thine health shall spring forth speedily: and thy righteousness shall go before thee; the glory of the Lord shall be thy rearward.

Then shalt thou call, and the Lord shall answer; thou shalt cry, and he shall say, Here I am. If thou take away from the midst of thee the yoke, the putting forth of the finger, and speaking vanity;

And if thou draw out thy soul to the hungry, and satisfy the afflicted soul; then shall thy light rise in obscurity, and thy darkness be as the noonday:

And the Lord shall guide thee continually, and satisfy thy soul in drought, and make fat thy bones: and thou shalt be like a watered garden, and like a spring of water, whose waters fail not.

And they that shall be of thee shall build the old waste places: thou shalt raise up the foundations of many generations; and thou shalt be called, The repairer of the breach, The restorer of paths to dwell in.

If thou turn away thy foot from the sabbath, from doing thy pleasure on my holy day; and call the sabbath a delight, the holy of the Lord, honorable; and shalt honour him, not doing thine own ways, nor finding thine own pleasure, nor speaking thine own words:

Then shalt thou delight thyself in the Lord; and I will cause thee to ride upon the high places of the earth, and feed thee with the heritage of Jacob thy father: for the mouth of the Lord hath spoken it.

Why is it important that we fast? What's that got to do with ministry? There are times when there is no other way to tap into the anointing of God than praying in the Spirit and fasting.

You remember the man that brought his son to Jesus? He said when the evil spirit comes on him, he casts himself into the fire. He said, "I brought him to Your disciples, and they could not cast him out." Jesus took control and brought deliverance to the man's son. Later the disciples said, "Why couldn't we do this?" Jesus said, "It's only through prayer and fasting."

The problem with the disciples was that they had not been fasting. So Jesus was saying, "If you had been properly prepared through prayer and fasting, then this wouldn't have happened. You would have had success." (Author's paraphrase.)

Let me give you some hints about fasting. When you come off of a fast, regardless of how long it is, it's not wise to go out and eat your biggest meal immediately. When you start eating again, do it gradually; do it moderately. You may want to start with juices and then a salad or something light and then work your way back up to what you normally eat.

I would also suggest when you go on a fast to write down what you're believing God for during your fast. What are your goals for this fast? What are your purposes? What are you expecting to hear from God? I write down what I expect to gain by fasting. In addition to those rewards in Isaiah 58, I'm very specific about what I expect to gain.

If you want to see results in your ministry, then become deeply committed. God will use you mightily to bring deliverance to hurting people and to set the captives free.

39
The Purpose of Your Ministry

1. There must be a singleness of purpose in your ministry, and that is to meet the needs of the people. That is why God has called you. I heard Brother Copeland say it this way: God doesn't create churches just to give the pastor a place to preach. He creates churches so He can meet the needs of the people. God's not going to establish a ministry for you just so you'll have a job. The purpose for the ministry is to meet the needs of the people. That's what it's all about. And if you ever lose sight of that, then you become a hireling and not a true minister of the Gospel.

Keep that in the forefront of your thinking at all times. If you do this, and this is what motivates you, then your ministry is going to be sustained. It's going to be supported. It will be taken care of.

Brother Copeland taught me years ago, don't seek more ways to get money; seek more ways to get the Word out, and the money will come. A lot of preachers spend most of their time trying to figure out how to get more money. And if you do that, then there's a possibility you will lose sight of your singleness of purpose. And if you lose sight of your singleness of purpose, (to meet the needs of the people), then you're going to wind up becoming a fundraiser, always having to come up with some project to generate more funds. But if your singleness of purpose is to meet the needs of the people and constantly seek God for more ways to get the Word into the lives of people, then your ministry is going to be sustained. You won't have to take advantage of people; you won't have to become a religious con artist, and you won't have to stay up all night worrying about where the money is going to come from.

I didn't say you won't be faced with challenges. I didn't say you won't be forced to believe God financially. You will. But, in the long run, you're going to be sustained and taken care of because you have a singleness of purpose.

In Matthew 9, we see what's on the mind and heart of Jesus.

Matthew 9:35-38– *And Jesus went about all the cities and villages, teaching in their synagogues, and preaching the gospel of the kingdom, and healing every sickness and every disease among the people.*

But when he saw the multitudes, he was moved with compassion on them, because they fainted, and were scattered abroad, as sheep having no shepherd.

Then saith he unto his disciples, The harvest truly is plenteous, but the labourers are few;

Pray ye therefore the Lord of the harvest, that he will send forth labourers into his harvest.

Notice verse 36 once again. What happened when He saw the multitudes? Something happened when Jesus looked into the eyes of the people. He didn't just see statistics; He didn't just see a crowd. What He saw was humanity hurting and in need. And He was moved with compassion toward them. You have to get to the place in your life, if you're going to be involved in full-time ministry, where you love what Jesus loves. And Jesus loves people. He cares about people. That's got to be the heartbeat of your ministry. You've got to be a people person.

You may say, "Well, that's strange that you would say something like that. Don't all preachers love people?" No, they don't. They like their position, they like the prestige, they like being looked upon as a person of God, but some of them don't like people. They don't like having to deal with people.

Be Willing to Make an Investment

Discipling people is time consuming. You've got to be willing to make an investment. You've got to be willing to lay down your life, so to speak, and invest in someone else. Obviously, the larger the ministry gets, and the more demand there is on it, then the less time you have for every person. I mean, I certainly can't sit in my office and answer every individual letter. I can't do that. I don't have the time for that. But because I care for them, I see to it that they do get a response. That's the reason I have a Prayer Department. That's the reason I have Associate Ministers.

You've got to care for people. You've got to love people. And sometimes people can drain you. Sometimes, no matter how much of yourself you invest in them, it's never enough.

I remember an elderly lady who was widowed and who also had a daughter who was about forty years old and had never been married. It seemed like every time I saw them, they were in need. There was never a conversation where they would say, "Brother Jerry, everything's going well. Thank you for your prayers." It was always, "Brother Jerry, can you help us?"

I helped them financially many times. I got a letter from them one time, and they needed $1,400 to take care of this pressing situation they had. And so when I read the letter, I wrote them, and I sent them a check from me personally for $200. It was seed to help. I got a letter back from them, and they were mad at me. They said, "You don't practice what you preach. You don't walk in love. We needed $1,400, and all you sent us was $200."

Now what they didn't know was that I had sent seed to about ten different people that day, all of whom had a large need, so I was able to invest into ten lives instead of just one. Instead of being thankful, they were mad that I hadn't totally met their need. And then they came to the office, unannounced, and demanded to see me. I happened to be in that day, so I saw them. And they said, "We just can't believe that you didn't send us $1,400."

I said, "Did it ever occur to you that your letter was not the only letter with a need that I received in the mail that day? Did it ever cross your mind that there may have been nine other people who had a need just like you? I'll tell you what I'll do. Why don't I write those nine other people, tell them that I've got one person here who is mad at me because I didn't totally underwrite their whole need, and I'll ask those other nine to send their money back so we can meet your need, and their need can go unmet. Will that be all right with you?"

"Well, no. We wouldn't want you to do that," they said.

They were mad. Here I was able to help ten people instead of just one person, but they wanted it all. Now I can't stop being compassionate toward people just because of this bad experience.

Don't Get Offended at People

If you allow it, you could become calloused, and you could think, "What's the use? I'm believing God, let them believe God themselves! I'm not their source." You could think, "I'm not going to help anybody ever again."

No, you can't do that. There will be some people who are going to be unlovely no matter how much you help them. And all they ever tell people is what you didn't do. They forget to tell them all the things you did do.

When I had a church years ago, it was not uncommon that from time to time on a Sunday night in particular, as the Spirit of God would lead me, I would receive a special offering to go toward the needs of people in the church. We'd have them come and tell us what they needed, and then we would help them. We didn't totally underwrite every need they had, but just to get some of the pressure off of them. I did that several times.

One particular family was always in need. We were always helping them. However, I must have said something one Sunday that made them mad, and they left and never came back. That almost makes you want to forget who you are, sin, and get forgiveness later. Well, you can't do that. If you're going to be in the ministry, then you're going to have to face the reality that some people, no matter how much you help them, are going to turn on you. You're going to be the one they blame for their failures and their mistakes.

Jesus was constantly faced with people that hated Him. He never sinned, He never made a mistake, and yet, not everybody loved Him. Not everybody received His ministry. Yet when He would see people, He was deeply moved by the fact that they were human beings; they had hurts; they had needs, and He still loved them.

We've got to care about people like Jesus did. Jesus saw them like wheat at harvest time, and He said that He needed laborers. He needs people with compassion to move out and touch them and care for them. When Jesus looked at the masses of people, He saw people aimlessly wandering about without any direction, without any sense of purpose, without any real fulfillment. And what He saw affected Him personally.

You Have What It Takes

What do you see when you see people? How does it make you feel when you see hurting people? Can you look at them and just walk away and say, "I wish there was something we could do?" You and I are filled with the Holy Ghost. There is something we can do. We may not have all the money they need, but we do have what it takes to help them.

Peter and John at the Gate called Beautiful said to the lame man, "Silver and gold have we none, but such as we have, give we thee." What did they have? The anointing of God. The Name of Jesus. The power of God. Well, as long as you've got that, then you can do something. You can help. You can pray.

No other people on earth have the opportunity to change the direction of a lost and dying world more than you and I do. It's not politics that's going to change their lives. It's not a better economy. There are a lot of people that are doing well financially, and yet they are still wandering aimlessly through life. It's going to take the power of God. It's going to take the anointing of God. And that's what you and I are here for. We are carriers of the anointing of God.

When we think of nations, we often think of geographical locations. But when God talks about nations, He's talking about people. What God is saying is, "I'll not only give you all the geographical locations on this planet, but I will give you the people that reside in those geographical locations." God expects you to have a vision for people.

How to Pray for Others

As I mentioned earlier, when I first began preparing for the ministry, and I had no place to preach, the Lord told me to start interceding for all the people that I would someday be preaching to.

I said, "Where are they?"

He said, "You pray for them now, and they'll come."

I started spending hours praying for all the people that I was eventually going to preach to. I said, "Lord, where do they live?"

He said, "How big is your vision?"

I said, "The world."

He said, "Then pray for people all over the world."

And I did. I started praying every day for people all over the world. It wasn't long after that, a little home Bible study group two streets over from where I lived, asked me if I'd come and share my testimony with them. The next thing I knew, they wanted me to teach them the Word.

Eventually, I had a network of home Bible studies that were asking me to come and teach. Soon, I had somewhere to teach every night. But it all started with me praying for the people that I was going to preach to when I didn't have a soul that wanted to hear me. Now I am preaching to people on every continent.

If you believe God's called you into full-time ministry, and if you believe in your heart that there is a particular city or state or nation that God's called you to, then don't wait until that door opens for you to go there. Start praying for them right now.

You say, "Well, how do you pray?"

I started praying the same prayers that Paul prayed in Ephesians. I prayed that the eyes of their understanding will be enlightened. I started binding the god of this world, Satan, who had blinded their minds, and that when the Gospel comes, the blinders will be removed, and they shall be saved according to 2 Corinthians 4. I was interceding for them that they would receive the Word, that their minds and their hearts would be illuminated when the Word came forth.

Don't wait until you have more invitations than you can get to before you start praying for people. Pray now while you're believing God for an invitation. Pray now while you're believing God for the doors of your ministry to be opened. Start praying for hurting people everywhere. And once again, if you have a particular area that you believe God's going to eventually send you to, then start interceding for all the people in that area right now. If it's a specific nation that God's laid on your heart that you believe you'll eventually go to, then don't wait until that door opens; get your atlas out. Get a map of that nation. Lay your hands on it every day. Pray. Intercede. God's going to honor that, and a door's going to open, and one day, you're going to be standing there in that place, preaching to those people that you have been praying for.

Stand in the Gap

When God spoke to me about the continent of Africa in 1973, He said, "You're going to establish your ministry in ten African nations." So I started praying for all ten of those nations, and I still do. I pray for those nations everyday. And then the door began to open. It was not until 1978 before I actually went to Africa. Today I've invested over twenty years of my life into that continent. I'm standing in my dream.

In Ezekiel 22:30 God says, *And I sought for a man among them, that should make up the hedge, and stand in the gap before me for the land, that I should not destroy it: but I found none.*

We see throughout Bible history that God has always looked for someone who would stand in the gap and believe God for the people of those nations.

You Have a Part

God is asking today, "Will you be a people person?" Will you have in your heart what's in His heart? The theme of my Bible School is: A Passion for God and a Passion for Souls. That's what it's all about. God wants to know that He can count on you. Will you catch the vision for multitudes of people to come into the Kingdom of God? Can you catch the vision of seeing lives transformed by the power of God? Are you willing to be that intercessor? Are you willing to go to them? Are you willing to stand in the gap for them? That's what ministry's all about. Ministry is not about having your name on the side of a building, it's about meeting the needs of people.

Do you remember in the Book of Acts where it talks about the need to replace Judas? It says that "he had his part in this ministry."

Well, all I am is "a part in the ministry of Jesus." I have my part. Brother Copeland has his part. Brother Oral Roberts has his part. You have your part. But it's still about Jesus. It's still about touching lives and winning people to Jesus.

God needs people who are willing to go. The Word says that He sought for a man and He found none. That's got to be one of the saddest verses in the entire Bible. God was looking for someone, and He couldn't find them. God forbid that He has to say the same thing about our generation. Is there anyone? Is there a man? Is there a woman?

Let's not disappoint God. Let's stand up and say, "Here am I. Search no more."

Stand in the gap and be consumed with compassion for people. You're the only hope that masses of people around the world have today.

Just think of the lives that may never, ever hear the Gospel if you don't do your part. Think of the people that may never come into the knowledge of the truth if you don't catch the vision. You have a part to play, and your part is vital to the Kingdom of God.

What Is "Power from on High?"

In Luke 24:49 Jesus said, *And, behold, I send the promise of my Father upon you: but tarry ye in the city of Jerusalem, until ye be endued with power from on high.*

What's this "power from on high" all about? Is it just to meet our need? Is that the reason God filled us with the Holy Ghost just so we could have all our needs met? I don't think so. I think the reason for our being consumed and filled with power from on high is so that we can meet the needs of others. Jesus said that we must possess this power from on high if we are going to be effective. This power from on high is what enables us to affect other lives. Without it, there's not a thing we can do for anyone else.

Acts 4:33 – *And with great power gave the apostles witness of the resurrection of the Lord Jesus.*

With great power they gave witness to the fact that Jesus is alive.

Acts 5:12 – *And by the hands of the apostles were many signs and wonders wrought among the people.*

What was it that enabled them to affect the lives of so many people? It was the fire of the Holy Ghost, it was the compassion of the Lord Jesus. The early church refused to sit back and be idle and allow multitudes of people to go to hell. The early church refused to sit back and be idle and allow people to continue to wander aimlessly. They had a fire on the inside of them that could not be quenched.

Romans 1:14 and 15 are some of my favorite verses. The Apostle Paul says, *I am debtor both to the Greeks, and to the Barbarians; both to the wise, and to the unwise. So, as much as in me is, I am ready to preach the gospel to you.*

Notice he said, I am a debtor. I'm in debt to every man. The Lord said it to me this way several years ago, "Because of everything I have imparted into you and everything you've seen, you now have an obligation to share it with every man."

Whether you ever go to another nation or not, whether you ever enter into full-time ministry or not, you're in debt to somebody. It may be your next door neighbor. It may be the people that you work with. They have a right to hear what you've learned.

Do You Have Passion?

When you're a passionate person, then you are able to believe God for big things. Passion ignites your imagination and your creativity. God ideas will begin to flood your mind and your heart for how to reach more people. When you're consumed with passion, you just simply believe that God can do anything. No matter how impossible it may seem, no matter how much it may cost. Your passion for touching people and changing lives just enables you to look beyond the obstacles and dare believe that God can do this! We can get this done!

People of passion cannot keep from going and doing. They are people who are on the go, and they are people who are doing something all the time in order to reach humanity. Passion wakes them up in the morning, keeps them rejoicing during the day, and causes them to dream big dreams when they go to sleep.

2. Seek more ways to get the Word out. When I first left Brother Copeland's organization and launched out into my part of Jesus' ministry, he said, "Jerry, don't spend all your time seeking ways to get more money. Spend your time seeking more ways to get the Word out, and the money will come."

That's good advice.

2 Timothy 4:1-5 – *I charge thee therefore before God, and the Lord Jesus Christ, who shall judge the quick and the dead at his appearing and his kingdom;*

Preach the word; be instant in season, out of season; reprove, rebuke, exhort with all longsuffering and doctrine.

For the time will come when they will not endure sound doctrine; but after their own lusts shall they heap to themselves teachers, having itching ears;

And they shall turn away their ears from the truth, and shall be turned unto fables.

But watch thou in all things, endure afflictions, do the work of an evangelist, make full proof of thy ministry.

Notice Paul's instructions to this young man, Timothy. He said, "I charge you to preach the Word." That's what the ministry is all about: preaching the Word. It's the Word that's going to make the difference in people's lives. It's not programs, it's not gimmicks, it's not buildings; it's the Word. The reason for television is to get the Word out. The reason for crusades is to get the Word into people. The reason for a Believers' Convention is to get the Word into more people.

The reason for the printed page is to get the Word out. The reason for the magazine is to get the Word out. The purpose for the books is to get the Word in people. The purpose for the audio tapes, the video tapes, is to get the Word into people. That's what it's all about.

I've watched Brother Copeland all these years, constantly receiving God ideas on how to get the Word into more people. If you develop that in your ministry, then you can't help but grow. God will entrust you with more people to minister to.

3. Give and it shall be given unto you. When you have a singleness of purpose to meet the needs of the people and you're constantly looking for more ways to get the Word into the lives of people, then there is a spiritual law released, and that law is simply this: give and it shall be given unto you.

You might say, "Well, how does that work?" If you impart into their lives something that changes their lives forever, it's highly probable that they will become a supporter of your ministry.

Just stop and think about it. That's exactly what happened to me. Kenneth Copeland came to my home town in 1969, preached the Word that changed my life forever, and I became a partner with him, and have remained a partner with him for thirty years. Why? Because he brought to me the message that changed my life.

This is one of the ways that God will take care of your ministry financially so you don't have to spend all your time seeking more ways to get more money. You're making an investment in people; and the Spirit of God will move on them to make an investment in your ministry.

Be very careful. There's a fine line. Make sure that the reason you're imparting into them is not for the money, but to change their lives. Whether they give back to you or not, whether they invest a dime in your ministry or not, your purpose is to minister to them.

Living to Give

If someone asked me what is the most important thing that Kenneth Copeland ever taught you, I would have to say: Living to give.

The spirit of giving that is on Kenneth and Gloria Copeland was imparted into my life. I had never met people then, nor to this day, who give like Kenneth and Gloria Copeland.

From the day that I met them, they have been givers. And as a result, their ministry is very successful. Everything's paid for; no debts in their ministry; no one can come and put a padlock on the gate. It all came from giving.

If you want your ministry to be sustained financially and you want it to be strong financially, then be a giving ministry. Brother Copeland takes the top 10 percent of his ministry income, puts it into a tithe account and invests it into other ministries. I do the same thing. I've done it for years and years. That means that we demand that our ministries operate on 90 percent of their income.

I'm operating on Spiritual Laws that I believe are not only applicable to an individual, but also to a ministry or a business. Do you want your business blessed? Then tithe out of it. Do you want your church blessed? Then tithe out of it.

You Were Born to be a Blessing

Living to give is one of the greatest revelations that Brother Copeland imparted into my life, and I attribute that revelation to the success I enjoy in the ministry today and the financial stability that we have in our ministry.

Mark 10:17-22 – *And when he was gone forth into the way, there came one running, and kneeled to him, and asked him, Good Master, what shall I do that I may inherit eternal life?*

And Jesus said unto him, Why callest thou me good? there is none good but one, that is, God.

Thou knowest the commandments, Do not commit adultery, Do not kill, Do not steal, Do not bear false witness, Defraud not, Honour thy father and mother.

And he answered and said unto him, Master, all these have I observed from my youth.

Then Jesus beholding him loved him, and said unto him, One thing thou lackest: go thy way, sell whatsoever thou hast, and give to the poor, and thou shalt have treasure in heaven: and come, take up the cross, and follow me.

And he was sad at that saying, and went away grieved: for he had great possessions.

Jesus is endeavoring to teach this man what I like to refer to as the Essence of Living is Giving. Giving is the cardinal law of God. John 3:16 says, *For God so loved . . . that he gave.*

Life is not about how much you can get before you die; it's really about how much you can give before you die. Jesus said, *A man's life consisteth not of the things which he possesses.* The world measures success by how much people acquire before they die. God measures success by how much a person gives.

1 Timothy 6:17-18 says, *Charge them that are rich in this world, that they be not highminded, nor trust in uncertain riches, but in the living God, who giveth us richly all things to enjoy; That they do good, that they be rich in good works, ready to distribute, willing to communicate.*

God is saying, when you're blessed, then you need to be a blessing. You need to be willing to distribute. God wants you and me to become "distribution centers." He wants us to be blessed, obviously, but the reason that He wants us to be blessed is so that we can bless other people.

In order to be a blessing, you have to be blessed. But when you're blessed, then God expects you to be ready to distribute, willing to communicate or to give.

Ephesians 4:28 says, *Let him that stole steal no more: but rather let him labour, working with his hands the thing which is good, that he may have to give to him that needeth.*

God is saying, the very reason that we earn money with our own hands is so that we'll have seed to sow.

Luke 6:38 says, *Give, and it shall be given unto you; good measure, pressed down, and shaken together, and running over, shall men give into your bosom. For with the same measure that ye mete withal it shall be measured to you again.*

If you increase the measure of your giving, then God will increase the measure of the return. And that enables you to be able to give more.

Genesis 12:2 says, *And I will make of thee a great nation, and I will bless thee, and make thy name great; and thou shalt be a blessing.*

This is what God told Abraham and his seed. What was God saying? I not only want to bless you, but the purpose in blessing you is so that you can become a blessing.

I like to define a blessing as this: An instrument through which God's divine favor flows; bringing joy, happiness, healing, and prosperity, and preventing misfortune in the lives of those needing to be blessed.

In other words, when I'm blessed, then I become a blessing, that is: I become God's instrument. His divine favor is now flowing through me to the person needing to be blessed.

For instance, if you're in need financially, and I have the means to assist you and to bless you, then I am nothing more than an instrument. God's divine favor is flowing through me to you, and my meeting your need now brings joy, happiness, prosperity, and it prevented a misfortune in your life.

If you show God you're willing to be that instrument, then He will put you in position to do more and help more people. That's what I've watched happen in Brother Copeland's life all these years.

God's looking for somebody who will express a deep commitment to help people, to bless people. And when God finds a person like that, then He increases their resources for sowing.

Make up your mind that from here on out, your life does not consist of how much you can get, but how much you can give.

God's not interested in people who only want to be blessed so they can hoard it up. God's not interested in people who only want to be blessed so that they can brag about how blessed they are and never distribute.

2 Corinthians 8:7 says, *Therefore, as ye abound in every thing, in faith, and utterance, and knowledge, and in all diligence, and in your love to us, see that ye abound in this grace also.*

If you'll study this chapter closely, you'll realize that the grace he was talking about there was the grace of giving. See that you abound in this grace also. He's saying, if you're going to abound in faith, and if you're going to abound in knowledge, then abound in this grace also. And the grace he was referring to was the grace of giving. God blesses those who live to give.

40
Establishing Covenant Relationships

If there is any one thing I've noticed that is lacking in the Body of Christ, it is understanding and honoring covenant relationships.

There are just not enough people in the Body of Christ who are "covenant relationship-minded." Brother Copeland and I have enjoyed covenant relationship for thirty years. God brought us together by divine appointment, and we've honored that relationship. We've come to one another's aid in times of trouble. We've prayed over one another's situation, trials and adversities. We've stood with one another when all of hell's power broke loose against us. And we've rejoiced over each other's victories. That's a covenant relationship.

1 Samuel 18:1 says, *And it came to pass, when he had made an end of speaking unto Saul, that the soul of Jonathan was knit with the soul of David, and Jonathan loved him as his own soul.*

Notice it says, *the soul of Jonathan was knit with the soul of David.*

In your lifetime, you're going to meet a lot of people, and you're going to develop friendships, but from time to time, God is going to cause your path to cross the path of another person in which that relationship is going to be special. It's not something that you make happen; it's not something that you necessarily pursue. It's simply a divine appointment.

I shared the story earlier of how I met Brother Copeland back in 1969, when he came to my home town.

Obviously, nothing "clicked" between Brother Copeland and me right then. As far as I knew, that was probably the last time I would ever see him.

But later, when I completely surrendered my life to the call of God, and I began to study his tapes, then I felt more connected to him. But it never dawned on me that I'd ever really get to know him or go to work for him, much less become a "team" with him. I just knew that I could identify with him.

But then when he came back to Shreveport and stated, "God showed me while I was praying today that you and I would become a team and that we would preach the Gospel around the world together for the rest of our lives. And it will be your responsibility to believe God for the perfect timing for this team to begin," I was surprised. But I also knew right then that there was a connection in the spirit.

Later, I read this Scripture from 1 Samuel about the soul of David and the soul of Jonathan being knit together, and I knew that's what had happened to Brother Copeland and me. It was more than just an acquaintance; it was more than just a friendship, it was a covenant relationship. Neither of us knew the extent of it, nor did we know how it was going to develop, but apparently, the Spirit of God said to him that it would be for the rest of our lives.

Relationships are very important to me, and when I enter into a relationship, I consider it to be for the rest of my life. I just think that way. And when he said, "Together for the rest of our lives," then to me that meant *together for the rest of our lives*.

When I eventually moved to Fort Worth and I went to work for Brother Copeland, he became my boss. There was an employer-employee relationship; but it began to develop into something deeper than that. I still recognized him as my superior, as my boss, but yet there was a kindred spirit, and I knew, after a period of time, that he trusted me, and that he had great confidence in me. He believed in me, and he was willing to invest his life into me.

So when God started dealing with me about going into my own ministry, I was not in favor of that. All I could see was that it would split up the team. I couldn't see how the team would stay together if I left. Being in covenant relationship with Brother Copeland was more important to me than having my own ministry.

Finally, the Lord was able to get it across to me that the team would not split up if I left. It would enable the team to cover twice as much territory. The team didn't split up. Our souls had been knit together.

What I'm sharing with you is very rare in the Body of Christ. It's a shame, but it's true. It's very rare in the Body of Christ. One of the major reasons we don't see more preachers in covenant relationship is because of competition, fear and jealousy. Most preachers cannot have a covenant relationship with another preacher because they're competitive. They're afraid they're going to get more attention; they're afraid they're going to have bigger crowds; they're afraid they might take some of *their* people and *their* money.

I deeply believe that if any preacher has to compete with another preacher, then he's not too sure he's called. There's never been any competition between Brother Copeland and me, and never will be.

I represent Kenneth Copeland Ministries when I stand behind his pulpit. How does he know I'm not going to go up to the platform and say, "Send all donations to Jerry Savelle." He trusts me. He knows that I would not promote myself nor my ministry because I'm in covenant relationship with him.

Brother Jesse Duplantis said to me one time, "I've never seen preachers like you and Brother Copeland. I can't believe that Brother Copeland just turns his ministry over to us like this and trusts us."

I said, "Jesse, it's rare, but it's an example of true covenant relationship."

1 Samuel 18:1-4 . . . the soul of Jonathan was knit with the soul of David, and Jonathan loved him as his own soul.

And Saul took him that day, and would let him go no more home to his father's house.

Then Jonathan and David made a covenant, because he loved him as his own soul.

And Jonathan stripped himself of the robe that was upon him, and gave it to David, and his garments, even to his sword, and to his bow, and to his girdle.

In covenant relationship, you are willing to give your best. I've watched Brother Copeland do that many times with me, and I've done it with him. There are times when I may be shopping, and I buy myself something, and immediately, I think of my covenant partner. I want to buy him something, too.

One night, while Brother Copeland and Gloria were in our home fellowshipping, the Lord said, "I want you to show Kenneth how much your covenant relationship with him means to you." I said, "Okay."

He said, "Go to your study and get one of your most prized possessions."

Well, I have a few things that I would consider prized possessions, so I went into my study and started looking. I enjoy collecting commemorative pistols, and I had a commemorative John Wayne 45.

It is one of the most beautiful pistols I've ever seen. So, I unlocked my cabinet and got that pistol out. Brother Copeland was in another room and didn't know what was going on.

I came out with that pistol, walked up to him and said, "Brother Copeland, my covenant relationship with you is a high priority in my life."

I said, "In 1969, you came to my home town and preached the Gospel, and it absolutely changed my life. I have never been the same since that day. Kenneth Copeland, your feet will always be beautiful in the Savelle household. I strip myself of this possession, and I give it to you as a token of our covenant relationship."

He was deeply moved. That's covenant.

1 Samuel 20:4 says, *Then said Jonathan unto David, Whatsoever thy soul desireth, I will even do it for thee.*

Verse 11 says, *And Jonathan said unto David, Come, and let us go out into the field. And they went out both of them into the field.*

And Jonathan said unto David, O Lord God of Israel, when I have sounded my father about tomorrow any time, or the third day, and, behold, if there be good toward David, and I then send not unto thee, and show it thee;

The Lord do so and much more to Jonathan: but if it please my father to do thee evil, then I will show it thee, and send thee away, that thou mayest go in peace: and the Lord be with thee, as he hath been with my father.

And thou shalt not only while yet I live show me the kindness of the Lord, that I die not:

But also thou shalt not cut off thy kindness from my house for ever: no, not when the Lord hath cut off the enemies of David every one from the face of the earth.

So Jonathan made a covenant with the house of David, saying, Let the Lord even require it at the hand of David's enemies.

What's he saying? This covenant goes further than just Jonathan and David. It even goes to their families.

One of my covenant partners, Buddy Harrison, just recently went home to be with the Lord. Buddy and I had been in covenant relationship for over twenty-five years, and I said to his family at his homegoing, "This covenant does not end because Buddy left. This covenant is to you and to your children and to your children's children. As long as there are Savelles, then we will come to your aid."

It's the same way with the Copeland and Savelle family. In fact, Kellie Copeland Kutz, Brother Copeland's daughter, came up to me recently in a meeting, threw her arms around me and said, "I just need a hug from my second Daddy." That's covenant relationship. She knows that Carolyn and I and our family would do anything for her.

John Copeland knows that the Savelle family would do anything for him. George and Terri (Copeland) Pearsons know that we would do anything for them. Why? My covenant is not just with Brother Copeland and Gloria; it's with their children and their children's children.

Any time there has been a hurt in their family, we're there. When there has been a hurt in our family, they're there for us. Our families are in covenant. There has never been one cross word between our families. We're in covenant with each other.

When there's been tragedy in their family, we're the first ones they call. When there has been a tragedy in our family, they're the first ones we call. "We need prayer. We need for you to stand in agreement with us." That's covenant.

Galatians 6:6 says, *Let him that is taught in the word communicate unto him that teacheth in all good things.*

The Amplified says, *Let him who receives instruction in the Word [of God] share all good things with his teacher [contributing to his support].*

Paul is emphasizing honoring covenant relationships. Brother Copeland has been a teacher to me, but he's also been a spiritual father to me. Paul says in 1 Corinthians 4:15-16 that you have many teachers, but not many fathers.

God expects you to honor your spiritual fathers. God expects me to honor Brother Copeland as my spiritual father. It would be a violation of spiritual law if I didn't. I say to Brother Copeland, as Elisha said unto Elijah, "As long as the Lord thy God liveth and thy soul liveth, I will not leave thee."

In other words, his vision is my vision. What he believes God has given him as a mandate, then I'm part of that. I'll never stop supporting Brother Copeland's vision simply because I have my own vision and my own ministry. No, he's the one who brought the message to me thirty years ago that revolutionized my life, and I'm not going to leave him now.

I believe every preacher should be in covenant relationship with someone else. I personally believe that. I believe there would be much less falling away in the ministry, less scandals, less loneliness in the ministry if preachers had someone that they trusted and would allow them to speak into their lives.

You need people who are willing to rebuke you when you're wrong, straighten you out when you're going the wrong way; do it in love; do it in faith, but keep you on the straight and narrow. Thank God I've got men like that. I have had a covenant relationship with Pastor Happy Caldwell for over twenty years, and I value that relationship. Jesse Duplantis is like a brother to me. I value his friendship.

Brother Copeland wouldn't hesitate a minute to get in my face and correct me when I'm wrong. He would be stern, but he would do it in love. Why? Because he cares. I know it's genuine. He wouldn't have done it if he didn't care.

Never Lose a Servant's Heart

Well, thirty years have come and gone, and Kenneth Copeland and Jerry Savelle are still a team. I think it's a testimony to the Body of Christ that two internationally known preachers can still love one another, serve one another, and not compete with each another.

Forever, I will be willing to serve this great man of God. Jesus said if you want to be great, then serve. That's the reason God has blessed Brother Copeland. I've seen him when he gets around Oral Roberts or Kenneth Hagin, he's there to serve.

Don't ever lose your servant's heart. God will bless you, and you'll never have to be self-promoting or self-exalting. There's no limit to where God will take you if you always look for opportunities to serve.

This has been the story of my life for the last thirty years. I've walked in the footsteps of a prophet, and what wonderful adventures in faith it has been.

About the Author

Dr. Jerry Savelle is a noted author, evangelist, and teacher who travels extensively throughout the United States, Canada, and around the globe. He is president of Jerry Savelle Ministries International, a ministry of many outreaches devoted to meeting the needs of believers all over the world.

Well-known for his balanced Biblical teaching, Dr. Savelle has conducted seminars, crusades and conventions for nearly thirty years as well as ministered in thousands of churches and fellowships. He is in great demand today because of his inspiring message of victory and faith and his vivid, and often humorous, illustrations from the Bible. He teaches the uncompromised Word of God with a power and an authority that is exciting, but with a love that delivers the message directly to the spirit man.

In addition to his international headquarters in Crowley, Texas, Dr. Savelle is also founder of JSMI-Kenya; JSMI-United Kingdom; JSMI-South Africa; JSMI-Tanzania; and JSMI-Australia. He is also the founder and President of JSMI Bible Institute and School of World Evangelism in the USA, Kenya and the United Kingdom. It is a two-year school for the preparation of ministers to take the Gospel of Jesus Christ to the nations of the world.

The missions outreach of his ministry extends to over 50 countries around the world. JSMI further ministers the Word of God through its prison ministry outreach.

Dr. Savelle has authored many books and has an extensive video and cassette teaching tape ministry and a worldwide television broadcast. Thousands of books, tapes, and videos are distributed around the world each year through Jerry Savelle Ministries International.

Other Books by Jerry Savelle

Take Charge of Your Financial Destiny

From Devastation to Restoration

Walking In Divine Favor

Turning Your Dreams Into Reality

Turning Your Adversity Into Victory

Honoring Your Heritage Of Faith

Don't Let Go Of Your Dreams

Faith Building Daily Devotionals

The Force of Joy

If Satan Can't Steal Your Joy,
He Can't Keep Your Goods

A Right Mental Attitude

The Nature Of Faith

The Established Heart

Sharing Jesus Effectively

How To Overcome Financial Famine

You're Somebody Special To God

Leaving The Tears Behind

For a complete list of tapes, books,
and videos by Jerry Savelle,
write or call:

Jerry Savelle Ministries International
P.O. Box 748
Crowley, Texas 76036
(817) 297-3155
www.jsmi.org